T0305793

Models of
Health Plan Payment
and Quality Reporting

Models of
Health Plan Payment
and Quality Reporting

Jacob Glazer
Tel Aviv University, Israel & The University of Warwick, UK

Thomas G McGuire
Harvard Medical School, USA

 **World Scientific**

NEW JERSEY · LONDON · SINGAPORE · BEIJING · SHANGHAI · HONG KONG · TAIPEI · CHENNAI · TOKYO

Published by

World Scientific Publishing Co. Pte. Ltd.
5 Toh Tuck Link, Singapore 596224
USA office: 27 Warren Street, Suite 401-402, Hackensack, NJ 07601
UK office: 57 Shelton Street, Covent Garden, London WC2H 9HE

British Library Cataloguing-in-Publication Data
A catalogue record for this book is available from the British Library.

MODELS OF HEALTH PLAN PAYMENT AND QUALITY REPORTING

ISBN 978-981-3202-87-0

Desk Editor: Sandhya Venkatesh

Typeset by Stallion Press
Email: enquiries@stallionpress.com

Printed in Singapore

CONTENTS

INTRODUCTION

All western countries regulate health insurance and health services markets. While the two main goals for such regulation are everywhere broadly similar — to achieve an efficient and equitable system — the regulatory strategies to achieve these goals are very different. One reason for these differences could be that in spite of the large share of national incomes devoted to health care and the large volume of research devoted to health insurance regulation, it is not yet clear what the optimal mechanism should look like. Our joint work over the past 30 years has sought a better understanding of how regulation of health plan payment should be designed and implemented in order to achieve these two goals. While our objective has always been practical, our approach has been theoretical: we develop models of managed competition among health plans in order to analyze market equilibrium under different regulatory regimes. In managed competition, private plans compete for enrollees subject to regulation of premiums and benefits. Some form of managed competition characterizes health policy in many countries, including Germany, Israel, the Netherlands, Switzerland, the U.S. and other countries where social policy is based on regulated private plans competing in a market for enrollees.

While one can think of many reasons for why unregulated competition among health plans can lead to inefficiency, there is no doubt that the most important one is adverse selection. "Adverse selection" refers to the tendency of consumers who will benefit more from more generous insurance — in our case, health insurance — to purchase more generous coverage. As a consequence, the seller of the more generous coverage is subject to an adverse selection from among the risk pool. Matching consumers with greater need to better coverage would seem like a good thing, and it is, but the pricing problems in health insurance that arise from this tendency can interfere with efficient market functioning.

If health insurance markets were left unregulated, prices to sick people would be very high, pricing many out of the market altogether, and offending most people's sense of social fairness. Keeping prices for health insurance for sick people at below market rates implies several things: sicker consumers will respond to the subsidy and seek to buy too generous health insurance; plans will seek to deter sick people from joining; as part of this deterrence, plans will tend to set quality too low for services used by the sick and too high for services used by the healthy. Obviously, if quality could be easily regulated, payers and regulators could simply "dictate" to health plans the efficient level of care each and every service they provide. The problem, however, is that for many services, quality is not easily measurable and verifiable, and regulators need to implement mechanisms, other than direct regulation, in order to induce plans to provide the efficient level of care. However, as both the theoretical and empirical literature has demonstrated again and again, any regulatory mechanism to address these problems is subject to some major negative side effects that could be costlier than the problem they aimed to solve and could cause more harm than good. In this volume, we focus on three such mechanisms: risk adjustment, quality reporting and premium design.

In what follows we briefly discuss each of the papers that appear in this volume. The chapters are organized in three sections according to the main policy instrument they analyze. The first section focuses on risk adjustment and plan design, the second on quality reporting mechanisms, and the third on premium and plan design policies to achieve an efficient and fair sorting of beneficiaries among plans.

RISK ADJUSTMENT AND PLAN DESIGN

Premiums charged to (expensive) sick people can be kept low if a regulatory authority gathers premiums from all consumers, possibly adding tax contributions, and restructures the payment out to plans using a risk adjustment formula. Risk adjustment refers to the practice of paying health plans a premium for each person or family based on a formula using risk adjuster variables, such as age, gender, or indicators of prior health care use, and weights on those adjusters. Paying plans more for consumers with higher anticipated costs means premiums charged do not need to reflect differences in expected costs. Chapters 1, 2 and 3 are all concerned with how economic forces stemming from risk-adjusted plan payments affect the efficiency of plan design. Early research on risk adjustment regarded the goal of risk adjustment design to be a statistical one — find a useable set of risk-adjustor variables that maximized the statistical fit (usually an R-squared) of the risk adjustment regression. Improving risk adjustment meant bettering the R-squared.

Chapter 1 is credited with initiating a literature on "optimal risk adjustment," which turns the problem from a statistical one to an economic one. The goal of risk adjustment is to improve the efficiency of health insurance markets. A model of health insurance market relating the nature of plan payment and risk adjustment to plan payment is therefore required. Chapter 1 adapts the Rothschild-Stiglitz two-good, two-consumer type model to managed health care, using conditions associated with a zero-profit competitive equilibrium. The answer for how to do risk adjustment differs when the goal is economic efficiency. This idea opens up a different way to think about the basic problem of plan payment, developed in our work theoretically and in work by us and others empirically.

More specifically, we argue that risk adjustment should be viewed as a way to set prices for different individuals to address adverse-selection problems. Solving for prices in an explicit optimizing framework, rather than simply paying according to average costs, magnifies the power of risk-adjustment policies. We show that conventional risk adjustment is never the optimal policy for a regulator, in a market with asymmetric information, and that optimal risk adjustment pays higher than conventional risk adjustment for persons who are likely to be costly (e.g., the old), and lower than conventional risk adjustment for the other (the young).

Chapter 2 studies the behavior of a single plan setting access to services of various types in response to incentives associated with adverse selection. The main contribution of Chapter 2 is to lay out a model of profit maximization of a health insurance plan. This essential tool of a mechanism-design approach to this sector had been missing in the literature. The model developed in that paper relates a plan's profit-maximizing choice of the strictness of service rationing (as represented by a "shadow price") to risk adjustment, demand elasticity, the predictability of services, and to how different services are correlated with financial gains and losses at the person level. This model has proved durable over the years and has formed the basis of many later theoretical and empirical papers.

Chapter 3 uses the model of plan behavior in Chapter 2 to derive a method for estimating risk adjustment weights based on a modification of an ordinary least squared regression. What would seem like an impossible empirical task, to derive weights on risk-adjustor variables to align plan profit maximization to incentives for social efficiency, turns out to be operational. Weights on risk adjustor variables appear as parameters in a plan's profit-maximization conditions. Correcting these conditions for selection-related inefficiencies leaves a set of equations in the risk-adjustment parameters that can be imposed as constraints on an OLS regression. The resulting estimates are the "minimum variance" estimators (in terms of residual variance from the regression) that satisfy the efficiency conditions for "optimal risk adjustment" of the title.

USING QUALITY REPORTS TO INDUCE EFFICIENT QUALITY OF CARE

Quality reporting mechanisms are becoming more and more popular among policymakers, regulators, managers and insurers. Certification of health care providers through healthcare report cards, and the use of pay for performance contracts, has become widespread. However, the jury is still out about whether they have caused more harm than good. In one well-known case — cardiac surgeon reports in New York State, Pennsylvania, and Massachusetts — physician reports have been shown to improve quality. Because these reports are inevitably both partial (not covering all elements of "output") and imperfectly adjusted for differences in severity across practices, once a quality report has power, providers may seek ways to game the reports by shifting activities within their practice or taking different patients. It is, therefore, surprising that very little theoretical work, in health economics, attempts to understand the full effect of such mechanisms on the various parties involved (i.e., doctors, patients, employers and insurers), and their optimal design.

A public report about the quality of physicians, hospitals, nursing homes and health plans has two purposes: equipping decision-makers (e.g., patients, managers, other doctors, regulators) with more information so they can choose the provider that best suits their needs, and motivating providers to improve the quality of the services they offer. The benefits of such reporting must be weighed against its costs, which include not only the costs to collect and distribute the information but also costs borne by the provider.

The starting point of Chapter 4 is the observation that markets in health care are subject to adverse selection-related inefficiencies even in the presence of complete information. More specifically, consumers' knowledge about the quality of services they anticipate receiving at a health plan drives the plan to "underprovide" (i.e., to set quality sub-optimally) services that will be used by enrollees whose expected costs exceed their expected revenue and to "overprovide" services that will be used by enrollees whose expected revenue expected their expected costs. In such a case, giving consumers more information about quality may in fact decrease market efficiency and harm consumers. In Chapter 4 we cast the decision of what information about quality to report to consumers as a policy instrument. We focus on markets for health plans, where a regulator supplies information to consumers about quality at the plans. Health plans provide a range of health care services and potential enrollees choose a plan partly on the basis of what they anticipate will be the quality of services they receive in the plan. Our main finding about reporting is intuitive and practical, but quite surprising: by providing information only about the average quality of services in a health plan, rather than the quality of each of the elements of service a plan provides, a payer or regulator can give consumers helpful information, but prevent a plan from setting quality of its services to try to attract a profitable mix of enrollees. The averaged report is powerful: the right weights for elements of quality in the averaged report induce a plan to produce the socially efficient quality of all services. Consumers' rationality plays a very important role in our analysis as it implies that even when they cannot observe the quality of each of the services a plan provides, and they can only observe the average quality of these services, in equilibrium, consumers can infer the quality of each of these services.

In Chapter 5 we study how to optimally report consumer satisfaction of health plans. One important component of such reports is that it often reports a simple average of consumers' rating, weighting each member equally, where each consumer's rating (often referred to as "global rating") is a simple average of the quality of the different services he uses. In this paper we first show that a simple averaging of global ratings gives a plan incentives to improve some services more than others. We then propose a simple way to fix incentives, and illustrate how this can be done with some data on Medicare beneficiaries. The solution we propose is straightforward and readily implementable on an ongoing basis.

A simple averaging of consumers' global ratings can be inefficient because of consumers' heterogeneity. If all patients had the same needs and the rating scale of "worst possible" to "best possible" could be interpreted as equivalent to "no healthcare benefit provided" to "all possible benefit provided", then a system that reports averaged ratings would convey incentives to provide services to all patients equally. However, when some patients have greater healthcare needs (and potential benefits of care) than others, but all report on the same scale, points on the scale no longer represent the same amount of benefit for different patients. Instead the benefit to less needy patients is overvalued (since a small potential benefit is stretched across the entire scale) while the benefit to needier patients is undervalued (since a large potential benefit is compressed into the same scale). A health plan attempting to maximize its reported ratings then has an incentive to undertreat needier patients and overtreat less needy patients. However, this distortion of the scale can be corrected by weighting reports by patients proportionally to their potential benefit from healthcare; this unequal weighting has the same effect as expanding the scale for the needier patients.

EFFICIENT AND FAIR SORTING AMONG PLAN TYPES

In Chapters 6 and 7, we shift analytic focus away from plan payment and risk adjustment to the premiums and the incentives faced by heterogeneous beneficiaries when they choose a health plan. Our approach is based on the observation that beneficiaries vary in their demand for health care for many reasons. One reason for such heterogeneity among beneficiaries, which has attracted most of the attention among both policy makers and researchers, is "health status." Risk adjustment technology is designed to deal precisely with this heterogeneity. Another reason, and one that we call attention to in these papers, is that factors other than health status — income, education, "taste" more generally, also influence demand for health care, and therefore choice of plan. From the standpoint of the beneficiary, anticipated demand for health care, together with the premiums individuals pay, determine the best plan option.

One public policy response to demand heterogeneity creates "Gold", "Silver" and possibly other plans representing different levels of coverage and generosity. This strategy was recently adopted by the U.S. in its health care reform of 2010. The design of efficient and equitable health policy in this policy context is the focus of Chapter 6. We carry out the analysis when two types of health plans can efficiently serve tastes, a basic plan which we term "Silver" and a more generous plan which we term "Gold." Chapter 6 studies how to efficiently and fairly implement a "Silver" and "Gold" health insurance plan within a policy context of managed competition. In managed competition, private plans compete for enrollees subject to regulation of premiums and benefits. Our "Silver Plan" covers a basic bundle of health care services. The "Gold Plan" offers better coverage/higher quality of care, but is more expensive. Efficiency calls for the groups with a higher willingness to pay for health care to be in the Gold Plan. For fairness, we want the sick and the healthy to pay the same for plan membership in both plans.

In our model consumers differ in two dimensions, health status and "taste" for health care, and are served by competing managed health care plans. A Regulator pays plans and may levy plan-specific taxes. Plans compete on services and premiums. In the case where both health status and "taste" are available as a basis of payment we show that incremental cost pricing of individual premiums is efficient but unfair, and that average cost premiums are fair but not efficient. By use of a new policy with an income-based tax on plan membership the Regulator can achieve both an efficient and fair allocation. However, if "taste" cannot be used as a basis for payment we show that no payment policy leads to both efficiency and fairness. When we weaken the solidarity principle to be that the sick pay no more for health insurance than the healthy, efficiency and fairness can be achieved.

In Chapter 7 we study how beneficiaries in Medicare, the U.S. federal health insurance program for the elderly and disabled, choose between two major options: traditional Medicare (TM) and a set of private health insurance plans, including managed care plans, referred to as Medicare Advantage (MA) plans. To address normative questions around beneficiary choice between MA and TM, we propose a formulation of the efficient division of beneficiaries between MA and TM. We argue that, from the standpoint of social welfare, MA should draw beneficiaries from the thick central part of the distribution of preferences for health care, and in this sense make MA a "middle class" program. To get there requires a redesign of premium policy.

Presently, premiums for TM depend on the circumstances of the beneficiary whereas MA plans choose the premium beneficiaries pay (subject to Medicare regulation), and this premium is the same for all beneficiaries. We argue that there is a fundamental problem with this approach. Any single premium for MA does a poor job of sorting beneficiaries between MA and TM. We argue that some form of premium discrimination by non-health status factors affecting demand is necessary to fundamentally improve the performance of the MA program.

ACKNOWLEDGEMENTS

We thank our coauthors, Zhun Cao, Richard Frank and Alan Zaslavsky, for permission to reprint our papers here. These colleagues, along with many other colleagues and students, have contributed to our thinking over the years. We continue to benefit from the collaboration of Randy Ellis, Tim Layton, Albert Ma, Joe Newhouse, Sherri Rose and others.

Some of the best health economists spanning generations work on the economics of health insurance. In addition to our colleagues mentioned above, some of the notable research reviewed in our papers include work by Mike Chernew, David Cutler, Liran Einav, Amy Finkelstein, Jon Gruber, Ben Handel, Igal Hendel, Jonathan Kolstad, Mark Pauly, Johannes Spinnwin, Richard Zeckhauser and others.

We have recently begun collaboration with researchers in the Netherlands, the country which arguably sets the standard for health financing policy based on an individual health insurance market. We are looking forward to work on theory, empirics and policy with Shuli Brammli-Greenberg, Richard van Kleef, Wynand van de Ven, Rene van Vliet and with other colleagues in the European-based Risk Adjustment Network.

We continue to work on health financing policy in the U.S. and Israel, with the goal of applying some of the theoretical ideas laid out here to improving the functioning of health insurance markets, particularly for persons with chronic illness. In the U.S., regulated individual health insurance markets in which plans are paid by risk adjustment are active in Medicare, Medicaid and in the state-level Marketplaces created by the Affordable Care Act. In Israel, the entire population chooses health insurance from among a set of private plans paid by risk adjustment.

Finally, we thank Zvi Ruder and Sandhya Venkatesh from World Scientific Publishers for their encouragement, guidance and assistance in putting this volume together.

ACKNOWLEDGEMENTS

Chapter 1: Optimal Risk Adjustment of Health Insurance Premiums
Reprinted from the *American Economic Review* (2000), 90(4): 1055–1071, with the permission of the American Economic Association.

Chapter 2: Measuring Adverse Selection in Managed Health Care
Reprinted from the *Journal of Health Economics* (2000), 19(6): 829–854, with the permission of Elsevier.

Chapter 3: Setting Health Plan Premiums to Ensure Efficient Quality in Health Care: Minimum Variance Optimal Risk Adjustment
Reprinted from the *Journal of Public Economics* (2002), 84: 153–173, with the permission of Elsevier.

Chapter 4: Optimal Quality Reporting in Markets for Health Plans
Reprinted from the *Journal of Health Economics* (2006), 25(2): 295–310, with the permission of Elsevier.

Chapter 5: Using Global Ratings of Health Plans to Improve the Quality of Health Care
Reprinted from the *Journal of Health Economics* (2008), 27(5): 1182–1195, with the permission of Elsevier.

Chapter 6: Gold and Silver Health Plans: Accommodating Demand Heterogeneity in Managed Competition
Reprinted from the *Journal of Health Economics* (2011), 30: 1011–1019, with the permission of Elsevier.

Chapter 7: Making Medicare Advantage a Middle-Class Program
Reprinted from the *Journal of Health Economics* (2013), 32: 463–473, with the permission of Elsevier.

Chapter 1

OPTIMAL RISK ADJUSTMENT IN MARKETS WITH ADVERSE SELECTION: AN APPLICATION TO MANAGED CARE

Jacob Glazer* and Thomas G. McGuire[†,‡]

*Faculty of Management, Tel Aviv University,
Gertner Institute for Health Policy Research,
Tel Aviv, Israel
glazer@post.tau.ac.il

[†]Department of Economics,
Boston University, Boston, MA 02215
tmcguire@bu.edu

It is well known that adverse selection causes distortions in contracts in markets with asymmetric information. Taxing inefficient contracts and subsidizing the efficient ones can improve market outcomes (Bruce C. Greenwald and Joseph E. Stiglitz, 1986), although regulators rarely seem to implement tax and subsidy schemes with adverse-selection motives in mind. Contracts are often complex and "incomplete," and it is the "inefficient" elements of the contract that are difficult to verify and hence tax or subsidize. This is precisely the reason that in health insurance markets, rather than subsidizing *contracts*, regulators and payers contend with adverse selection by taxing and subsidizing the price paid to insuring health plans on the basis of observable characteristics of the *persons* joining the plan — a practice known as "risk adjustment."

_____

[‡]McGuire's research was supported by Grant K05 MHO1263 from the National Institute of Mental Health. We thank Randy Ellis, Richard Frank, Marty Gaynor, Hsien-Ming Ling, Albert Ma, Joseph Newhouse, Michael Riordan, and Wynand P. M. M. van de Ven for helpful discussions. Advice from two referees is gratefully acknowledged. The authors alone are responsible for the analysis and conclusions.

Risk-adjusted premiums are paid to "managed-care" plans — plans that ration care by management, rather than by conventional approaches like coinsurance and deductibles, and offer a bundle of characteristics (quality, access for many services) that is fundamentally outside the scope of direct regulation. Selection-related incentives threaten the efficiency and fairness of this organization of health insurance markets by inducing plans to distort the quality of the services they offer to discourage high-cost persons from joining the plan. As managed care becomes the predominant source of health care for residents of the United States and many other countries, payers attempt to address this incentive by setting a risk-adjusted price that pays more for more-expensive enrollees.[1]

As it is conventionally practiced, risk adjustment sets prices for people proportional to their expected cost based on observable characteristics. The federal Medicare program, for example, has used age, sex, welfare status, and county-of-residence adjusters to set prices to managed-care plans.[2] To convey how what we term "conventional" risk adjustment works, suppose age is the risk adjuster for a Medicare population over 65. If it is determined that the 75- to 84-year-old population costs 20 percent more than the overall average in Medicare, the assumption in conventional risk adjustment is that the premium paid to plans for someone in this group should be 20 percent above the average.

We fundamentally disagree that this is the right way to think about and do risk adjustment. We argue that risk adjustment should be viewed

---

[1]For representative discussions in the U.S. contexts, see Joseph P. Newhouse (1994), David M. Cutler (1995), and Alain C. Enthoven and Sarah J. Singer (1995). Risk adjustment was to be part of President Clinton's proposed healthcare reform. See also Netanyahu Commission (1990) for Israel, Rene C. J. A. van Vliet and Wynand P. M. M. van de Ven (1992) for The Netherlands, and Donald W. Light (1998) for Ireland. Risk adjustment is an integral part of many state-based health-reform proposals centering on the poor and uninsured. For a discussion of these reforms, see John Holohan *et al.* (1995).

[2]Medicare's risk-adjustment system is called the average adjusted per capita cost (AAPCC), and is used to pay HMOs for Medicare beneficiaries that choose to join. Medicare calculates the expected cost in the unmanaged fee-for-service sector for a beneficiary based on the above- mentioned characteristics, and then pays 95 percent of this to the HMO. A substantial amount of favorable risk selection by HMOs not captured by these factors has taken place within the Medicare program. See Harold S. Luft (1995) and Katherine Swartz (1995). Medicare is revising its risk-adjustment policy to moderate the impact of geographic adjusters, and to add indicators of diagnosis from previous hospitalizations. See Medicare Payment Advisory Commission (1998).

as a way to set prices for different individuals, to address adverse-selection problems. Solving for prices in an explicit optimizing framework, rather than simply paying according to average costs, magnifies the power of risk-adjustment policies. Specifically, we show in this paper that conventional risk adjustment is never the optimal policy for a regulator in a market with asymmetric information. Furthermore, we solve for alternative weights on persons' observable characteristics that improve the efficiency of the market for health plans in relation to conventional risk adjustment.

This paper presents a model of the market for managed-care plans in which an individual's true health-cost risk, which we refer to as an individual's "type," is private information. A regulator can use observable characteristics (e.g., age), which are correlated with type and which we refer to as "signals," to pay plans. In these terms, conventional risk adjustment pays, for each enrollee, expected cost given the signal. Conventional risk adjustment attenuates the inefficiency that results from adverse selection, but does not make the best use of the information contained in the signal. Optimal risk adjustment pays higher than conventional risk adjustment for persons with the "bad" signal (the old), and lower than conventional risk adjustment for persons with the "good" signal (the young), a result that we contend is general and of practical importance to health policy in the United States and other countries. "Optimal" risk adjustment, of course, can fully solve the adverse-selection problem only in a simple model. We present such a model to clarify the properties of the idea we are proposing. The main point of the paper, however, is this: in comparison to conventional risk adjustment, the "overpayment" policy we advocate can improve the efficiency properties of health insurance markets in realistic contexts.

The intuition behind our finding is as follows: Consider a plan's incentive to provide a service that might attract the sick "types" in the population. The "service" might be care for cancer, which could be done at a higher or lower quality. The plan evaluates the costs and revenues brought in by providing a higher-quality service. Conventional risk adjustment, because of the weak empirical association of costs with signals at the individual level, cannot do much to raise the premiums paid for the high-cost types who value cancer care. (Medicare's four variables mentioned earlier, for instance, explain only about 1 percent of health cost variance in the elderly.) Under conventional adjustment, the plan is likely to have strong incentives to underprovide care for cancer to discourage high-cost types from joining. Note, however, that the group of high-cost types contains relatively more old people. Optimal risk adjustment can pay more for enrolling high-cost types by giving a heavy weight ("overpaying") for the old, thereby rewarding the plan for spending on cancer care. Our simple insight is that the payment weight on age may be chosen for its incentive properties, and need not — indeed should not — be the same as the coefficient on age from a regression explaining average cost.

1. RISK ADJUSTMENT AND MANAGED CARE

Recently, managed care has supplanted coverage policy (deductibles, copayments, limits, coverage exclusions) as the main control on moral hazard in employment-based health insurance and many public programs.[3] Managed care is a set of strategies health plans use to direct the quality and quantity of health care provided to their enrollees, including limitation of the hospitals and physicians a patient may see for treatment or drugs the patient may take, specification of clinical protocols to be followed in the case of certain illnesses, application of criteria for access to services, limitations on authorized length of stay or visits, and so on (Institute of Medicine, 1989). A managed-care plan integrates the health insurance and health care functions (Joseph P. Newhouse, 1996) and, as the name suggests, influences the quality of care through internal management processes largely immune from direct regulation.

Even though most of the literature emphasizes managed care as a device to control moral hazard [for a recent empirical study, see Dana Goldman *et al.* (1995)], a health plan can also use managed care to affect the plan's risk selection.[4] Newhouse (1996) writes that, in spite of regulations

---

[3]Virtually all private health insurance and Medicaid plans include some elements of managed care. About 75 percent of the privately insured population are in managed care according to Gail A. Jensen et al. (1997). The Health Care Financing Administration's website reports that as of 1996, 40 percent of the Medicaid population were in managed care, up from 29 percent just the year before. The largest group that has been slow to enter managed care is the elderly in Medicare, just 14 percent at the end of 1997 (Medicare Payment Advisory Commission, 1998) but this number also has been increasing rapidly of late.

[4]Attendees at a conference on risk selection noted that a health plan has an incentive to select professional staff (including type and number) and invest in facilities to encourage favorable selection (Anne K. Gauthier *et al.*, 1995). Luft (1995, p. 27) observes that regulation can deal with some elements of a plan's tactics to attract good risks, like coverage policy, but regulation cannot prevent competition for good risks on the basis of "quality."

requiring plans to offer "open enrollment," plans

> Can alter their product to influence [enrollee] choice.... Their staffing
> may discourage some types of risks and encourage others; for example,
> they may stint on oncologists (cancer specialists) but have numerous
> pediatricians (families with children are better risks). Staffing choices
> seem especially hard to regulate, because of numerous sensible opportu-
> nities for substituting less highly trained personnel for specialists. They
> could offer incentives to gatekeeper physicians not to refer patients to
> specialists, thereby discouraging enrollment by the chronically ill.

Another form of adverse selection takes place when a health plan discriminates in favor of or against particular applicants. If a plan knows that the expected costs of an applicant are different from the premium the plan gets if the person joins, the plan may encourage or discourage that individual from joining. An extreme example is simply denying enrollment to an applicant likely to be unprofitable. Seeking favorable risks is often referred to as "cream skimming" (see van de Ven and van Vliet, 1992), whereas seeking to shed bad risks is called "dumping" (Ching-to Albert Ma, 1994; Randall P. Ellis, 1998). Regulation can forbid these risk-selection activities, by, for example, requiring open enrollment, but subtle forms of risk selection of this form are probably hard to eradicate.

The presence of adverse selection in health insurance has been recognized for a long time, and evidence continues to accumulate attesting to its empirical importance. Data from the federal Medicare program indicate that the typical Medicare beneficiary joining a managed-care plan has costs 35 percent lower in the year before joining than his/her nonjoining counterpart; the typical beneficiary leaving a plan has costs 60 percent higher than a nonjoiner (Physician Payment Review Commission, 1997). In the case of a private employer, David M. Cutler and Sarah Reber (1998) contend that the most generous plan fell victim to an adverse-selection-induced "premium death spiral." At the same time, there have been few formal analyses of adverse selection in a context of competing health plans, and of the role of risk adjustment in correcting misallocations. Cutler and Richard Zeckhauser (1998), in an environment without risk adjustment, analyze the employer's problem of setting contributions to health plan choices, when employees differ in their costs and in their tastes for more- or less-generous plans. Plans' characteristics are regarded as given, and enrollment prices are assumed to be set by plans at the average cost of all enrollees in a plan. Employees joining a plan pay the difference between the plan's average cost and the employer's contribution to the plan. The

efficiency issue addressed in that paper is how the employer's subsidy policy
serves enrollees' taste to sort among more- or less-generous plans. In an
observation akin to Greenwald and Stigliz (1986), Cutler and Zeckhauser
note the efficiency value of an employer contribution that varies with plan
generosity. Subsidizing expensive plans substitutes for risk adjustment,
because it ends up paying more for more-expensive employees who tend
to choose the generous plan. Tracy Lewis and David Sappington (1996)
consider the incentives to cream skim when a health plan may gain private
information about a person's health risk by incurring a screening cost. If this
screening cost is sufficiently low, Lewis and Sappington show that it will be
optimal for the principal to offer a menu of contracts to the plan to induce
the plan to reveal the true "type" of its enrollees. Their analysis applies
to a much different information structure and regulatory environment than
that considered here.

The literature on risk adjustment consists almost exclusively of empirical research on the statistical determinants of health costs.[5] Current
research on risk adjusters focuses on clinical information such as diagnosis
and health care use in past periods as well as demographics. See, for
example, Ellis *et al.* (1996). Empirical models that use lagged values of
components of past health care costs explain less than 10 percent of the
variance in health care expenditures at the individual level, leaving many
observers pessimistic about how well conventional risk adjustment can deal
with selection incentives.[6]

2. THE MODEL

Suppose that there are two types of consumers L and H, who can contract
two illnesses a and c. Illness a we call an acute illness and both types of
people have the same probability of contracting this illness. To simplify the
presentation, we normalize the probability of each type contracting illness
a to 1. The two types are distinguished in their probability of contracting
the chronic illness, illness c. Let P_i, $i \in \{H, L\}$, denote the probability that
a person of type i contracts illness c. Then, $P_H > P_L > 0$. The proportion
of H types in the population is λ.

[5]For a summary of some of the empirical literature on risk adjustment, see van de Ven
and Ellis (2000).
[6]A risk-adjustment system needs to explain only the "predictable" part of the variance
in health costs. Consumers or insurers can act only on something they know. Existing
empirical risk adjusters, however, are not regarded as coming very close to this standard.
See Newhouse (1996) for review and discussion.

If a person (of either type) has illness j, $j \in \{a, c\}$, his/her utility from treatment will be increased by $v_j(m_j)$, where m_j is the dollar value of resources devoted to treat this illness, $v'_j > 0$ and $v''_j < 0$. Thus, we make the simplifying assumption that the benefits from treatment are independent of one another and the same for all people. If a person has both illnesses, utility will simply be increased by $v_a(m_a) + v_c(m_c)$.

We assume plans have no copayments to focus on the key aspect of managed care. A contract will thus be of the form (m_a, m_c, r), where r is the premium the consumer pays. Later on, we allow for a regulatory policy in which the consumers do not pay premiums directly to plans. In such a case, regulation can introduce a difference between the premium the *consumer pays* and the premium the *plan receives* for that consumer. In such cases, the "contract" (m_a, m_c, r) will always refer to the premium the consumer pays.

Given some contract (m_a, m_c, r), type i's expected utility, if he/she chooses this contract, will be

$$V_i(m_a, m_c, r) = v_a(m_a) + P_i v_c(m_c) - r, \quad \text{for } i = H, L. \tag{1}$$

We thus assume no income effects (and no risk aversion).[7]

2.1. *The Socially Desired Contract*

The regulator is concerned with the efficiency and equity of markets for health insurance. Efficiency will be judged in terms of the degree of managed care (which in turn determines treatment). The health plan sets the level of care that will be provided to a patient if he/she becomes ill. With respect to equity, the regulator's goal is to distribute the burden of health care costs equally among the healthy and the sick.[8] (We ignore differences in income in our model.) "Community rating" health insurance is one way to achieve this objective. Equalizing the cost of health insurance to all could be viewed as a form of social insurance, insuring individuals against the risk of being

---

[7]We disregard the option to buy no insurance contract at all, and simply assume that premiums never drive consumers out of the pool. Such an assumption readily applies to cases of national health policy where the "premium" to the consumer takes the form of a compulsory tax (and cannot be avoided by not choosing a plan) or to an employer's health benefit plan where the worker's "premium" takes the form of a fringe benefit (and also cannot be avoided).

[8]This involves a redistribution accomplished through taxes or some other collective financing mechanism between the healthy and the sick. Our results about optimal risk adjustment would continue to hold for other feasible redistributions, including no redistribution through regulation.

an unhealthy type, and reinterpreted as an efficiency objective. Having noted this interpretation, however, we will continue to refer to equalizing the financial burden of illness as an "equity" objective.

The efficient level of managed care equalizes the marginal benefit of treatment to its marginal cost, 1. Thus, we define m_a^* and m_c^*, the efficient levels of treatment for the two diseases as follows:

$$v_a'(m_a^*) = 1,$$
$$v_c'(m_c^*) = 1. \tag{2}$$

High- and low-risk types have different probabilities of becoming ill, but once ill, receive the same utility from treatment. Thus, the efficient level of managed care and treatment for each illness is the same for both types.

Next, define the premium r^*:

$$r^* = m_a^* + [\lambda P_H + (l - \lambda)P_L]m_c^*. \tag{3}$$

r^* is the cost of a contract offering managed care of (m_a^*, m_c^*) averaged across the entire population.

The efficient and fair allocation will be called the "socially desired" allocation. The *socially desired contract* is (m_a^*, m_c^*, r^*). This contract provides the efficient level of managed care. Both types pay the same premium r^*, and thus the equity goal is achieved as well. Low-risk types subsidize the high-risk types. It is easy to confirm that a plan attracting a random distribution of the population will break even with this contract.[9]

2.2. Risk Adjusters

Suppose that the regulator and the plans get some signal about each consumer's type. Some proposed risk adjusters, such as evidence of health care utilization in prior periods, could be controlled by an individual or a plan and, therefore, subject to moral hazard. We disregard this feature of some signals, and assume the signal is entirely exogenous. The signal s can take a value of 0 or 1. The signal contains information in the sense that a type H person is more likely than a type L person to get a signal of value 1. From time to time we refer to 0 as the "good" signal, and 1 as the "bad" signal. In general, the signal is imperfect. Some L types get

---

[9] As we later show, all of our results regarding optimal risk adjustment will hold if the regulator only wished to implement the efficient levels of care (m_a^* and m_c^*), ignoring redistribution.

a signal 1, and some H types get a signal 0. Let q_i, $i = H, L$, be the probability that consumer of type i gets a signal with a value of 1. We assume $1 \geq q_H > q_L \geq 0$. With a perfect signal, $q_H = 1$ and $q_L = 0$. The probability of getting signal of value 0 is just $1 - q_i$ for each type.

Let λ_s be the posterior probability the consumer is of type H given the signal s, $s = 0, 1$. Since the signal is informative, using Bayes' rule one can show that: $1 \geq \lambda_1 > \lambda > \lambda_0 \geq 0$. Thus, if a consumer got the signal 1, that person is more likely be of type H than if he/she got the signal 0. When the signal is fully informative, we have $\lambda_1 = 1$ and $\lambda_0 = 0$. Let

$$\mathbf{P_s} = P_H \lambda_s + P_L(l - \lambda_s), \quad \text{for } s = 0, 1 \tag{4}$$

and

$$\mathbf{r_s} = m_a^* + \mathbf{P_s} m_c^*, \quad \text{for } s = 0, 1. \tag{5}$$

$\mathbf{P_s}$ is the probability that a person with signal s will contract illness c and $\mathbf{r_s}$ is the expected health care costs of such a person at the efficient levels of care. Clearly, $\mathbf{P_1} > \mathbf{P_0}$ and $\mathbf{r_1} > \mathbf{r_0}$. Hereafter, variables representing probabilities and premia will be bold typeface when they refer to values conditioned on signals, and will be regular typeface when they refer to true types. $\mathbf{r_s}$ is what we later refer to as the "conventional" risk adjuster. One can readily confirm that if plans are paid in this way, and consumers are randomly distributed across plans, plans break even providing the optimal levels of care. This "pooling," however, does not constitute an equilibrium.

2.3. *Equilibrium*

We assume that each plan can offer only one contract, and that each consumer chooses only one contract. Our definition of competitive equilibrium is similar to that of Michael Rothschild and Stiglitz (1976). A *competitive equilibrium* is a set of contracts such that, when consumers choose contracts to maximize expected utility, (i) no contract in the equilibrium set makes negative expected profits; and (ii) there is no contract outside the equilibrium set that, if offered, will make a positive profit.[10]

---

[10]It is well known that in this type of model, if the proportion of the L types is large enough, a competitive equilibrium may not exist. We shall study the competitive equilibrium under several informational assumptions. In some cases an equilibrium may not exist, whereas in some others an equilibrium does exist but it is not the socially desired one. However, under the risk-adjustment policies we suggest, an equilibrium always exists, and it is always the socially desired one.

Consumers know their type, whereas the regulator and the plans observe only the signal defined previously about consumers' type. The assumption that consumers "know their type" is not at all restrictive. One need not interpret this assumption literally. A refined interpretation is that consumers have some additional signal about their expected health costs that is not available to the regulator. Consumers may know their family medical history, for example, and a regulator may be unable to use this in premium regulation.

Furthermore, it is not really important what the regulator knows or does not know — what is important is what is used in the risk adjustment system. Many informative signals about health care costs may be "known," but may not be suitable for use in premium regulation for various reasons. One important reason that a signal may not be used is that it is subject to moral hazard. Some empirical research on risk adjusters studies how health care use in past periods predicts health care use in the future. In general, past health care use is a better predictor than sociodemographic factors. The obvious problem with past health care use as a risk adjuster is that a plan or a consumer has incentives to manipulate use to affect the plan's payment. Although past use may not be suitable for a risk adjuster, it is known to the consumer (and plan), and even may be known to the regulator. It is irrelevant to the impact of premium regulation whether the regulator "knows" past use, so long as it is not part of the risk-adjustment system. Thus, our result in this section applies to a wide range of important and relevant situations in which the consumer knows more information about his/her expected health care costs than the regulator uses in a risk-adjustment system.

We start the analysis by examining the market equilibrium when no regulation takes place. We then consider the impact of the "conventional" form of risk adjustment, and finally, solve for the optimal risk-adjustment policy.

Since signals are observed by plans, in the unregulated case, plans can condition their contract on the consumer's signal. In principle, a plan can offer a contract only to those who got the signal 0 but not 1, or vice versa. One should, therefore, analyze separately the equilibrium contracts in each of the two "markets": the one that serves those who got the signal 0 and the one that serves those who got the signal 1. We show, however, that this separation is artificial since signals are completely ignored by plans in equilibrium and the only thing that affects the contract a consumer obtains in equilibrium is his/her type.[11]

Let us assume that there are two markets and consider first the market for those who got the signal 0. Equilibrium in the unregulated case will be similar to the standard Rothschild-Stiglitz one. Consumers of type H will purchase their best (full information) contract, namely the contract (m_a^*, m_c^*, r_H^*), where m_a^* and m_c^* have been defined previously and are the efficient levels of quality for the acute and chronic illness, respectively, and $r_H^* = m_a^* + P_H m_c^*$. The contract for the L types is their best separating contract — the zero-profit contract that maximizes the utility of the L types subject to the contract not being preferred by the H types. Solving this maximization problem (a complete proof is given in the Appendix), one can show that type L consumers purchase the contract (m_a^*, m_c', r_L'), where $m_c' < m_c^*$ and $r_L' = m_a^* + P_L m_c'$.

Note that the L types get a contract with the efficient level of acute care, but less than the efficient level of chronic care, and pay a premium lower than that paid by the high-cost types.[12] Even though the premium is lower, the H types do not purchase the contract that L types purchase, since the reduction in premium is not enough to compensate them for the reduction in the coverage for illness c.

One can see that the fact that consumers got signal 0 is completely ignored in equilibrium. In a similar way it can be shown that in the market for those who got signal 1, equilibrium contracts depend only on the consumer's type and are independent of the signal. Furthermore, the contracts are precisely the same contracts as those obtained in the 0 signal market. The reason that signals are ignored in equilibrium is that what really affects plans' profit and consumers' utility are consumers' types. The

---

[11]It should be mentioned, however, that the conditions for a separating equilibrium to exist are different in the presence of signals. Without signals, a separating equilibrium will exist if the proportion of the type L consumers, in the entire population, is not too large, since, otherwise, a plan may enter offering a contract that attracts both types and makes a positive profit. In the presence of signals, the condition for a separating equilibrium to exist is that *within each signal group* the proportion of the type L consumers is not too large.

[12]All the "distortion" in the contract for the low-cost types is in the level of managed care for the chronic illness here because of our assumption of separability of the benefits of the two illnesses and the absence of risk aversion. In general, the level of managed care would be distorted for both illnesses for the low-cost types. Some further analysis and discussion regarding these results are provided in the Appendix.

signal is nothing but a piece of information about the type. Since consumers know their type and since plans know that consumers choose contracts according to their type, signals are ignored.

This equilibrium is inefficient because the low-cost types do not get the efficient level of care, and unfair as we have defined it because the high-cost types are not subsidized by the low-cost types.

2.4. Regulation

Our next purpose is to see whether regulation can improve on the unregulated equilibrium and implement the socially desired outcome. As already noted, we assume that managed care cannot be regulated directly.[13]

Suppose, first, that the regulator does not use risk adjustment and simply sets the premium at r^*. The regulator stipulates that plans must accept all applicants. Thus, each plan chooses a combination (m_a, m_c), consumers choose plans, and each consumer pays r^* to the plan. In this case, if λ is sufficiently small, an equilibrium will not exist; however, if λ is sufficiently large, equilibrium will exist, and it will be characterized by two contracts: H types purchase the contract

$$(m_{aH}, m_{cH}, r^*) = \operatorname{argmax} v_a(m_a) + P_H v_c(m_c) \qquad (6)$$

subject to $m_a + P_H m_c - r^* = 0$, where r^* is given by (3), and L types purchase the contract

$$(m_{aL}, m_{cL}, r^*) = \operatorname{argmax} v_a(m_a) + P_L v_c(m_c) \qquad (7)$$

subject to $m_a + P_L m_c - r^* = 0$, where r^* is given by (3), and

$$V_H(m_a, m_c, r^*) = V_H(m_{aH}, m_{cH}, r^*).$$

The equilibrium is described in Figure 1. The lines $r^{*^i}, i = H, L$, represent all combinations of (m_a, m_c) that will break even if a plan attracts only consumers of type i, each paying premium r^*. The points $i, i = H, L$, depict the equilibrium levels of care of a person of type i. The point D

---

[13] Our approach in this respect is the same as James Baumgardner's (1991) model of a managed care organization, and similar to the many papers concerned with the regulation of health care that assume a hospital or a health plan offers a "quality" of care, which is prohibitively costly to regulate directly [e.g., Ma (1994) or William P. Rogerson (1994)]. This is obviously an extreme assumption; some elements of quality can be regulated. However, as long as some dimensions of quality cannot be regulated, our results will be of interest.

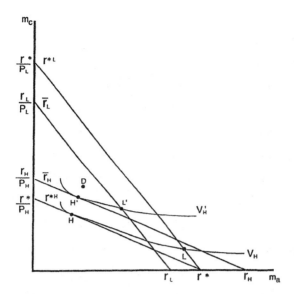

Figure 1. Equilibrium with conventional risk adjustment.

depicts the socially desired levels of care. We can see, therefore, that setting the premium at r^* does not implement the socially desired outcome.

Since setting the premium at r^* does not implement the socially desired outcome, the question arises as to whether risk adjustment can help. Risk adjusters will depend on the signal since this is the only additional information that the regulator can use about consumers' type. The natural risk-adjustment policy to consider first is conventional risk adjustment. We consider conventional risk adjustment in the case in which everyone pays r^* and the regulator enforces an open enrollment policy. To be explicit, the model of conventional risk adjustment we analyze can be described in the following four stages:

Stage 1. All consumers pay the regulator r^*.
Stage 2. Plans choose levels of care (m_a, m_c).
Stage 3. Consumers choose plans; plans must accept every applicant.
Stage 4. The regulator pays the plans; for each applicant who received signal s, $s = 0, 1$, the plan receives the conventionally risk-adjusted premium $\mathbf{r_s}$, where $\mathbf{r_s}$ is given by (5).

Under the preceding policy, equilibrium consists of two contracts. H-type consumers, like all consumers pay r^*, and get m'_{aH} and m'_{cH} defined as follows:

$$(m'_{aH}, m'_{cH}) = \operatorname{argmax} v_a(m_a) + P_H v_c(m_c), \tag{8}$$

subject to $m_a + P_H m_c - r_H = 0$, where r_H is given by [14]

$$q_H \mathbf{r_1} + (1 - q_H)\mathbf{r_0} = r_H.$$

L-type consumers get m'_{aL} and m'_{cL}, where

$$(m'_{aL}, m'_{cL}) = \operatorname{argmax} v_a(m_a) + P_L v_c(m_c), \tag{9}$$

subject to $m_a + P_L m_c - r_L = 0$, where r_L is given by

$$q_L \mathbf{r_1} + (1 - q_L)\mathbf{r_0} = r_L,$$

and

$$v_a(m_a) + P_H v_c(m_c) = v_a(m'_{aH}) + P_H v_c(m'_{cH}).$$

In Figure 1, the zero-profit line for a plan attracting only the high-cost types will shift outward relative to the no-risk adjustment case, and to compensate, the zero-profit line for a plan attracting only the low-cost types will shift inward by the risk adjustment. These lines are labeled $\bar{r}_H$ and $\bar{r}_L$, respectively, in Figure 1, with the "bars" over the premiums for the high- and low-cost types, indicating that these are the average premiums plans would receive in the presence of conventional risk adjustment. The new equilibrium will be a separating equilibrium, given the zero-profit lines altered by risk adjustment.

Because all consumers pay r^*, they will simply choose the plan that maximizes their expected benefits. All H-type consumers will choose the same plan in equilibrium, the plan that maximizes their expected utility given the average per-person payment to the plan r_H, which is greater than r^* because of risk adjustment and because H types are more likely to get the signal 1. A plan that attracts the H types will offer a combination of managed care levels that maximizes their expected utility given that it breaks even with an expected payment of r_H. A plan that attracts the

---

[14]Recall that q_i is the probability that a person of type i, $i = L, H$ gets a signal of value 1. A health plan getting consumers of type H only would have a share q_H of its enrollees with a signal of 1 and $(1 - q_H)$ with signal zero. With conventional risk adjustment paying premiums $\mathbf{r_0}$ and $\mathbf{r_1}$ for consumers getting the signals 0 and 1, respectively, the plan attracting H types would receive only an average payment of r_H, where this average premium is defined in the text. A similar formula applies to r_L. Since $q_H > q_L, r_H > r_L$.

L types will offer the best combination to those consumers, given that it breaks even at a premium of r_L, and given it does not attract the H types. Solving (8) one can see that $m'_{aH} < m^*_a$ and $m'_{cH} < m^*_c$. Thus, under conventional risk adjustment, H types get *less than* the efficient levels of care. Solving (9), one can see that $m'_{aL} > m^*_a$ and $m'_{cL} < m^*_c$. Thus, the L types also do not get the efficient levels of care.

We can see, therefore, that the forces that break the efficient pooling equilibrium when premiums are not risk adjusted will also break the efficient pooling equilibrium when premiums are conventionally risk adjusted. Since conventional risk adjustment does not pay expected cost given type, plans will try to attract the low-cost types within each signal group.

In Figure 1, the points H' and L' depict the levels of care of types H and L, respectively, in equilibrium under the conventional risk adjustment, and V'_H is the indifference curve of a type H consumer in equilibrium. Although conventional risk adjustment can improve the efficiency of the equilibrium in insurance markets with managed care, it is not the best the regulator can do with the information available.

2.5. *Optimal Risk Adjustment*

As just shown, conventional risk adjustment redistributes some, but not enough, resources from the low-cost to the high-cost types. In Figure 1, this redistribution appears as a shift in the zero-profit lines relative to the zero-profit lines in the no-risk adjustment case. As we now go on to show, the regulator may shift the zero-profit lines even further than is implied by conventional risk adjustment, by "overpaying" for a consumer who got the signal 1, compensated by "underpaying" for consumers who got the signal 0, and by so doing, bring the market closer to the socially desired outcome. "Overpaying" and "underpaying" are in comparison to the conventional risk-adjustment premiums. In fact, an optimal risk adjustment can be constructed so as to implement precisely the socially desired bundle of services.

Let

$$r^*_H = m^*_a + P_H m^*_c \tag{10}$$

$$r^*_L = m^*_a + P_L m^*_c, \tag{11}$$

where r^*_H and r^*_L are the expected costs of the efficient levels of managed care provided to consumers of types H and L, respectively. Let $\mathbf{r^*_o}$ and $\mathbf{r^*_1}$

be the solution of the following two equations:

$$q_H \mathbf{r_1^*} + (1 - q_H)\mathbf{r_o^*} = r_H^*, \tag{12}$$

$$q_L \mathbf{r_1^*} + (1 - q_L)\mathbf{r_o^*} = r_L^*. \tag{13}$$

These are two linear equations with two unknowns, $\mathbf{r_1^*}$ and $\mathbf{r_o^*}$. So long as $q_H > q_L$, which will be the case so long as the signal is at all informative, there will be a solution for $\mathbf{r_1^*}$ and $\mathbf{r_o^*}$. The premiums $\mathbf{r_s^*}$, $s = 0, 1$, are the optimal risk-adjustment premiums, as is proven in the following proposition.

Proposition 1. *The regulator can achieve the socially desired outcome by the following policy.*[15]

Stage 1. All consumers pay the regulator r^*.
Stage 2. Plans choose levels of care (m_a, m_c).
Stage 3. Consumers choose plans; plans must accept every applicant
Stage 4. The regulator pays the plans; for each applicant who received signal s, $s = 0, 1$, the plan receives the risk-adjusted premium $\mathbf{r_s^*}$ defined in (12) and (13).

Proof. We show that under the preceding policy, the market equilibrium is such that all plans offer the socially desired bundle of services. □

Suppose all plans offer the socially desired bundle of services (m_a^*, m_c^*) and consumers randomly choose a plan. Each plan breaks even since its expected cost per person equals the expected premium it receives per person, r^*. (A formal proof of this claim is contained in the next section.) Is there another bundle of services a plan can offer and make a positive profit? There are three cases to consider:

1. A plan can introduce another bundle that will attract both types and will make a positive profit. This, however, is impossible by the efficiency of (m_a^*, m_c^*, r^*).
2. A plan can introduce another bundle of services that will attract only the H-type consumers and will make a positive profit. By (12), if a plan attracts only the H-type consumers, the premium the plan expects to receive for each consumer is r_H^* since with probability q_H each consumer gets the signal 1 and with probability $(1 - q_H)$ he/she gets the signal 0.

---

[15]If the regulator just wishes to implement the efficient levels of care, and disregards equity objectives, stage 1 of Proposition 1 could be eliminated, and consumers would pay r_s^* directly to the plans.

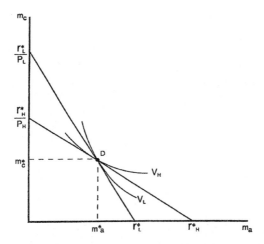

Figure 2. Equilibrium with optimal risk adjustment.

However, since the bundle (m_a^*, m_c^*) is the solution to the following problem:

$$\text{Max } V_H(m_a, m_c) \quad \text{subject to } m_a + P_H m_c - r_H^* = 0, \qquad (14)$$

a profitable deviation does not exist. [In Figure 2, the line connecting r_H^* on the horizontal axis and r_H^*/P_M on the vertical axis represents the zero-profit line of a plan that attracts only the H-type consumers and the point D is the solution to the maximization problem (14).]

3. A plan can offer a contract that will attract only the L-type consumers and will make a positive profit. If a plan attracts only the L types, the premium it expects to receive for each consumer is r_L^*, since with probability q_L each consumer gets the signal 1 and with probability $(1 - q_L)$ he/she gets the signal 0. By (13), the expected premium for each type-L consumer is r_L^*. However, since (m_a^*, m_c^*) is the solution to the following problem:

$$\text{Max } V_L(m_a, m_c) \quad \text{subject to } m_a + P_L m_c - r_L^* = 0, \quad \text{and}$$

$$V_H(m_a, m_c, r^*) = V_H(m_a^*, m_c^*, r^*), \qquad (15)$$

a profitable deviation that attracts only the L-type consumers also does not exist. [In Figure 2 the line connecting r_L^* and r_L^*/P_L represents the zero-profit line of a plan that attracts only the L types and the solution to the maximization problem (15) is at the point D.]

The essence of Proposition 1 is that it is possible to compensate for a weak signal by a tax/subsidy scheme. If signal perfectly captured type, $q_H = 1$ and $q_L = 0$, and equations (12) and (13) reduce to $\mathbf{r_1^*} = r_H^*$ and $\mathbf{r_0^*} = r_L^*$. In general, however, we can solve (12) and (13) for the optimal risk adjustment as

$$\mathbf{r_0^*} = [q_H r_L^* - q_L r_H^*]/[q_H - q_L] \tag{16}$$

and

$$\mathbf{r_1^*} = [(1 - q_L)r_H^* - (1 - q_H)r_L^*] \div [q_H - q_L]. \tag{17}$$

As the signal weakens (q_H gets closer to q_L), $\mathbf{r_1^*}$ gets larger and $\mathbf{r_0^*}$ gets smaller.[16]

Intuitively, this result can be understood as follows: If the signal is not very precise, the difference in premiums conventional risk adjustment pays for a consumer who got the signal 1 and a consumer who got the signal 0 will be small. Furthermore, the proportion of consumers who got the good signal 0 among the type-L consumers is not much larger than the proportion of consumers who got this signal in the entire population. Thus, by offering a contract that attracts only the L-type consumers, a plan can reduce its costs by a significant amount — as the L-type consumers are much cheaper — without sacrificing much on the premium it is paid per enrollee. If, on the other hand, the premium for a consumer who got the good signal is much smaller than the premium for a consumer who got the bad signal (as our optimal risk-adjustment policy dictates), the plan is severely punished for attracting only the L types, enough so as to deter the plan from taking such an action.

An important assumption in our equilibrium is that when all plans offer the same contract, consumers randomly choose a plan. This is a standard assumption under a "pooling" equilibrium but it deserves some discussion. Obviously, if consumers' preferences over plans do not depend only on the contracts the plans offer but also on some other plans' characteristics (e.g., distance), the equilibrium may not survive, as some plans may not break even. An analysis of this case is discussed later in Section III. However, it is important to observe that consumers having different preferences over

---

[16]Indeed, if q_H is too close to q_L, (16) can call for $\mathbf{r_0^*}$ to be negative. If plans must accept all applicants, there is nothing to stop the regulator within the context of our model from requiring a negative payment for consumers with the good signal, though it would obviously cause protest in a real-world context!

plans alone is not sufficient to break our equilibrium; plans must know these preferences, since, otherwise, all plans break even *ex ante* and our equilibrium survives.

One should also notice that the assumption that consumers are indifferent among plans (with the same contract) is common to most adverse-selection models that aim to abstract from issues other than asymmetric information problems. In fact, we view our assumption here as much weaker than the assumption needed for a separating equilibrium to exist under the conventional risk adjustment policy. There, it is absolutely necessary that H types and L types do not mix, even though, from the H type's point of view, all plans offer them contracts with the same expected utility.

Finally, one should observe that there exists another equilibrium under our optimal risk-adjustment policy, one that also implements the socially desired bundle of services. Under this equilibrium, all plans offer the efficient bundle (m_a^*, m_c^*), and consumers fully separate according to type: all H-type consumers go to one (or several) plans and all L types go to another (or several other). We do not view this equilibrium as interesting by itself, but rather as a demonstration of one of the main contributions of our paper. Note that this separating equilibrium is, in fact, the limit of the separating equilibria that emerge under the risk-adjustment overpayment/underpayment policy. Starting with no risk adjustment at all, a separating equilibrium exists, which is far away from the socially desired one. Conventional risk adjustment results in another separating equilibrium, which is closer to the socially desired one. (Refer to Figure 1.) By increasing the payment for the bad signal, 1, and decreasing payment for the good signal, 0, even further, the regulator can induce a separating equilibrium that is even closer to the socially desired one, and the limit of all these equilibria is the separating equilibrium with the optimal contracts.

In practical terms, this is the main point of our paper. Conventional risk adjustment moves us in the right direction, but not far enough. The empirical research that underlies conventional risk adjustment tells the regulator the good and bad signals, and gives the regulator a benchmark, the *minimum* adjustments warranted by the data. The economic reasoning laid out in this paper adds this: magnifying the adjustments implied by conventional risk adjustment further improves matters, by sharpening plans' incentives to provide the efficient level of services.

A problem with our optimal risk-adjustment mechanism is that if risk adjustment does not pay expected cost on the basis of a signal, plans have an incentive to select consumers on the basis of the signal itself. This was not possible in our analysis so far as we assumed that the regulator could enforce an open enrollment policy and a plan could compete for persons only on the basis of their type, not on the basis of their signal. However, in general, if overpayment on some signal were in place, one could assume that plans would try to provide services attractive to the "old," say, to attract these people. We do not address this problem here, because our main objective was not so much to solve for the optimal risk adjustment, but rather to show that some overpayment is desirable. We have carried out some preliminary analysis of the case where plans can also attract consumers on the basis of signals, and not only on the basis of types. One can show that this boils down to a situation where there are more types than signals, where a risk-adjustment policy that implements the first best may not exist. Conventional risk adjustment, however, will not generally be second best. Competition on the basis of the signal can be viewed as imposing a cost on the overpayment policy, but this cost is very small as "over" payment begins to be made, implying that at least some overpayment is part of the second-best policy.

3. HETEROGENEOUS CONSUMERS

In this section we dispense with the assumption that, if all plans offer the same contract, consumers are indifferent among plans. As Cutler and Zeckhauser (1998) point out, one function of a market for health plans is to accommodate consumers' tastes for different plans. In general, we can expect that consumers' choices are a function not only of the contracts plans offer, but also of some other (plans' or consumers') characteristics (e.g., distance).

In what follows we do not provide a general theory of equilibrium under consumer heterogeneity. Instead, we use results regarding optimal risk adjustment from Section II to address a much narrower question: Suppose an equilibrium exists, and in this equilibrium all plans offer the same bundle of services, but consumers do not necessarily randomize across plans. In other words, the proportion of consumers with the signal 0 (1) is not the same in all plans. How should premiums be risk adjusted so that all plans break even?[17] We show that the risk adjustment required for the

---

[17] For an equilibrium to be sustained, two conditions must hold: (1) all plans break even and (2) there is no profitable deviation. In this section, we study the risk adjustment implied by the first necessary condition alone.

plans to break even depends on the distribution of consumers (defined by types and signals) across plans. We show that except for some special cases, conventional risk adjustment will not be optimal (i.e., plans will not break even) and overpayment on one signal, compensated by underpayment on another, is generally necessary.

Suppose there is some equilibrium with two plans A and B.[18] Let a denote the number of consumers that choose plan A and let b denote the number of consumers in plan B in equilibrium. Let a_s denote the number of consumers that choose plan A and got signal s, a_i the number of consumers of type i that choose plan A, and a_{is} denote the number of type i consumers who got signal s choosing plan A in equilibrium, where $s = 0, 1$, and $i = H, L$. Define similar notation for plan B.

Let r_i denote the expected cost of type i consumers in equilibrium. We assume that all consumers in all plans receive the same levels of care in equilibrium, and hence the expected cost of a type i consumer is independent of which plan he/she purchases. Given this equilibrium, our purpose is to find the values of r_0 and r_1 so that the plans break even.

For plan A to break even, the following condition must hold:

$$a_0 r_0 + a_l r_l = a_H r_H + a_L r_L. \tag{18}$$

The left-hand side of (18) is the total premiums the plan receives, and the right-hand side is total expected cost. Since

$$a_s = a_{Hs} + a_{Ls} \quad \text{for } s = 0, 1, \tag{19}$$

and

$$a_i = a_{i0} + a_{i1} \quad \text{for } i = H, L, \tag{20}$$

we can plug (19) and (20) into (18) and get

$$a_{H0}(r_0 - r_H) + a_{L0}(r_0 - r_L) + a_{H1}(r_1 - r_H) + a_{L1}(r_1 - r_L) = 0, \tag{21}$$

and similarly for plan B we get

$$b_{H0}(r_0 - r_H) + b_{L0}(r_0 - r_L) + b_{H1}(r_1 - r_H) + b_{L1}(r_1 - r_L) = 0. \tag{22}$$

---

[18]The basic insight obtained by the analysis below will be true also in the more general case when there are more than two plans.

Equations (21) and (22) are the generalizations of equations (16) and (17) from the previous section for any distribution of types and signals across plans. The two unknowns are the risk-adjusted premiums r_0 and r_1 and the given parameters are the distribution of types across plans, $\{a_{is}, b_{is}\}$, $i = H, L$, $s \in 0, 1$, and the expected cost of the contracts for each type, r_H and r_L.

A special case to mention is when consumers are homogeneous. In this case, consumers randomize between plans, and each plan gets the same share of consumers of each type-signal combination. Thus, $a_{ij} = kb_{ij}$, where $i = H, L$ and $j = 0, 1$, and $k > 0$. Hence, equations (21) and (22) are the same equation, and become just one equation with two unknowns. This one equation has many solutions, including, as is easy to show, the conventional and optimal risk adjustment discussed earlier in Proposition 1.[19]

A simple manipulation of (21) will give us the following condition:

$$a_0 \left(\frac{a_{Ho}}{a_0} r_H + \frac{a_{Lo}}{a_0} r_L - r_0 \right) + a_1 \left(\frac{a_{H1}}{a_1} r_H + \frac{a_{L1}}{a_1} r_L - r_1 \right) = 0. \qquad (21')$$

From (21') we can report the following:

Proposition 2.   *If $(a_{H0}/a_0) = \lambda_0$, and $(a_{H1}/a_1) = \lambda_1$, then r_0 and r_1 that satisfy (21') are the conventional risk-adjusted premiums.*

The proof of Proposition 2 (and of Proposition 3 below) follows directly from equation (21'). Proposition 2 says that if in a plan, the distribution of types given a signal is the same as the distribution of types given the signal in the entire population, then conventional risk adjustment will cover the plan's costs.

Two cases that satisfy Proposition 2 are:

(i) complete pooling; and
(ii) one plan gets all consumers that have the signal 0, and the other plan gets all consumers that have the signal 1.

One can see, however, that if the condition in Proposition 2 about the distribution of types within plans does not hold, then r_0 and r_1 will not generally be the conventional risk-adjusted premiums. We now discuss this case.

One special case where the preceding condition does not hold is when $a_L = 0$ and $b_H = 0$. This is the separating equilibrium, and equations (21)

---

[19]We are grateful to a referee for insight on this point.

and (22) reduce to the equations (16) and (17) from the previous section. In equations (16) and (17), optimal risk adjustment "overpaid" for the "bad" signal, 1, and "underpaid" for the "good" signal, 0. The question we address now is whether this result is special to the case studied in Section II, or whether it is more general. In what follows, we demonstrate that overpayment for the bad signal and underpayment for the good signal is a general property of optimal risk adjustment.

Denote $(a_H/a) \equiv \lambda_a$ and $(b_H/b) \equiv \lambda_b$.

Proposition 3. *If* $\lambda_i > \lambda_j$, $i,j = a,b$, $i \neq j$, *and,* $a_{H1} = q_H a_H$, $a_{L1} = q_L a_L$, $b_{H1} = q_H b_H$, *and* $b_{L1} = q_L b_L$; *then in equilibrium* r_0 *and* r_1 *must satisfy:*

$$r_1 - r_0 = \frac{r_H - r_L}{q_H - q_L}. \tag{23}$$

Proposition 3 says that if the fraction of type H people in one plan is larger than the fraction of type H people in the other plan ($\lambda_i > \lambda_j$) and, given a type, the distribution of signals in the plan is the same as the distribution of signals given a type in the entire population, then condition (23) holds. A special case of the previous results is when $\lambda_i = 1$ and $\lambda_j = 0$, $i,j = a,b$, i.e., equilibrium is fully separating. In this case, r_0 and r_1 will satisfy (16) and (17).

Since r_H and r_L are given, condition (23) says that the smaller the difference $q_H - q_L$ (i.e., the less informative the signal), the larger the difference $r_1 - r_0$ (i.e., the greater the difference in payment between the bad signal and the good signal). We can therefore conclude that "overpayment" for the bad signal is general to the form of equilibrium.

4. DISCUSSION

Risk adjustment of health insurance premiums is part of virtually all market-based proposals to reform health care markets, in the United States and internationally. Weak correlation between observable characteristics, such as gender and age, and health costs at the individual level limit how effectively conventional risk adjustment — paying a plan in proportion to a person's expected costs conditional on the observable signals — can remedy adverse-selection-created incentives. With this paper we hope to suggest that risk adjustment is a more powerful tool than previously thought. A regulator need not confine itself to paying in proportion to expected costs. Indeed, as we have shown, conventional risk adjustment proportional to expected costs is not the best policy of risk adjustment. By viewing risk adjustment as a tax/subsidy scheme based on signals, risk adjusters can improve the allocation over that which can be achieved with conventional risk-adjustment policy. The weakness of empirical signals about health costs can be compensated for by overpaying on the basis of a bad signal, and underpaying for a good signal.

Our paper contains a model of health insurance with managed care within which we formally solve for the optimal risk-adjustment policy. Although we regard this theoretical characterization of the optimal policy to be a contribution to the analysis of risk adjustment, we want to stress here the practical importance of the idea of overpayment in relation to conventional adjusters. Starting with conventional risk adjustment, helpful but hardly dispositive, public and private regulators can take the information contained in conventional risk adjusters and improve the efficiency of health insurance markets by magnifying the weights. We want to be clear that we are not claiming that our proposed method for risk adjusting is a substitute for conventional risk adjustment. Indeed, to be implemented, our ideas rely on the existence of reliable empirical associations between signals and cost. Better conventional risk adjustment improves matters on its own (see Section II) and, furthermore, increases the confidence we would have in the overweighting of the signals correlated with higher costs implied by the theory of optimal risk adjustment developed here.

The most direct application of the ideas developed here would be to some state Medicaid programs for the poor in the United States, to countries such as Israel, or many employers, which require employees to choose a managed care plan paid by risk-adjusted capitation payments. For practical reasons, the present and likely future risk adjusters available to regulators in these systems are simple and few (Israel, for example, uses only "age"). We contend that increasing the weight on the bad signal from that derived from conventional risk adjustment would improve the efficiency of the health care system by redistributing health care spending away from services the healthy are likely to use and toward services likely to be used by the less-healthy members of the pool.

Medicare, the federal program for the elderly, has been beset by selection-related problems since the government opened the choice of managed care plans to the elderly about ten years ago. Medicare continues to experiment with the formula with which to pay plans, currently beginning a downweighting of geographical adjusters, and introducing a new more powerful signal, categories of prior health care use. (See Medicare Payment Advisory Commission, 1998.) Medicare's main complaint about its risk adjustment/managed care policy is that since the healthy elderly tend to join the managed care plans, and conventional adjusters pay only the mildly adjusted average, Medicare pays too much to managed care plans. Though not designed to address Medicare's expenditure minimization perspective, our proposed policy of over- and underpaying would help Medicare, too: the healthy will come disproportionately from those with the good signal (the young elderly), and underpaying for this group will at least partially alleviate Medicare's budget woes.

Stepping back to the more general literature on adverse selection, a tax/subsidy based on a signal is new for this literature, and may have promise for applications outside of health care. The "privatization" of public education and other social services shares key features with the market for managed health care. Fairness and efficiency of schooling would seem to matter in much the same manner as these criteria do in health care, motivating governments to subsidize consumption and to equalize ability to pay for education through voucherlike mechanisms. Students' true differences in "cost" (viewed in terms of either management costs or costs to educate to a certain standard) will be imperfectly correlated with signals like ability scores. In a recent paper, Dennis Epple and Richard Romano (1998) characterize the equilibrium of private and public schools when government sets a (non-risk-adjusted) voucher paid on behalf of heterogeneous students. Lower ability/income students get lower-quality education. A student-based tax/subsidy scheme, amounting to "risk-adjusted vouchers," seems, on the basis of our analysis, to be a promising approach to improving the efficiency and fairness of the market outcome in that case, too.

APPENDIX

In this Appendix we solve for the equilibrium contracts in the unregulated case and show that only the c service is distorted. We also provide an intuition for this result. In the unregulated case, the equilibrium contract for the L types solves the following problem:

$$\text{Max } v_a(m_a) + P_L v_c(m_c) - r \quad \text{subject to } m_a + P_L m_c - r = 0 \quad \text{(A1)}$$

$$v_a(m_a) + P_H v_c(m_c) - r = v_a(m_a^*) + P_H v_c(m_c^*) - r_H^*. \quad \text{(A2)}$$

J. Glazer and T. G. McGuire

The first-order conditions are:

$$v'_a(m_a) - \alpha - \delta v'_a(m_a) = 0 \tag{A3}$$

$$P_L v'_c(m_c) - \alpha P_L - \delta P_H v'_c(m_c) = 0 \tag{A4}$$

$$-1 + \alpha + \delta = 0. \tag{A5}$$

Substituting (A5) into (A3) we get:

$$\alpha(v'_a)(m_a) - 1) = 0. \tag{A6}$$

If $\alpha = 0$, (A4) and (A5) imply $P_L = P_H$, which is a contradiction. Thus, by (A6) it must be that $v'_a(m_a) = 1$ and hence, $m_a = m_a^*$. Substituting $m_a = m_a^*$, $r^* = m_a^* + P_H m_c^*$ and (A1) into (A2) we obtain

$$P_H v_c(m_c) - P_L m_c = P_H v_c(m_c^*) - p_H m_c^*. \tag{A7}$$

Since $P_L < P_H$, (A7) implies

$$m_c^* - m_c < v_c(m_c^*) - v_c(m_c). \tag{A8}$$

Since $v''_c < 0$ and $v'(m_c^*) = 1$ we obtain $m_c < m_c^*$.

The intuition for this result is as follows: when consumers are risk neutral, the contract (m_a, m_c, r) can, in fact, be viewed as an integration of two contracts, (m_a, r_a) and (m_a, r_c), where the first one covers acute care and the second one covers chronic care, and $r_a + r_c = r$. Since there is no asymmetry of information with respect to acute care, its contract must be the efficient one for both types, namely $m_a = m_a^*$. As for chronic care, since there is asymmetric information regarding the consumer's type, equilibrium here will take the standard Rothschild-Stiglitz form: type H consumers get the efficient contract and pay premium accordingly and the type L consumers are separated by a contract that provides less chronic care and requires a lower premium. One should note, however, that risk neutrality is what enables us to treat the contract (m_a, m_c, r) as an integration of two contracts for the two services. In the presence of risk aversion, the marginal utility depends on the premium and, hence, the premium paid for one treatment, r_c, say, may affect the consumer's utility from treatment of the other illness, m_a.

REFERENCES

Baumgardner, James. "The Interaction Between Forms of Insurance Contract and Types of Technical Change in Medical Care." *Rand Journal of Economics*, Spring 1991, *22*(1), pp. 36–53.

Cutler, David M. "Cutting Costs and Improving Health: Making Reform Work." *Health Affairs*, Spring 1995, *14*(1), pp. 161–72.

Cutler, David M. and Reber, Sarah. "Paying for Health Insurance: The Trade-Off between Competition and Adverse Selection." *Quarterly Journal of Economics*, May 1998, *113*(2), pp. 433–66.

Cutler, David M. and Zeckhauser, Richard. "Adverse Selection in Health Insurance," in Alan M. Garber, ed., *Frontiers in Health Policy Research*, Vol. 1, Cambridge, MA: MIT Press, 1998, pp. 1–31.

Ellis, Randall P. "Creaming, Skimping and Dumping: Provider Competition on the Intensive and Extensive Margins." *Journal of Health Economics*, October 1998, *17*(5), pp. 537–56.

Ellis, Randall P.; Pope, Gregory C.; Iezzoni, Lisa I; Ayanian, John Z.; Bates, David W.; Burstein, Helen and Ash, Arlene S. "Diagnosis-Based Risk Adjustment for Medicare Capitation Payments." *Health Care Financing Review*, Spring 1996, *17*(3), pp. 101–28.

Encinosa, William E. and Sappington, David E. M. "Competition Among Health Maintenance Organizations." *Journal of Economics and Management Strategy*, Spring 1997, *6*(1), pp. 129–50.

Enthoven, Alain C. and Singer, Sara J. "Market-Based Reform: What to Regulate and by Whom." *Health Affairs*, Spring 1995, *14*(1), pp. 105–19.

Epple, Dennis and Romano, Richard E. "Competition Between Private and Public Schools, Vouchers, and Peer-Group Effects." *American Economic Review*, March 1998, *88*(1), pp. 33–62.

Gauthier, Anne K.; Lamphere, Jo and Barrand, Nancy L. "Risk Selection in the Health Care Market: A Workshop Overview." *Inquiry*, Spring 1995, *32*(1), pp. 14–22.

Goldman, Dana; Hosek, Susan D.; Dixon, Lloyd S. and Sloss, Elizabeth M. "The Effects of Benefit Design and Managed Care on Health Care Costs." *Journal of Health Economics*, October 1995, *14*(4), pp. 401–18.

Greenwald, Bruce C. and Stiglitz, Joseph E. "Externalities in Economies with Imperfect Information and Incomplete Markets." *Quarterly Journal of Economics*, May 1986, *101*(2), pp. 229–64.

Holohan, John; Coughlin, Teresa; Ku, Leighton; Lipson, Debra J. and Rajan, Shruti. "Insuring the Poor Through Section 1115 Medicaid Waivers." *Health Affairs*, Spring 1995, *14*(1), pp. 199–216.

Institute of Medicine. *Controlling Costs and Changing Patient Care? The Role of Utilization Management.* Washington, DC: National Academy Press, 1989.

Jensen, Gail A.; Morrisey, Michael A.; Gaffney, Shannon and Liston, Derek K. "The New Dominance of Managed Care: Insurance Trends in the 1990's." *Health Affairs*, January/February 1997, *16*(1), pp. 125–36.

Lewis, Tracy and Sappington, David. "Cream Skimming, Cost Sharing, and Subjective Risk Adjustment in the Health Care Industry." Unpublished manuscript, University of Florida, June 1996.

Light, Donald W. "Keeping Competition Fair for Health Insurance: How the Irish Beat Back Risk-Rated Policies." *American Journal of Public Health*, May 1998, *88*(5), pp. 745–48.

Luff, Harlod S. "Potential Methods to Reduce Risk Selection and Its Effects," *Inquiry,* Spring 1995, *32*(1), pp. 23–32.

Ma, Ching-to Albert, "Health Care Payment Systems: Cost and Quality Incentives." *Journal of Economics and Management Strategy,* Spring 1994, *3*(1), pp. 93–112.

Medicare Payment Advisory Commission. *Report to Congress: Medicare Payment Policy.* Washington, DC, 1998.

Netanyahu Commission. *Report of the State Commission of Inquiry into the functioning and efficiency of the health care system.* Jerusalem: The State of Israel, August 1990.

Newhouse, Joseph P. "Patients at Risk: Health Reform and Risk Adjustment." *Health Affairs,* Spring I 1994, *13*(1), pp. 132–46.

_____. "Reimbursing Health Plans and Health Providers: Efficiency in Production Versus Selection." *Journal of Economic Literature,* September 1996, *34*(3), pp. 1236–63.

Pauly, Mark V. "Is Cream-skimming a Problem for the Competitive Medical Market?" *Journal of Health Economics,* April 1984, *3*(3), pp. 87–95.

Physician Payment Review Commission. *Risk Selection Remains Problem in Medicare.* PPRC Update No. 21, Washington, DC, July 1997.

Rogerson, William P. "Choice of Treatment Intensities by a Nonprofit Hospital under Prospective Pricing." *Journal of Economics and Management Strategy,* Spring 1994, *3*(1), pp. 7–51.

Rothschild, Michael and Stiglitz, Joseph E. "Equilibrium in Competitive Insurance Markets: An Essay in the Economics of Imperfect Information." *Quarterly Journal of Economics,* November 1976, *90*(4), pp. 629–49.

Swartz, Katherine. "Reducing Risk Selection Requires More Than Risk Adjustments." *Inquiry,* Spring 1995, *32*(1), pp. 6–10.

van de Ven, Wynand P. M. M. and Ellis, Randall P. "Risk Adjustment in Competitive Health Plan Markets," in A. J. Culyer and J. P. Newhouse, eds., *Handbook in Health Economics.* Amsterdam: North-Holland, 2000.

van de Ven, Wynand P. M. M. and van Vliet, Rene C. J. A. "How Can We Prevent Cream Skimming in a Competitive Health Insurance Market? The Great Challenge for the 90's." in Peter Zweifel and H. E. Frech, III, eds., *Health Economics Worldwide.* Dordrecht: Kluwer Academic, 1992, pp. 23–46.

van Vliet, Rene C. J. A. and van de Ven, Wynand P. M. M. "Towards a Capitation Formula for Competing Health Insurers: An Empirical Analysis." *Social Science and Medicine,* 1992, *34*(9), pp. 1035–48.

Chapter 2

MEASURING ADVERSE SELECTION IN MANAGED HEALTH CARE

Richard G. Frank

Harvard University, Harvard Medical School,
Department of Health Care Policy,
180 Longwood Avenue, Boston, MA 02115, USA
frank@hcp.med.harvard.edu

Jacob Glazer*

Tel Aviv University, Tel Aviv, Israel

Thomas G. McGuire

Boston University, Boston, MA, USA

Received 1 September 1999
Received in revised form 1 May 2000
Accepted 12 May 2000

Health plans paid by capitation have an incentive to distort the quality of services they offer to attract profitable and to deter unprofitable enrollees. We characterize plans' rationing as a "shadow price" on access to various areas of care and show how the profit maximizing shadow price depends on the dispersion in health costs, individuals' forecasts of their health costs, the correlation between use in different illness categories, and the risk adjustment system used for payment. These factors are combined in an empirically implementable index that can be used to identify the services that will be most distorted by selection incentives. ©2000 Elsevier Science B.V. All rights reserved.

JEL classification: I10

Keywords: managed health care; capitation; shadow price

*Corresponding author. Tel.: +1-617-432-0178; fax: +1-617-432-1219.

29

1. INTRODUCTION

Many countries are turning to competition among managed care plans to make the tradeoff between cost and quality in health care. In the U.S., major public programs and many private health insurance plans offer enrollees a choice of managed care plans paid by capitation.[1] Recent estimates are that 40% of the poor and disabled in Medicaid and 14% of the elderly are enrolled in managed care plans paid by capitation (Medicare Payment Advisory Commission, 1998). Medicaid figures are increasing rapidly. In private health insurance, about three-quarters of the covered population is already in some form of managed care, though in many cases, employers continue to bear some or all of the health care cost risk (Jensen *et al.*, 1997). Health policy in the Netherlands, England, and other countries shares similar essential features. Israel, for example, recently reformed its health care system so that residents may choose among several managed care plans which all must offer a comprehensive basket of health care services set by regulation. A common feature of such reforms is for plans to receive a capitation payment from the government or private payers for each enrollee.[2]

The capitation/managed care strategy relies on the idea that costs are controlled by the capitation payment and the "quality" of services is enforced by the market. The basic rationale for this health policy is the following: the capitation payment plans receive gives them an incentive to reduce cost (and quality), while the opportunity to attract enrollees gives plans an incentive to increase quality (and cost). Ideally, these countervailing incentives lead plans to make efficient choices about service quality.

Competition in the health insurance market has well known drawbacks, the most troubling one being adverse selection. As competition among managed care plans becomes the predominant form of market interaction in health care, adverse selection takes a new form which is much harder for policy to address than in conventional health insurance. With old-fashioned fee-for-service insurance arrangements, a health plan might provide good

---

[1] For representative discussions in the U.S. context, see Cutler (1995), Newhouse (1994), Enthoven and Singer (1995). See also Netanyahu Commission (1990) for Israel, and van Vliet and van de Ven (1992) for the Netherlands. For a discussion of state-level reforms in the United States, see Holohan *et al.* (1995). Van de Ven and Ellis (2000) contain a recent and comprehensive review.

[2] For a recent survey of how health plans are paid in the U.S. by all major payer groups, see Keenan *et al.* (2001).

coverage for, say, child-care, to attract young healthy families, and provide poor coverage for hospital care for mental illness. If it appeared that refusing to cover hospital care for mental illness was motivated by selection concerns, public policy could force private insurers to offer the coverage through mandated benefit legislation. As health insurance moves away from conventional fee-for-service plans, where enrollees have free choice of providers, and becomes "managed care", the mechanisms a health insurance plan uses to effectuate selection change from readily regulated coinsurance, deductibles, limits and exclusions, to more difficult-to-regulate internal management processes which ration care in a managed care plan.

Researchers focusing on the economics of payment and managed care are well aware of the issue. Ellis (1998) labels underprovision of care to avoid bad risks as "skimping." Newhouse *et al.* (1997) call it "stinting." Cutler and Zeckhauser (2000) call it "plan manipulation." As Miller and Luft (1997, p. 20) put it:

> Under the simple capitation payments that now exist, providers and plans face strong disincentives to excel in care for the sickest and most expensive patients. Plans that develop a strong reputation for excellence in quality of care for the sickest will attract new high-cost enrollees....

The flip side, of course, is that in response to selection incentives the plan might provide too much of the services used to treat the less seriously ill, in order to attract good risks. "Too much" is meant in an economic sense. A plan, motivated by selection, might provide so much of certain services that the enrollees may not benefit in accord with what it costs the plan to provide them (Newhouse *et al.*, 1997, p. 28). An important implication of this observation is capitation and managed care can be expected to generate too little care in some areas and too much in others.[3]. This leads, then, to the questions: How does a regulator know which services a managed care plan is skimping on or over-providing to affect risk selection? Even if the regulator did know, what could he or she do about it?

Motivated by these questions, public regulatory bodies and private payers have recently become interested in monitoring the quality of care

---

[3]Miller and Luft (1997) reviewed 37 studies meeting research standards of quality of care in managed care organizations paid by capitation. In comparison to care outside of capitation/managed care, quality was found to be sometimes higher and sometimes lower. However, the authors called attention to several studies showing systematically lower quality for Medicare enrollees with chronic conditions, reflecting a concern for chronic illnesses expressed by others, such as Schlesinger and Mechanic (1993)

in managed care plans. Monitoring consists of identification of measurable standards (consumer satisfaction, health outcomes, quality of inputs) against which a plan's performance is compared. There are many drawbacks to this approach from a policy and an economic standpoint. At a recent conference, observers noted that standards have proliferated, and it is difficult to find standards that are sensitive to system characteristics (Mitchell *et al.*, 1997). The standards are at best imperfect indicators of value to enrollees. Ranking the importance of different standards is largely arbitrary. Quality can be too high, as well as too low, and existing approaches are all oriented to a minimum, not a maximum standard.[4] Gathering information on many standards for many plans in a timely fashion is very expensive. Plans do not all have adequate administrative capability (Gold and Felt, 1995). Enrollees move in and out of plans, making measures based on performance at the person level difficult to implement. Rewarding a subset of quality indicators may distort performance by health plans.

In this paper we take a very different approach to address the question of how to monitor selection-related quality distortions in the market for health insurance with managed care. We start from the assumption that plans maximize profit. We show that to do so, each plan rations by, in effect, setting a service-specific "shadow" price for each service. We interpret the shadow price as characterizing the *incentives* a plan has to distort services away from the efficient level. The shadow price captures how tightly or loosely a profit maximizing plan should ration services in a particular category in its own self-interest. Once costs are normalized, we can compare shadow prices across services. Services that the plan should restrain will be characterized by higher shadow prices than services that the plan should provide generously. The shadow price is an operational concept, measurable with data from a health plan. We take the ratio of the shadow price for a particular service to some numeraire service to create a "distortion index."

The shadow price is a device to capture the myriad of strategies a plan uses to ration care, other than by demand-side cost sharing (literal prices). Shadow prices can reflect plan decisions about capacity in various

---

[4]This paper discusses selection-related incentives that could lead to quality for various services to be too high or too low. Another well-established argument from health economics also applies to the health insurance options considered here. The federal tax subsidy provided through the tax-free employer contribution to employee health insurance may lead to too high quality across the board.

service areas, such as the number of specialists in a physician network or the number of staff hired in a plan department. They could reflect the makeup of networks or payment to providers, including supply-side cost sharing or the stringency of utilization review.

After developing the shadow price measure of selection distortions and discussing the properties of services that will be over and underprovided (Section 2), we illustrate how these shadow prices can be calculated with data from a health plan (Section 3). Our purpose at this stage is not to draw conclusions about which services are distorted. To do so one needs data, just now emerging, on the behavior of managed care plans. Our purpose here is to illustrate how to calculate the shadow prices with health plan data, and to confront the issues involved in an empirical application. We go on to illustrate how our measures can be used to evaluate the efficiency properties of various strategies to deal with adverse selection, such as risk adjusting payments to managed care plans.

An analogy might be helpful at this point. Another question about the efficiency of markets is more familiar: Which firms' outputs are most distorted by monopoly power? The direct approach to answering this would be to compare the existing price of each firm to an estimate of what the price would be in a competitive market. However, since hypothesized competitive prices cannot be easily observed, more common is an indirect approach: estimate each firm's elasticity of demand. Following Lerner (1934), we could use demand elasticities to rank firms according to where output is likely to be distorted most. Demand elasticity does not *directly* measure the distortion; it simply is a measure of how bad the distortion would be under the assumption that the firm maximizes profit. In the market for managed care, the condition for profit maximization involves more than an elasticity-driven markup, but the method we use for exposing distortions is exactly analogous to Lerner's for flagging monopoly. We do not measure the distortion directly, but we do measure the strength of the economic forces creating the distortion.

Our analysis is based on a model of a profit-maximizing managed care plan competing for enrollees. We assume that the plan cannot select enrollees based on their future health care costs, either because the plan does not have this information or because there is an "open enrollment" requirement. Consumers, however, have some information about their future health care costs. The plan sets the quality of services in light of its beliefs about consumers' knowledge. We analyze the incentives of the plan to distort quality in order to attract "good" enrollees — those with low expected future health care costs in relation to the capitated payment plans are paid. We find that incentives to a plan to devote resources to services depend on the demand for that service among the plan's current enrollees, how well potential enrollees can forecast their demand for the service, whether the distribution of those forecasts is uniform or skewed in the population, the correlation of those forecasts with forecasts of other health care use, and on the risk-adjustment system used to pay for enrollees. We show how all these factors fit together into an index for each service the plan provides.

Many papers have shown that consumers choose health plans on the basis of their anticipated spending. Medicare's program for paying HMOs by capitation has been studied repeatedly in this regard. In a representative analysis, Hill and Brown (1990) find that individuals choosing to join HMOs for the first time were spending 23% less than those who do not choose to join in the period immediately prior to joining, and had a lower mortality rate in the period after joining (see also Eggers and Prihoda, 1982; Garfinkel et al., 1986; Brown et al., 1993). The finding of significant adverse selection in Medicare continues to be borne out by more recent studies (Medicare Payment Advisory Commission, 1998). Numerous other studies have also found among other populations that those choosing to join HMOs are "healthier" in some ways than those not joining (Cutler and Reber, 1998; Cutler and Zeckhauser, 2000; Glied et al., 2000; Robinson et al., 1993; Luft and Miller, 1988).

Risk-adjustment of payments to managed care plans is intended to counteract incentives to distort services. The basic idea behind risk adjustment is the following: If plans are paid more for enrollees likely to be costly, the plan will not shun these enrollees. Individuals choose plans based on what they (the individuals) can predict. A risk adjustment system that picks up the predictable part of the variance in health costs is thus able to address dangers of selection.[5] We will show below, how risk adjustment

---

[5]How much of the health care cost variance individuals can anticipate is not known. To get some idea, empirical researchers have assumed that individuals know the information contained in certain potential explanatory variables, and then investigate how much of the variance is explained by these covariates. In the most well-known of these studies, Newhouse (1989) assumes that individuals know the information contained in their individual time invariant contribution to the variance and the autoregressive component of their immediate past spending. With these assumptions individuals can predict about a quarter of the variance. He regarded this as a reasonable "minimum" of what individuals could predict. Currently available risk adjusters miss a good deal of this predictable variance. Medicare's current risk adjusters explain about 2% of total

works to affect plans' incentives to detect service quality in order to affect the risks the plan draws in a population.

2. PROFIT MAXIMIZATION IN MANAGED CARE

We describe the behavior of a health plan (such as an HMO) in a market for health insurance in which potential enrollees choose their health plan. The health plan is paid a premium (possibly risk-adjusted) for each individual that joins. Individuals differ in their need/demand for health care, and choose a plan to maximize their expected utility. "Health care" is not a single commodity but a set of services — maternity, mental health, emergency care, cardiac care, and so on. A health plan chooses a rationing or allocation rule for each service. The plan's choice of rules will affect which individuals find the plan attractive and will therefore determine the plan's revenue and costs. We assume that the plan must accept every applicant, and we are interested in characterizing the plan's incentives to ration services.

2.1. *Utility and Plan Choice*

A health plan offers S services. Let m_{is} denote the amount the plan will spend on providing service s to individual i, if he joins the plan, and let: $\boldsymbol{m}_i = \{m_{i1}, m_{i2}, \ldots, m_{iS}\}$. The value of the benefits individual i gets from the plan, $u_i(\boldsymbol{m}_i)$, is composed of two parts, a valuation of the services an individual gets from the plan, and a component of valuation that is independent of services. Thus,

$$u_i(\boldsymbol{m}_i) = v_i(\boldsymbol{m}_i) + \mu_i \tag{1}$$

where,

$$v_i(\boldsymbol{m}_i) = \sum_s v_{is}(m_{is})$$

The term v_i is the service-related part of the valuation and is itself composed of the sum of the individual's valuations of all services offered by the plan. The term $v_{is}(\cdot)$ is the individual's valuation of spending on service

---

variance; proposed refinements improve the explanatory power considerably, but only to about 9% (Ellis *et al.*, 1996; Weiner *et al.*, 1996). There remains considerable room for systematic selection that would not be captured by a payment system based on existing risk adjusters.

s, also measured in dollars, where $v'_{is} > 0$, $v''_{is} < 0$. For now, we proceed by assuming that the individual knows $v_i(\boldsymbol{m}_i)$ with certainty. Later, we consider the case when the individual is uncertain about his $v_i(\boldsymbol{m}_i)$. The non-service component is μ_i, an individual-specific factor (e.g. distance or convenience) affecting individual $i's$ valuation, known to person i. From the point of view of the plan, μ_i is unknown, but is drawn from a distribution $\Phi_i(\mu_i)$. We assume that the premium the plan receives has been predetermined and is not part of the strategy the plan uses to influence selection. Premium differences among plans (if premiums are paid by the enrollees) can be regarded as part of μ_i.

The plan will be chosen by individual i if $u_i > \bar{u}_i$, where $\bar{u}_i$ is the valuation the individual places on the next preferred plan. We analyze the behavior of a plan which regards the behavior of all other plans as given, so that $\bar{u}_i$ can be regarded as fixed. Given $\boldsymbol{m}_i$ and $\bar{u}_i$, individual i chooses the plan iff:

$$\mu_i > \bar{u}_i - v_i(\boldsymbol{m}_i).$$

For now, we assume that, for each i, the plan has exactly the same information as individual i about the individual's service-related valuation of its services, v_i, and the utility from the next preferred plan, $\bar{u}_i$. For each individual i, the plan does not know the true value of μ_i but it knows the distribution from which it is drawn. Therefore, for a given $\boldsymbol{m}_i$ and $\bar{u}_i$, the probability that individual i chooses the plan, from the point of view of the plan is:[6]

$$n_i(\boldsymbol{m}_i) = 1 - \Phi_i(\bar{u}_i - v_i(\boldsymbol{m}_i)). \tag{2}$$

2.2. Managed Care

Managed care rations the amount of health care a patient receives with minimal demand-side cost sharing, and thus without imposing much financial risk on enrollees.[7] Two approaches have been employed to model the rationing process.

In an early model of managed care, Baumgardner's (1991) plan sets a common quantity of care for persons with the same illness but who

---

[6] An alternative interpretation is that index i describes a group of people with the same $v_i(\boldsymbol{m}_i)$ function and $n_i(\boldsymbol{m}_i)$ is then the share of this group that joins the plan.

[7] Although health plans that are managed care may also use some demand-side cost sharing.

differ in severity, an approach later employed by Pauly and Ramsey (1999). These papers consider only a single illness and are concerned with the properties of quantity rationing compared to demand-side cost sharing for purposes of controlling moral hazard. Pauly and Ramsey (1999) show that some quantity setting is always part of the optimal combination of demand-side cost sharing and rationing. The plans of Glazer and McGuire (2000a) also set quantity in a two-illness model focused on adverse selection. They characterize equilibrium in the insurance market with managed care to solve for the optimal risk adjustment policy to counter selection incentives.[8]

An alternative approach to modeling managed care, used by Keeler *et al.* (1998), is to regard the plan as setting a "shadow price" — the patient must "need" or benefit from services above a certain threshold in order to qualify for receipt of services. In Keeler *et al.* (1998), demand is for one service, "health care," and the plan sets just one shadow price.[9] Here, we adopt the shadow-price approach to managed care but allow for many services in order to study selection incentives.

Let q_s be the service-specific shadow price the plan sets determining access to care for service s. A patient with a benefit function for service s of $v_{is}(\cdot)$ will receive a quantity of services, m_{is} determined by:

$$v'_{is}(m_{is}) = q_s. \tag{3}$$

Let the amount of spending determined by the equation above be denoted by $m_{is}(q_s)$. Note that (3) is simply a demand function, relating the quantity of services to the (shadow) price in a managed care plan. See Fig. 1.

The use of a shadow price as a description of rationing in managed care permits a natural interpretation of the division of responsibility between the "management" of a plan, presumably most interested in profits, and the "clinicians" in a plan who face the patients. Cost-conscious management allocates a budget or a physical capacity for a service. Clinicians working in the service area do the best they can for patients given the budget by rationing care so that care goes to the patients that benefit most. In this

---

[8]Risk adjustment can be viewed as a tax-subsidiary scheme used to equalize incentives to ration all services equally. This idea is developed in the general case of many services in Glazer and McGuire (2002).
[9]In Keeler *et al.* (1998) plans are characterized by a single price, but do not choose its level. Plans do not choose premiums or level of care and are thus inactive in terms of selection.

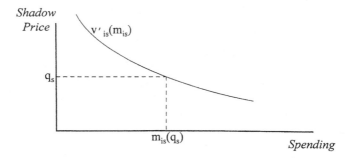

Figure 1.   Determination of spending on service s for individual i.

environment, management is in effect setting a shadow price for a service through its budget allocation. It is evident in data that individuals with the same disease get different quantities of service. The constant shadow price assumption is consistent with managed care rationing but with more care being received by patients who "need" it more.[10]

2.3. Profit and Profit Maximization

Let $q = \{q_1, q_2, \ldots, q_s\}$ be a vector of shadow prices the plan chooses and $m_i(q) = \{m_{i1}(q_1), m_{i2}(q_2) \ldots, m_{is}(q_s)\}$ be the vector of spending individual i gets by joining the plan. Define $n_i(q) \equiv n_i(m_i(q))$. Expected profit, $\pi(q)$, to the plan will depend on the individuals the plan expects to be members, the revenue the plan gets for enrolling these people, and the costs of each member. Thus,

$$\pi(q) = \sum_i n_i(q) \left[r_i - \sum m_{is}(q_s) \right], \qquad (4)$$

where r_i is the (possibly risk-adjusted) revenue the plan receives for individual i. The plan will choose a vector of shadow prices to maximize expected profit, (4). Define $\pi_i(q)$ to be the gain or loss on individual i:

$$\pi_i(q) = r_i - \sum_s m_{is}(q_s). \qquad (5)$$

---

[10] In this way the shadow price approach seems superior to the quantity setting approach in a context of a distribution of demands for a service. The shadow price method is also the "efficient" way to ration a given budget.

Given this, for one such service s (dropping the arguments q and q_s from all functions), the condition for profit maximization is:

$$\frac{d\pi}{dq_s} = \sum_i \left[\left(\frac{dn_i}{dq_s} \right) \pi_i - n_i m'_{is} \right] = 0 \tag{6}$$

Condition (6) has two parts. Consider the term $-n_i m'_{is}$. If the shadow price q_s is raised, the plan will spend less by m'_{is} on individual i if he joins the plan. This term is always positive, reflecting the savings the plan can achieve by rationing more stringently. The other term, $(dn_i/dq_s)\pi_i$, may be positive or negative for any individual. The term dn_i/dq_s is always negative, reflecting the fact that everyone will find the plan somewhat less attractive as q_s is raised. The π_i will be positive or negative, depending on whether the risk-adjusted revenue is above or below the costs the individual will incur given the rationing in the plan. The idea behind competition among managed care plans is that the first term must after summation be negative — the plan by rationing too tightly will lose profitable customers — to balance the plan's incentive to reduce services to the existing enrollees.

To see what (6) implies for various services, we make some substitutions. The change in the probability of joining can be written as the product of two derivatives:

$$\frac{dn_i}{dq_s} = \frac{dn_i}{dv_{is}} \frac{dv_{is}}{dq_s}. \tag{7}$$

From (2), dn_i/dv_{is} is simply ϕ'_i, and from (1) and (3), dv_{is}/dq_s is $q_s m'_{is}$. Assuming that the elasticity of demand for service s is the same for all individuals for every q_s, and denoting this elasticity by e_s, we get:

$$m'_{is} = \frac{e_s m_{is}}{q_s}, \tag{8}$$

for every i. Note that the assumption that for every shadow price q_s the elasticity of demand for service s is the same for all individuals does not imply, of course, that all individuals have the same demand curve for that service. It only implies that demand curves of different individuals, for a certain services, are "horizontal multiplications" of some "basic" demand function for the service. Individuals will differ in their relative demands. One interpretation of this assumption, as in Glazer and McGuire (2000), is that given someone is sick, a common function describes valuation of a service, but people differ in the probability that they become ill.

Substituting for m'_{is} from (8), we can rewrite (6) as:

$$\sum_i \left[\Phi'_i e_s m_{is} \pi_i - \frac{n_i e_s m_{is}}{q_s} \right] = 0. \tag{9}$$

Multiplying through by (q_s/e_s) and summing the terms separately,

$$q_s \sum_i \Phi'_i m_{is} \pi_i - \sum_i n_i m_{is} = 0,$$

or

$$q_s = \frac{\sum\limits_i n_i m_{is}}{\sum\limits_i \phi'_i m_{is} \pi_i}. \tag{10}$$

From (10) we can make some observations about q_s in profit maxi-mization. The numerator of (10) reflects the incentive the plan has to save money on its expected enrollees. The greater is the numerator, the larger will be q_s. The denominator describes the expected gains a plan sacrifices by losing enrollees. The denominator contains a product $m_{is}\pi_i$ weighted by the change in enrollment probability, Φ'_i. Some enrollees will be profitable, with $\pi_i > 0$ given the risk adjustment formula in use, and some will be unprofitable, with $\pi_i < 0$. The association between these gains and losses and spending will determine the value of the denominator.

For any service provided in profit maximization, the denominator of (10) must be positive, implying that in profit maximization, provision of all services on average attracts profitable enrollees. This observation echoes a conclusion from the health care payment literature where under prospective payment systems, the enrollment response, or more generally, demand response, induces a provider to supply a noncontractible input (corresponding here to q_s). See Rogerson (1994), Ma (1995), or Ma and McGuire (1997). Creating profits on the margin in this way to induce firm "effort" is inconsistent with zero profitability unless marginal costs are less than average costs or the payer uses a two-part tariff of some kind to reimburse the provider.

In a first-best allocation, a payer or regulator would induce the plan to set $q_s = 1$, leading to an equality between the marginal benefit of spending on a service and its marginal cost. Eq. (10) shows how a payer could do this for this one service by manipulating the payment r_i. For a given level of payment r_i, if q_s were too high, for example, the payer could simply increase r_i by some factor, paying more for every potential enrollee. That would raise the denominator of (10) and induce more spending. In the one service case, risk adjustment is not necessary, simply paying more for all enrollees will do. It is only if a plan manipulates quality in more than one dimension of quality that risk adjustment of premiums paid to the plan has a role in countering selection incentives.[11]

2.4. *Uncertainty*

So far we have assumed that each individual i knows with certainty his valuation of each of the s services $v_{is}(m_{is})$, and, hence, given some q, the dollar amount of the different services that will be provided to him upon joining the plan. In order to make our model more realistic and to prepare for empirical application, we shall now allow for each individual to be uncertain about his future demands for the different services. Let us suppose that each individual has a set of prior beliefs about his possible health care demands, and that the plan shares these beliefs.

Let T denote the set of possible health states of each individual and let t denote an element of T. Let $v_t = \{v_{t1}(m_{t1}), v_{t2}(m_{t2}), \ldots v_{ts}(m_{ts})\}$ denote the vector of S valuation functions for the S services, if the health state is realized to be t. We assume that for each t and s, $v_{ts}()$ satisfies the properties discussed earlier.

Each individual i is uncertain about his health state t, but has some prior distribution (beliefs) f_i over the set of possible states.[12] Let $\tilde{x}_t$ be some random variable, the value of which depends on the state t, and let f be a distribution function defined over T. Let $E_f[\tilde{x}_t]$ denote the expected value of $\tilde{x}_t$ with respect to the distribution f.

The modified model has three moves: first, the plan chooses its level of shadow prices $q = (q_1, q_2, \ldots, q_s)$, second, the individual chooses whether or not to join the plan (in a manner studied below), and finally the individual's health state is realized and services are provided.

---

[11]Risk adjustment might also need to deal with individual-specific discrimination, such as, in the extreme, outright denial of enrollees. Glazer and McGuire (2002) consider the questions of how best to design risk adjustment when quality discrimination and individual selection are both concerns.

[12]To use conventional terminology, individual i's prior beliefs, f_i, can be thought of as the individual's "type." As will be discussed in Section 3, one can make different assumptions about how an individual's prior beliefs are formed. Under some of these assumptions (e.g., beliefs are on the basis of "age" and "sex" only), several individuals may have the same prior beliefs, and hence be of the same "type." Thereafter, we will continue using the terminology "individual i", but one can think of this as "individual of type i."

For a given shadow price q_s and a valuation function v_{ts}, the plan's expenditures on this individual on service s will be $m_{ts}(q_s)$, given by:

$$v'_{ts}(m_{ts}(q_s)) = q_s.$$

$$\text{Let } \boldsymbol{v}_t(\boldsymbol{q}) = \sum_s v_{ts}(m_{ts}(q_s))$$

The individual's expected utility is:

$$\mu + E_f[\boldsymbol{v}_t(\boldsymbol{q})].$$

Let $\bar{u}_t$ denote the individual's utility if his health state is t and he chooses the next best plan. Thus, $E_f[\bar{u}_t]$ is the individual's expected utility if he chooses the alternative plan.

We assume no asymmetry of information between the plan and the individual regarding the individual's health state. Thus, the plan knows the individual's prior beliefs, f, about his future health state.[13] The plan, however, does not know the true value of μ, although it holds beliefs $\Phi(\mu)$ about its cumulative distribution.

A plan imposing shadow price $\boldsymbol{q}$ gauges the individual's likelihood of joining the plan as:

$$n_f(\boldsymbol{q}) = 1 - \Phi(E_f[\bar{u}_t - \tilde{v}_t(\boldsymbol{q})]). \tag{2'}$$

yielding an expected profit on the individual of:

$$\pi_f(\boldsymbol{q}) = n_f(\boldsymbol{q}) \left(r - E_f\left[\sum_s \tilde{m}_{ts}(q_s) \right] \right). \tag{5'}$$

The plan chooses each $\boldsymbol{q}$ to maximize expected profit. To find profit-maximizing values of $\boldsymbol{q}$, we differentiate the above with respect to $q_{s'}$:

$$\frac{d\pi_f(\boldsymbol{q})}{dq_{s'}} = \Phi' E_f[\tilde{v}'_{ts}\tilde{m}'_{ts'}] \left(r - E_f\left[\sum_s \tilde{m}_{ts} \right] \right) - n_f E_f[m'_{ts'}] \tag{6'}$$

---

[13] Although it simplifies the exposition, the assumption that the plan knows each individual's prior beliefs is much too strong for what we need. It is easy to show that all of our results will go through under a much weaker assumption: that the plan only knows the distribution of prior beliefs over the population, or, in other words, that the plan only knows the distribution of "types" in the population. This is a standard assumption in the asymmetric information literature.

Using the fact that $v'_{ts} = q_s$ for all t, and assuming that $m'_{ts} = (e_s m_{ts}/q_s)$ for all t, we get that the right-hand side of Eq. (6') becomes:

$$e_{s'}\left(\Phi'\hat{m}_{s'}\left(r - \sum_s \hat{m}\right) - \frac{n_f \hat{m}}{q_{s'}}\right), \quad \text{where } \hat{m} = E_f[\hat{m}].$$

We can now show how the plan chooses its profit maximizing shadow prices in this case. Assume a population of N individuals. Each individual i has some prior beliefs f_i over the set of possible health states. Restoring the subscript i to Eq. (6'), summing Eq. (6') over all i and setting it equal to zero, the profit maximizing q_s will be:

$$q_s = \frac{\sum_i n_i \hat{m}_{is}}{\sum_i \Phi'_i \hat{m}_{is}\left(r_i - \sum_{s'=1,\ldots,s} \hat{m}_{is'}\right)} \tag{10'}$$

where $\hat{m}_{is} = E_{fi}[\tilde{m}_{ts}]$ is individual i's *predicted* expenditures on service s, where the prediction is with respect to the individual's prior beliefs about his future expenditures on service s. Define $\hat{\pi}_i = r_i - \sum_{s=1,\ldots,s} \hat{m}_{is}$.

To investigate which shadow prices are set high relative to other shadow prices, we use Eq. (10') to construct a ratio of q_s to q'_s where s' is some other service. We simplify by abstracting from individual differences in enrollment response by assuming that $\Phi'_i = \Phi'$. This amounts to saying that an increase in the value of plan i increases the likelihood of joining for all individuals equally. Eq. (10') can now be used to write the ratio of two shadow prices, q and q'. Note that the Φ' term cancels out of this expression:

$$\frac{q_s}{q'_s} = \frac{\sum_i \hat{m}_{is'}\hat{\pi}_i \sum_i n_i \hat{m}_{is}}{\sum_i \hat{m}_{is}\hat{\pi}_i \sum_i n_i \hat{m}_{is'}}. \tag{10''}$$

There is no particular reason to expect (10'') to be equal for all service pairs unless the risk adjustment system is so good as to equalize the relative incentives to supply each service.

2.5. *The Effect of Individuals' Information*

Information plays an important role in creating distortions of adverse selection. We are now ready to study how individuals' information (beliefs) about their future health care needs affect the plan's profit maximizing shadow prices. Let

$$\hat{m}_s = \frac{\sum_i \hat{m}_{is}}{N} \quad r = \frac{\sum_i r_i}{N}$$

$$\hat{\sigma}_s = \sqrt{\frac{\sum_i (\hat{m}_{is} - \hat{m}_s)^2}{N}} \quad \sigma_r = \sqrt{\frac{\sum_i (r_i - r)^2}{N}}$$

$$\hat{\rho}_{s,s'} = \frac{\sum_i (\hat{m}_{is} - \hat{m}_s)(\hat{m}_{is'} - \hat{m}_{s'})}{N \hat{\sigma}_s \hat{\sigma}_{s'}} \quad \hat{\rho}_{rs} = \frac{\sum_i (r_i - r)(\hat{m}_{is} - \hat{m}_s)}{N \hat{\sigma}_s \sigma_r}$$

$$\hat{M} = \sum_{s=1,\dots,s} \hat{m}_s$$

and assume that $n_i = n$, and $\Phi'_i = 1$ for all i.[14] Eq. (10′) can then be written as

$$q_s = \frac{n\hat{m}_s}{(r\hat{m}_s + \hat{\rho}_{rs}\hat{\sigma}_s\sigma_r) - \left(\hat{\sigma}_s^2 + \sum_{\substack{s'=1,\dots,s \\ s' \neq s}} \hat{\rho}_{s,s'}\hat{\sigma}_s\hat{\sigma}'_s + \hat{m}_s\hat{M}\right)} \tag{11}$$

The effect of an individual's information on the choice of q_s enters through $\hat{\sigma}_s$. Suppose, initially, that all individuals are identical in their beliefs about their health care needs of all services for the coming period. In such a case, $\hat{\sigma}_s = 0$ for all s and $q_s = (n/r - \hat{M})$ for all s. Thus, in this case all shadow prices are the same and no distortion occurs. This result is independent of the risk adjustment system and of correlation of predicted spending for different illnesses.

Suppose, now, that individuals have some information that makes them differ from each other with respect to their beliefs about their need of some service s. In such a case, $\hat{\sigma}_s > 0$. Suppose that there is no risk adjustment, so $r_i = r$. We can see that the more heterogeneous are individuals with respect to their $\hat{m}_{is}$, the larger will be $\hat{\sigma}_s$ and the higher will be the shadow price q_s. This is the standard adverse selection result. The better the information that individuals have about their future needs, the bigger will be the distortion created by the plan in order to attract the profitable individuals.

---

[14]This is true with a uniform distribution.

The effect of correlation among spending on different services on the shadow price can also be observed in (11). If needs are not at all correlated, then $\hat{\rho}_{s,s'} = 0$ and the only effect on the shadow price comes from individuals' information $\hat{\sigma}_s$. If, however, needs are correlated, $\hat{\rho}_{s,s'} > 0$ and the larger $\hat{\rho}_{s,s'}$, the higher will be the shadow price of services s and s'.

As is also evident from (11), risk adjustment can counter the distortive forces discussed above. The larger is the correlation between predicted spending on service s and risk adjustment payment, $\hat{\rho}_{r,s}$, the higher will be the denominator of (11), and the lower the shadow price.

3. MEASURING SHADOW PRICES: AN EMPIRICAL ILLUSTRATION

In this section we illustrate how to use our measure. As we noted in the introduction, the data we will use are from an "unmanaged" plan, so the findings are merely an example of how to implement our framework. In other words, our purpose here is to illustrate how to use presently available data to calculate a distortion index. The elements that feed into incentives to distort, such as predictability of various services, and correlation among use in various categories of service, are likely to be largely common to managed and unmanaged patterns of care. Our use of Medicaid data means that the population is not representative, but our findings are at least suggestive.

Recall from (11) that the profit maximizing shadow prices depend on the individuals' *expectations* regarding their future health needs. Therefore, the empirical building blocks for measuring shadow prices are the expected spending of individuals by service class and the correlation of expected spending across services under differing information assumptions. Our main strategy here is aimed at obtaining estimates of future spending, conditional on the information assumptions, which minimize the forecast error. The performance of a number of estimation strategies for health care spending data has been assessed over the past 15 years. Duan *et al.* (1983, 1984) and Manning *et al.* (1981) contend that two-part models minimize mean forecast errors under distributional assumptions commonly exhibited by health spending data. Two-part models consist of one equation, typically a logit, for the yes/no decision about use, and a second equation, typically estimated by OLS, describing the extent of use, given some use. We use a two-part model for estimation under differing information assumptions. An "informational assumption" means, operationally, which covariates to include in the models. The pieces of Eq. (11) are computed from the predicted values generated from these estimated models.

3.1. *Data*

The data are health claims and enrollment files from the Michigan Medicaid program for the years 1991–1993. We chose a subset of the data for application of our model. It is therefore important to highlight that the data we use consists largely of spending by poor women (90%); thus, calculated shadow prices may differ from those for other populations. The sample consists of individual adults who were eligible for Medicaid in 1991 through the Aid to Families with Dependent Children (AFDC) program, and who were continuously enrolled in this or another Medicaid program through the end of 1993. We excluded individuals who joined an HMO during the study time-period. The resulting sample consisted of 16,131 individuals, with a mean age of 32 years.

3.2. *Defining Services*

There are a variety of approaches one could take to identifying "services," ranging from very specific treatments, such as angioplasty, to groups of treatments which would be associated with an illness, such as care for hypertension. In this paper we define a "service" as all the treatments received in connection with certain diagnostic classifications. We identify nine classes of services: (1) birth related, (2) cancer care, (3) gastrointestinal problems, (4) heart care, (5) hypertension, (6) injuries/poisonings, (7) mental health/substance abuse, (8) musculoskeletal problems, and (9) an "all other category." Each of the services is defined by a grouping of ICD-9-CM diagnostic codes.[15] We chose groups of conditions according to several criteria. At least 7.5% of the population was treated for each condition in a year. We included conditions that were a mix of chronic (cancer, hypertension, mental health care) and acute conditions (gastrointestinal, injuries, and birth-related). Treatments for some conditions are likely to be expensive, some much less so. Some treatments for included conditions are arguably quite predictable, such as birth-related spending, while others might be considered more random, such as injuries and poisonings. We classify all health care claims according to the primary diagnosis attached to the claim.

---

[15]Our grouping of services by ICD-9 codes is available from the authors.

3.3. *Patterns of Spending*

Table 1 describes patterns of utilization and spending for the sample in 1993. The sixth and seventh columns of Table 1 indicate some of the key elements of the formula for shadow prices (11). The sixth column reports the intertemporal correlation between spending on each of our nine service categories and the sum of spending on all other services. None of the correlations exceeds 0.20, with the exception of the "other" category. Correlation with spending in the previous year for each category is a measure of the persistence of spending, reported in the seventh column. Persistent spending is probably more predictable. Several of the illnesses thought to be more chronic in character, hypertension, mental health/substance abuse and musculoskeletal conditions, display relatively high correlations in service-specific spending over time. Mental-health spending has the highest year-to-year correlation.

3.4. *Estimation of Components of the Ratio of Shadow Prices*

3.4.1. *Risk-Adjusted Premiums*

We first calculate the premium assuming that a single payment is made for all enrollees. This premium is based on the simple average level of spending across all enrollees and corresponds to a case with no risk adjustments. We next construct two sets of true "risk-adjusted" premiums, one based on the Ambulatory Diagnosis Group (ADG) classification system (Weiner *et al.*, 1996) and one based on the DCG classification system (Ellis *et al.*, 1996).[16] In each case we adjusted the risk-adjusted premium upward to make the marginal profit per enrollee positive on average, as it must be if plans are to be induced to compete for enrollees by service quality for all services.[17] The increase in premium was 50%.

---

[16]We used publicly available algorithms to implement these risk adjustment systems. The ADG algorithm is the 1997 version of the software provided by Jonathan Weiner at Johns Hopkins University. The HCC algorithm is the 1997 version of the software provided by Randy Ellis of Boston University.

[17]One alternative would be to introduce some fixed cost assumption. If AC=MC and AC is close to average premium, there will be some services the plan will not wish to provide at all! To be willing to provide some of a service, a plan must make some expected profit on it. Another alternative would be to assume a plan is required to offer at least some minimum of every type of service.

R. G. Frank, J. Glazer and T. G. McGuire

Table 1. Use and Cost in Michigan Medicaid AFDC 1993

Service	Probability of any use	Expected spending given use (US$)	Expected costs (US$)	Percent of total costs	Correlation with all other costs	Correlation with own costs last year
Birth-related	0.167	3904	653	19.2	0.007	0.122
Cancer care	0.109	1159	126	3.7	0.155	0.127
Gastrointestinal	0.204	1186	242	7.1	0.167	0.166
Heart care	0.070	1542	108	3.2	0.089	0.079
Hypertension	0.093	249	23	0.7	0.114	0.317
Injuries/poisonings	0.344	701	241	7.1	0.189	0.033
Mental health/ substance abuse	0.143	1671	239	7.0	0.032	0.385
Musculoskeletal	0.306	683	209	6.1	0.115	0.215
Other/missing	0.926	1692	1567	45.9	0.313	0.288

3.4.2. *Expected Spending*

The variable $\hat{m}_{is}$ is the expected level of spending by each individual for each category of service. Estimating expected spending requires assumptions about the information available to individuals. The literature reflects a wide range of conceptions of what consumers might know about their health risks. Newhouse (1989) suggests that individuals know some of the information contained in measurable aspects of health status plus the time invariant-person specific component of the unobserved factors contributing to variation in health care spending. Welch (1985) makes a similar assumption, referring to a "permanent" component of health spending that is individual-specific. Welch speculates that individuals might know more than this and be able to forecast use of some acute services such as births and some other illnesses. Some empirical work on plan choice confirms the presence of considerable individual knowledge. Ellis (1985) and Perneger *et al.* (1995) show that an individual's historical pattern of spending affects health plan choice. Other research points to the fact that individuals appear to select plans on the basis of information not contained in risk adjustment systems (Cutler, 1994; Ettner *et al.*, 1998).

We consider the implications of several informational assumptions. Recall that if individuals can predict nothing, there is no selection problem, so no simulation needs to be done for this case. We start with the assumption that individuals can predict based on age and sex. That is, we assume all individuals predict they will spend the average for a person of their age and sex for each service category. Alternatively, we assume individuals can also use the information contained in prior use. As will be seen shortly, if individuals know *all* the information contained in prior use, existing risk adjusters cannot cope with the selection-induced inefficiencies, and some services would have very high or very low q's in profit maximization. In the simulations, we therefore equip individuals with some of the information in prior use, 40%, to illustrate the impact of more information. In order to construct these estimates under different information conditions, we estimate a series of two-part models. Each two-part model uses right-hand side variables at their 1991 values to explain service-specific spending in 1992. Variables included in the model correspond to information individuals are assumed to be able to use to predict spending. We estimate two sets of regressions, one with age and sex as right-hand variables and one with age, sex, and prior spending. The estimated coefficients from each pair of service specific regressions are then applied to 1992 values of the right hand side variables to generate estimates of expected spending for each individual in 1993.

Following Duan *et al.* (1983) and Manning *et al.* (1981), each two-part model is specified as:

$$\text{logit}(\Pr(\text{Spending on services } s > 0))_i = \beta_1' X_i + \varepsilon_{i1} \qquad (12)$$

$$\sqrt{(\text{Spending on services } s \mid \text{spending} > 0)_i} = \beta_2' X_i + \varepsilon_{i2} \qquad (13)$$

where i indexes the individual enrollee, X is a vector of individual characteristics (either age, sex, or age, sex, and prior use), β is a vector of coefficients to be estimated and ε is a random error term. Eq. (12) is a logit regression. Eq. (13) is a linear regression that estimates the impact of the X's on the square root of the level of spending on each service for individuals with positive spending on that service. We chose the square root transformation to deal with skewness in the distribution of spending rather than the more common logarithmic transformation because the smearing estimator for the square root model is less sensitive to heteroskedasticity than the log transformation.[18] The difficulties in retransforming the two-part model have been treated in detail by Manning (1998) and Mullahy (1998).[19] Since this application calls for predicting 1993 spending using 1992 data and coefficients from the two-part model of 1992 spending on 1991 right side variables, a "smearing factor" is taken from the error term of the 1991–1992 regressions. Because we use a square root transformation, the smearing factor is additive as opposed to the multiplicative form in the case of the logarithmic transformation. The resulting empirical analysis consists of a set of 18 regressions for each of the two informational assumptions we make.

3.4.3. *Plan Enrollment*

We assume that competing managed care plans are in a symmetric equilibrium, and the plan therefore enrolls a representative sample of the

---

[18]We tested for heteroskedasticity logarithmic of the specification using the Breusch-Pagan test and rejected homoskedasticity. Moreover, the heteroskedasticity was not a simple function of any right hand variable such as previous spending. The heteroskedasticity was attenuated, but still present, under the square root specification using the Breusch-Pagan test.

[19]Those papers show the sensitivity of expected spending estimates to distributional properties such as heteroskedasticity. The use of a transformation to account for skewness in the spending data necessitates use of the "smearing" estimator to retransform the predicted values of spending to the expected levels of spending consistent with the original distributions of spending (Duan *et al.*, 1983).

Table 2.   **Correlations Between Actual and Predicted Spending with Different Information Assumptions**

Service	Model[a]	
	Age-sex	Age-sex prior spending
Birth-related	0.210	0.216
Cancer care	0.035	0.104
Gastrointestinal	0.031	0.184
Heart care	0.075	0.104
Hypertension	0.055	0.227
Injuries/poisonings	0.002	0.014
Mental health/substance abuse	0.019	0.306
Musculoskeletal	0.073	0.178
Other/missing	0.052	0.099

[a]All correlations are significant at $p < 0.01$.

population. To estimate plan spending on each service, the $\sum_{is} n_i m_{is}$ in the numerator of (10), we will simply use the average spending in the sample.

3.5. *A Welfare Index*

The welfare loss associated with a set of q's can be approximated by:

$$L = \sum_s 0.5(\triangle q_s)(\triangle m_s) \tag{14}$$

where $\triangle q_s$ is the absolute value of the discrepancy between the q for service s and the second best q, and $\triangle m_s$ is the change in spending induced by the discrepancy in q. For purposes of this analysis we define $\triangle q_s$ as the difference between q_s and the weighted average q for all service types contained in Table 3. Thus, for each service s, we take the expenditure-weighted average q for each information/risk adjustment combination, and compute $\triangle q_s$ based on that. Since $\triangle q_s$ is in percentage terms, $\triangle m_s$ is simply $\triangle q_s$ multiplied by demand elasticity, which we assume for simplicity is 0.25 for all services, except for mental health which we set at 0.5, based on Newhouse *et al.* (1997).

3.6. *Results*

We summarize the predictions of the 18 two-part models in Table 2 by reporting the correlations between actual and predicted service specific spending levels. This correlation is negatively and monotonically related to the absolute prediction error of the spending model. As expected, correlations between actual and predicted spending are generally quite

Table 3. Shadow Prices for Three Information Assumptions and Three
Risk Adjustment Systems

	Information assumption					
	Age, sex			Age, sex 40% of prior use		
	Risk adjuster			Risk adjuster		
Service	None	ADGs	HCCs	None	ADGs	HCCs
Birth-related	1.15	1.25	1.23	0.19	0.35	0.43
Cancer care	0.99	0.98	0.98	0.17	0.28	0.34
Gastrointestinal	0.99	0.99	0.99	0.18	0.29	0.36
Heart care	1.00	0.90	0.89	0.19	0.27	0.33
Hypertension	1.01	0.87	0.87	0.27	0.26	0.28
Injuries/poisonings	1.00	1.02	1.02	0.31	0.45	0.52
Mental health/substance abuse	0.99	0.98	0.98	3.73	0.67	0.76
Musculoskeletal	0.97	0.94	0.95	0.18	0.27	0.33
Other/missing	1.00	1.00	1.00	1.00	1.00	1.00
Weighted average of q's	1.03	1.04	1.04	0.82	0.67	0.70
Welfare loss (%)	0.6	1.1	1.0	9.7	3.9	3.6

Note: All shadow prices are relative to Other/Missing Category. Welfare loss is in
terms of percent of total expenditures.

low for all services when only age and sex related information is known
by consumers. The birth-related correlation between actual and predicted spending is, however, relatively large at 0.21 (probably a result
unique to a Medicaid sample). With prior use included, the correlation
between predicted and actual spending improves markedly for most
services.

The shadow prices implied by individuals' predictions and a risk
adjustment policy are contained in Table 3. Two information assumptions
are combined with three risk-adjustment policies to produce six sets
of profit-maximizing shadow prices. The q for the "other" category is
normalized to 1.00 in all cases, so each entry in the table needs to be
read as the shadow price relative to this numeraire. Begin with the first
three columns of results, computed for the assumption that individuals
can forecast health costs based only on their own age and sex. The
very first column shows the consequences of no risk adjustment with
this informational assumption. Individuals cannot forecast very well at
all, so the incentives plans have to distort are small, even with no risk
adjustment. All estimated q's are close to 1.00 with the exception of birth-
related expenditures. Risk adjustment using ADGs and HCCs magnifies

the distortion in the cases of birth-related services, heart care and care for hypertension. The explanation is that people who anticipate using these services are paid for relatively generously in these two risk adjustment formulae.

The welfare loss measure at the bottom of the table corroborates the q results. When there is no risk adjustment and people forecast on age and sex, there is not much distortion, as indicated by the welfare loss as a percentage of spending. Risk adjustment exacerbates the welfare loss, though the magnitude is not high.

The second panel of three columns presents calculated q's, assuming individuals can predict spending based on 40% of the information contained in prior spending. Note that with no risk adjustment, mental health and substance abuse services are quite distorted as evidenced by the q of 3.73. Risk adjustment attenuates the distortions, moving all q's toward unity. Mental health and substance abuse services continue to have the largest service-specific q.

The two risk-adjustment systems studied, ADGs and HCCs, have very similar effects on incentives. For some services, notably birth-related expenditures, risk adjustment improves matters, moving the profit-maximizing q closer to the overall average, but a favorable effect of risk adjustment is not uniform. The incentives to overprovide care for hypertension are exacerbated by risk adjustment. Mental health and substance abuse changes from a service that tends to be underprovided to one much closer to the average with either risk adjustment system. Without risk adjustment, the welfare loss due to selection in the case when individuals know 40% of the information in prior use has risen to almost 10% of spending.[20] Risk adjustment appears to be quite effective, reducing the measured distortion to about 50% of its original magnitude.[21] A similar analysis could be conducted to examine how shadow prices change if we were to "carve-out" any of the service from the overall insurance contract. The obvious

---

[20]This is likely to be a conservative measure because of the way we construct elasticity.
[21]A next step in this analysis would be to find the "optimal risk adjustment." Given a set of variables available for risk adjusting, Eq. (14) could be minimized with respect to the weights on the risk adjusters. It turns out it is possible to fully "solve" the optimal risk adjustment problem for the services if there are enough degrees of freedom in the variables available for risk adjustment (Glazer and McGuire, 2002). This solution, or the minimization of Eq. (14), requires information on what plans believe individuals can predict.

candidate for a carve-out, based on Table 3, is mental health and substance abuse.

As Table 3 shows, the calculations for shadow prices are sensitive to how much information individuals have in making their predictions. When we examined a scenario with individuals knowing as much as 50% of prior use, profit-maximizing the q's went "off the charts," signaling that incentives to over and underprovide are very strong.

4. CONCLUSION

Health plans paid by capitation have an incentive to distort the quality of services they offer to attract profitable and deter unprofitable enrollees. Characterizing plans' rationing as imposing a "shadow price" on access to care, we show that the profit maximizing shadow price for each service depends on the dispersion in health costs, how well individuals forecast their health costs, the correlation among use in illness categories, and the risk adjustment system used for payment. We further show how these factors can be combined to form an empirically implementable index that can be used to identify the services that will be most distorted in competition among managed care plans. A simple welfare measure is developed that measures the distortion caused by selection incentives. We apply our ideas to a Medicaid data set to illustrate how to calculate distortion incentives, and we conduct policy analyses of risk adjustment.

From the practical standpoint of health policy, our paper shows how the incentives to distort services depend in a relatively straightforward way on means and correlations among predicted values of health care services in a population. Several interesting findings emerge from the small data set we analyze. The most striking is the importance of individuals' knowledge and their ability to forecast their health expenses. This factor has been appreciated in abstract terms in earlier writing, but the dramatic effect that information has on incentives has not been empirically demonstrated. According to our preliminary analysis, if people know what they are sometimes commonly assumed to know (age, sex and prior spending), selection incentives would be very severe. Study of what individuals forecast is a key area of empirical research.

In our models if individuals know "too much," some services are not provided at all. We therefore analyze hypothetical cases in which individuals are not allowed to know "too much." Within this limitation, we illustrate how risk adjustment can be assessed. Two proposed risk adjustment systems have significant and similar effects in terms of cutting the magnitude of distortion incentives.

ACKNOWLEDGEMENTS

Research support from the Health Care Financing Administration Cooperative Agreement #18-C-9034/1, grant # K05-MH01263 from the National Institute of Mental Health (NIMH), and grant #23498 from the Robert Wood Johnson Foundation is gratefully acknowledged. We thank Randy Ellis, Arleen Leibowitz, Joseph Newhouse and participants in the BU-Harvard-MIT Health Economics Seminar for comments on an earlier draft. Pam Berenbaum provided very capable programming and statistical assistance.

REFERENCES

Baumgardner, J., 1991. The interaction between forms of insurance contract and types of technical change in medical care. *RAND Journal of Health Economics* 22(1), 36–53.

Brown, R., Bergeron, J.W., Clement, D.G., 1993. Does managed care work for medicare. Working paper, Mathematica Policy.

Cutler, D.M., 1994. A guide to health care reform. *Journal of Economic Perspectives* 8(3), 13–29.

Cutler, D.M., 1995. Cutting costs and improving health: making reform work. *Health Affairs* 14(1), 161–172.

Cutler, D.M., Reber, S., 1998. Paying for health insurance: the trade-off between competition and adverse selection. *Quarterly Journal of Economics* 113(2), 433–466.

Cutler, D.M., Zeckhauser, R.J., 2000. The Anatomy of health insurance. In: Culyer, A., Newhouse, P. (Eds.), *Handbook of Health Economics.* North Holland.

Duan, N., Manning, W.G., Morris, C.N., Newhouse, J.P., 1983. A comparison of alternative models for the demand of medical care. *Journal of Business and Economic Statistics* 1(2), 115–126.

Duan, N., Manning, W.G., Morris, C.N., Newhouse, J.P., 1984. Choosing between the sample selection model and the multi-part model. *Journal of Business and Economic Statistics* 2(3), 283–289.

Eggers, P., Prihoda, R., 1982. Pre-enrollment reimbursement patterns of medicare beneficiaries enrolled in at-risk HMOs. *Health Care Financing Review* 4(1), 55–74.

Ellis, R.P., 1985. The effect of prior-year health expenditures on health coverage plan choice. In: Scheffler, R.M., Rossiter, L.F. (Eds.), *Advances in Health Economics and Health Services Research: Biased Selection in Health Care Markets.* JAI Press, Greenwich, CT, pp. 149–170.

Ellis, R.P., 1998. Creaming, skimping and dumping: provider competition on the intensive and extensive margins. *Journal of Health Economics* 17(5), 537–556.

Ellis, R.P., Pope, G.C., Iezzoni, L.I. *et al.*, 1996. Diagnosis-based risk adjustment for medicare capitation payments. *Health Care Financing Review* 17(3), 101–128.

Enthoven, A.C., Singer, S.J., 1995. Market-based reform: what to regulate and by whom. *Health Affairs* 14(1), 105–119.

Ettner, S.L., Frank, R.G., McGuire, T.G., Newhouse, J.P., Notman, E.H., 1998. Risk adjustment of mental health and substance abuse payments. *Inquiry* 35(2), 223–239.

Garfinkel, S.A. *et al.*, 1986. Choice of payment plan in the medicare capitation demonstration. *Medical Care* 24(7), 628–640.

Glazer, J., McGuire, T.G., 2000. Optimal risk adjustment in markets with adverse selection: an application to managed health care. *American Economic Review* 90(4), 1055–1071.

Glazer, J., McGuire, T.G., 2002. Regulating premium payments to managed care plans: minimum variance optimal risk adjustment. *Journal of Public Economies* 84(2), 153–173.

Glied, S., 2000. Managed care. In: Culyer, A., Newhouse, J. (Eds.), *Handbook of Health Economics*. North Holland.

Gold, M., Felt, S., 1995. Reconciling practice and theory: challenges in monitoring medicare managed care quality. *Health Care Financing Review* 16, 85–105.

Hill, J.W., Brown, R.S., 1990. Biased selection in the TEFRA HMO/CMP Program. Mathematica Policy Research, Princeton, MPR Reference Number 7786–503.

Holohan, J., Coughlin, T., Ku, L., Lipson, D.J., Rajan, S., 1995. Insuring the poor through Section 1115 medicaid waivers. *Health Affairs* 14(1), 199–216.

Jensen, G.A., Morrisey, M.A., Gaffney, S.L., Derek, K., 1997. The new dominance of managed care: insurance trends in the 1990s. *Health Affairs* 16(1), 125–136.

Keeler, E.B., Newhouse, J.P., Carter, G., 1998. A model of the impact of reimbursement schemes on health plan choice. *Journal of Health Economics* 17(3), 297–320.

Keenan, P., Beeuwkes-Buntin, M., McGuire, T., Newhouse, J., 2000. Prevalence of risk adjustment in the U.S., 2001. *Inquiry* 38(3), 245–259.

Lerner, A.P., 1934. The concept of monopoly and the measurement of monopoly powers. *Review of Economic Studies*, 157–175.

Luft, H.S., Miller, R.H., 1988. Patient selection and competitive health systems. *Health Affairs* 7(3), 97–119.

Ma, C.A., 1995. Health care payment systems: cost and quality incentives. *Journal of Economics and Management Strategy* 3(1), 93–112.

Ma, C.A., McGuire, T.G., 1997. Optimal health insurance and provider payment. *American Economic Review* 87(4), 685–704.

Manning, W.G., 1998. The logged dependent variable heteroskedasticity and the retransformation problem. *Journal of Health Economics* 17(3), 283–296.

Manning, W.G., Morris, C.N., Newhouse, J.P., 1981. A two-part model of the demand for medical care: preliminary results from the health insurance study.

In: van der Gaag, J., Perlman, M. (Eds.), *Health, Economics, and Health Economics*. North Holland Publishing, Amsterdam, pp. 103–124.

Medicare Payment Advisory Commission, 1998. Report to the Congress: Medicare Payment Policy, Washington, DC.

Miller, R.H., Luft, H.S., 1997. Does managed care lead to better or worse quality of care? *Health Affairs* 16(5), 7–25.

Mitchell, P.H., Heinrich, J., Moritz, P., Hinshaw, A.S. (Eds.), 1997. Outcome Measures and Care Delivery Systems Conference. *Medical Care* 35(11) pp. NS1–NS5.

Mullahy, J., 1998. Much ado about two: reconsidering retransformation and the two part model in health econometrics. *Journal of Health Economics* 17(3), 247–282.

Netanyahu Commission, August 1990. Report of the State Commission of Inquiry into the Functioning and Efficiency of the Health Care System, Israel.

Newhouse, J.P., 1989. Adjusting capitation rates using objective health measures and prior utilization. *Health Care Financing Review* 10(3), 41–54.

Newhouse, J.P., 1994. Patients at risk: health reform and risk adjustment. *Health Affairs* 13(1), 132–146.

Newhouse, J.P., Buntin, M.J., Chapman, J.D., 1997. Risk adjustment and medicare: taking a closer look. *Health Affairs* 16(5), 26–43.

Pauly, M.V., Ramsey, S.D., 1999. Would you like suspenders to go with that belt? An analysis of optimal combinations of cost sharing and managed care. *Journal of Health Economics* 18(4).

Perneger, T.V., Allaz, A.F., Etter, J.F., Rougemont, A., 1995. Mental health and choice between managed care and indemnity health insurance. *American Journal of Psychiatry* 52(7), 1020–1025.

Robinson, J.C., Gardner, L.B., Luft, H.S., 1993. Health plan switching and anticipated increased medical care utilization. *Medical Care* 31(1), 42–51.

Rogerson, W.P., 1994. Choice of treatment intensities by a nonprofit hospital under prospective pricing. *Journal of Economics and Management Strategy* 3(1), 7–52.

Schlesinger, M., Mechanic, D., 1993. Challenges for managed competition from chronic illness. *Health Affairs* 12, 123–137.

van de Ven, W.P.M.M., Ellis, R., 2000. Risk adjustment in competitive health plan markets. In: Culyer, A., Newhouse, P. (Eds.), *Handbook of Health Economics*. North Holland.

van Vliet, R.C.J.A., van de Ven, W.P.M.M., 1992. Towards a capitation formula for competing health insurers: an empirical analysis. *Social Science and Medicine* 34(9), 1035–1048.

Weiner, J.P., Dobson, A., Maxwell, S.L., Coleman, K., Starfield, B.H., Anderson, G.F., 1996. Risk-adjusted capitation rates using ambulatory and inpatient diagnoses. *Health Care Financing Review* 17(3), 77–99.

Welch, W.P., 1985. Medicare capitation payments to HMOs in light of regression toward the mean in health care costs. In: Scheffler, R.M., Rossiter, L.F. (Eds.), *Advances in Health Economics and Health Services Research: Biased Selection in Health Care Markets*. JAI Press, Greenwich, CT, pp. 75–96.

Chapter 3

SETTING HEALTH PLAN PREMIUMS TO ENSURE EFFICIENT QUALITY IN HEALTH CARE: MINIMUM VARIANCE OPTIMAL RISK ADJUSTMENT

Jacob Glazer*

Tel Aviv University, Faculty of Management, Tel Aviv, Israel
glazer@post.tau.ac.il

Thomas G. McGuire

Harvard Medical School, Boston, USA

Risk adjustment refers to the practice of paying health plans a premium per person (or per family) based on a formula using risk adjusters, such as age or gender, and weights on those adjusters. One role of risk adjustment is to make sure plans have an incentive to accept all potential enrollees. Another role, at least as important in our view, is to lead health plans to choose the efficient level of quality of care for the various services they offer. Most of the research and policy literature on risk adjustment focuses on the first problem. This paper proposes a new way to calculate weights in a risk adjustment formula that contends with both problems. For a given set of adjusters, we identify the weights that minimize the variance in plan predictable health care costs that are not explained by risk adjustment (addressing the access problem), subject to the payments satisfying conditions for an optimal risk adjuster (making sure plans provide the efficient quality). We call the formula minimum variance optimal risk adjustment (MVORA). ©2002 Elsevier Science B.V. All rights reserved.

1. INTRODUCTION

Managed health care plans — insurance and service organizations responsible for providing 'medically necessary' health care — enroll about

---

*Corresponding author.

75 percent of the U.S. population and large shares of European populations. These health plans receive individual or family premiums, paid by governments (e.g. Medicare or Medicaid in the U.S.), or by a combination of employers and consumers in U.S. employment-based health insurance. One of the major concerns with the health insurance/managed care health care policy is adverse selection (Enthoven, 1993). Generally, plans may take actions to discourage or encourage potential enrollees. For one thing, they may refuse some applicants, although overt actions to discourage individuals are normally prohibited and may be readily monitored. More troublesome is that plans may distort the mix of the quality of health care they offer to discourage high-cost persons from joining the plan. As a number of papers have observed, decisions about what care is medically necessary are fundamentally outside the scope of direct regulation (Miller and Luft, 1997; Newhouse, 1996). In this paper, we consider how risk adjustment of premiums paid to health plans can address what we refer to as the individual access problem and the quality problem.[1]

Risk adjustment refers to the practice of paying health plans a premium for each person or family based on a formula using risk adjuster variables, such as age, gender, or indicators of prior health care use, and weights on those adjusters. Risk adjustment researchers have sought to find the formula that does the best job of 'fitting' the distribution of health care costs in a population. Risk adjuster variables are chosen that are likely to be related to costs, and weights on those variables are chosen by regression techniques to minimize the sum of the squared residuals, a practice we will refer to

---

[1]A comprehensive discussion of health insurance premiums and risk adjustment would include analysis of the setting of the premiums charged to enrollees. Except in some individual insurance markets, individuals receive some 'subsidy' of this premium. In the case of government programs in the U.S. and some European countries, this subsidy is complete and the person or family pays nothing. In the employment-related health insurance context in the U.S., the employer pays a portion of the premium. Authors have considered how to set the consumer contribution in order to give consumers the incentives to join the right plans. This issue can also be considered within an adverse selection framework and may involve risk adjusting consumer premium contributions. The most immediate effect of the person-paid component of premiums is to influence the consumer's choice of plan. In this paper, as will be made clear in the next section, we will analyze a situation in which the consumer's contribution is zero. This is empirically accurate for many people in the U.S., including a large share of the employed population, as well as the entire population enrolling in managed health care in Medicare and Medicaid. It is also common in Europe.

here as 'conventional risk adjustment.'[2] The intuitive appeal of regression coefficients as weights on risk adjusters derives from a desire to address the individual access problem. Matching payments with individual costs as closely as possible may discourage plans from denying membership to some and aggressively recruiting others.

When the problem being addressed is plans' distortion of the quality of services to affect the decisions of groups of potential applicants, however, the regression-based approach lacks intuitive foundation. Figuring risk adjustment weights to mitigate quality distortions requires a conception of how health plans set the quality of services, and a conception of what 'optimal' quality means in this context. In this paper we propose an approach to deriving weights on risk adjuster variables that begins with an explicit statement of health plan behavior in a market with heterogeneity in the demand for health care services, and an explicit statement of the economic efficiency problem.

With two efficiency problems in view, individual access and quality distortions, and one policy instrument, the formula for the premium paid to plans, it is natural to expect there to be some trade-off in meeting the two competing objectives. Although it has inspired most empirical risk adjustment research, 'individual access' to health plans is not the major social efficiency problem in the health plan market. In the U.S., Europe, Israel and Latin America, governments and employers require contracting plans to offer periodic 'open enrollments'. During open enrollment periods (once a year for most U.S. employers, and every month in Medicare), plans must accept any applicant. It seems clear that open enrollment regulation works well to ensure access. Simulation research demonstrates that existing risk adjustment systems leave some individuals as big 'losers' or winners (Chapman, 1997; Shen and Ellis, 2000), but there is no evidence that plans act to deny membership to individuals. By way of contrast, quality of care in managed care health plans is the major policy focus in the U.S. and elsewhere. We believe that the quality distortion problem is more important

---

[2] Age and gender are commonly used in regression formulae, but alone explain only about 1% of the variance in actual costs. Research on improving the explanatory power of these regressions has focussed on using sophisticated clinical algorithms to define new variables based on the diagnoses from prior health care use. Researchers have been able to run regressions explaining up to 10% of the variance in actual costs, but risk adjustment systems presently in use explain much less. See van de Ven and Ellis (2000) for a review of the empirical literature. Keenan *et al.* (2001) describes risk adjustment practices by major public and private payers in the U.S.

and less amenable to other regulatory solutions than the individual access problem, and is therefore the proper primary target of risk adjustment policy. Therefore, in the analysis below, when it comes to a tradeoff between policy objectives, we put more weight on maintaining quality than on individual access.

Plans' incentives to overprovide the quality of some services and underprovide the quality of others derives from the distribution of health care demands in the population. With data about the distribution of those demands, the regulator can anticipate plans' incentives, and impose a system of corrective taxes and subsidies at the person level, using the many observable variables available for each individual. Within this framework we derive a simple rule that characterizes optimal risk adjustment: the relation between the covariance between spending on a service and the risk adjusted premium and the covariance between spending on that service and the sum of spending on all services must be the same for all services that the plan provides. In general, there will be many combinations of weights on risk adjuster variables that satisfy the rule for optimal risk adjustment. By choosing from among the set of optimal risk adjustment weights the combination that leads to the best fit of premiums to costs, we integrate our approach with traditional regression-based methods, in effect designing a risk adjustment formula that contends with the two forms of adverse selection problems identified above. We will refer to our proposed method for risk adjustment as minimum variance optimal risk adjustment (MVORA), 'optimal' because it solves the quality distortion problem, and 'minimum variance' because it does so in a way that minimizes the sum of the squares of the deviations between premiums and costs at the individual level. In line with the literature on risk adjustment, we argue that this statistical criterion is motivated by a concern for individual access.

Our paper is related to several lines of research in health and public economics. Many papers in health economics are concerned with efficiency problems due to selection in insurance markets (see Cutler and Zeckhauser, 2000; Encinosa, 1999 and van de Ven and Ellis, 2000 for reviews). Researchers have long been aware that one significant adverse selection-related problem associated with competition among health plans is service competition to attract the good risks/deter the bad (Newhouse, 1996). Little research has been done, however, on the implications of this concern for a risk adjustment formula. So far, risk adjustment of this type has only been characterized in simple cases. Glazer and McGuire (2000) consider the two-service case and one risk adjuster, and show that the best risk adjustment weights are the solution to a pair of equations. The weights obtained by this procedure are generally different from those obtained from regression coefficients.

From the perspective of public economics, it is natural to view risk adjustment as a question of optimal taxes and subsidies on the prices paid for health insurance, a framework adopted in several papers (Glazer and McGuire, 2000; Neudeck and Podczeck, 1996; Selden, 1999). By explicit characterization of the distortions emerging in markets for health plans, we are able to identify, Pigouvian fashion, the set of taxes and subsidies necessary to align private incentives to maximize profit with the social objective of production of the efficient quality of health care.

In the context of risk adjustment, the taxes and subsidies to correct incentives work in an unusual fashion. Normally, a tax or subsidy applies directly to the activity intended to be affected: for example, a tax on the volume of pollution is intended to reduce pollution. Obviously though, there are other ways to tax/subsidize to hit a particular pollution target. If the actual level of pollution were not verifiable, for example, a regulator familiar with the effect of pollution (on, say water quality) could put a tax on this effect in order to manipulate the firm into choosing the target level of pollution. The idea in this paper is the same. Quality provided by health plans is usually not verifiable and, hence, cannot be taxed or subsidized directly. However, the regulator can magnify or diminish the revenue consequences to the health plan's quality choices by choice of the risk adjustment formula. If older people value and join a plan in response to good care for cardiac problems and the regulator is concerned that the quality offered for these diseases is too low, the regulator can induce higher quality by 'subsidizing' older people.[3]

A central insight of this paper is that there is an instruments/targets feature of risk adjustment policy. A plan sets quality for many services. The regulator has many variables in a risk adjustment formula. When the regulator has more instruments than it needs, the quality problem can be addressed. The final choice of risk adjustment formula can then be made in order to contend also with individual access.

---

[3]The health payment literature has used this insight previously, as in Rogerson (1994) where the optimal hospital per discharge payment was figured in order to induce the desired non-verifiable quality. In this case, quality is one-dimensional, and the level of the payment was the only instrument necessary. Another early paper along the same lines is Ma (1994).

The paper is organized as follows: Section 2 presents our basic model of health plan behavior in an environment with no uncertainty and symmetric information. In Section 3 we present the conditions for optimal risk adjustment and in Section 4 we solve for the Minimum Variance Optimal Risk Adjustment formula. An example of how to figure MVORA is contained in Section 5. Section 6 extends our analysis to the case of uncertainty and asymmetric information.

2. HEALTH PLAN BEHAVIOR

Assume there are N individuals. Each one of them is about to choose a health plan. In this section, we will analyze the behavior of one (representative) health plan, taking the behavior of the others as given. In Section 3 we will analyze this behavior within a symmetric equilibrium. The model presented in this section is based on that in Frank *et al.* (2000), hereafter referred to as FGM. The health plan is paid a premium (possibly risk-adjusted) for each individual that enrolls. Individuals differ in their need/demand for health care, and choose a plan which maximizes their expected utility. 'Health care' is not a single commodity, but a set of services — maternity, mental health, emergency care, cardiac care, and so on. A health plan chooses a rationing or allocation rule for each service. The plan's choice of rules will affect which individuals find the plan attractive and will therefore determine the plan's revenue and costs. We assume that the plan must accept every applicant, and we are interested in characterizing the plan's incentives to ration services.

2.1. *Utility and Plan Choice*

The health plan offers S services. Let m_{is} denote the amount the plan will spend on providing service s to individual i, if he joins the plan, and let: $m_i = \{m_{i1}, m_{i2}, \ldots, m_{iS}\}$. The dollar value of the benefits individual i gets from a plan, $u_i(m_i)$, is composed of two parts, a valuation of the services an individual gets from the plan, and a component of valuation that is independent of services. We assume these enter additively in utility. Thus,

$$u_i(m_i) = v_i(m_i) + \mu_i \qquad (1)$$

where,

$$v_i(m_i) = \sum_s v_{is}(m_{is})$$

is the service-related part of the valuation and is itself composed of the sum of the individual's valuations of all services offered by the plan $v_{is}(\cdot)$ is the individual's valuation of spending on service s, also measured in dollars, where $v'_{is} > 0$, $v''_{is} < 0$. Assume for the moment that the individual knows $v_i(m_i)$ with certainty. (This assumption will be relaxed in Section 6). The non-service component is μ_i, an individual-specific factor (e.g. distance or convenience) affecting individual i's valuation, known to person i. From the point of view of the plan, μ_i is unknown, but is drawn from a distribution $\phi_i(\mu_i)$. We assume that the premium the plan receives has been predetermined and is not part of the strategy the plan uses to influence selection.

The plan will be chosen by individual i if $u_i > \bar{u}_i$, where $\bar{u}_i$ is the valuation the individual places on the next preferred plan. We analyze the behavior of a plan which regards the behavior of all other plans as given, so that $\bar{u}_i$ can be regarded as fixed. Given m_i and $\bar{u}_i$, individual i chooses the plan if:

$$\mu_i > \bar{u}_i - v_i(m_i).$$

For now, we assume that, for each i, the plan has exactly the same information as individual i regarding the individual's service-related valuation of its services, v_i, and regarding the utility from the next preferred plan, $\bar{u}_i$. For each individual i, the plan does not know the true value of μ_i but it knows the distribution from which it is drawn. Therefore, for a given m_i and $\bar{u}_i$, the probability that individual i chooses the plan, from the point of view of the plan, is:[4]

$$n_i(m_i) = 1 - \phi_i(\bar{u}_i - v_i(m_i)) \tag{2}$$

2.2. Managed Care

Managed care rations the amount of health care a patient receives. Following Keeler *et al.* (1998) and FGM, let q_s be the service-specific shadow price the plan sets determining access to care for service s. A patient with a benefit function for service s of $v_{is}(\cdot)$ will receive a quantity of services, m_{is} determined by:

$$v'_{is}(m_{is}) = q_s \tag{3}$$

---

[4] An alternative interpretation is that index i describes a group of people with the same $v_i(m_i)$ function and $n_i(m_i)$ is then the share of this group that joins the plan.

Let the amount of spending determined by the equation above be denoted by $m_{is}(q_s)$. Note that Eq. (3) is simply a demand function, relating the quantity of services to the (shadow) price in a managed care plan.

2.3. *Profit and Profit Maximization*

Let $q = \{q_1, q_2, \ldots, q_S\}$ be a vector of shadow prices the plan chooses and $m_i(q) = \{m_{i1}(q_2), m_{i2}(q_2), \ldots, m_{iS}(q_S)\}$ be the vector of spending individual i gets by joining the plan. Define $n_i(q) \equiv n_i(m_i(q))$. Expected profit, $\pi(q)$, to the plan will depend on the individuals the plan expects to be members, the revenue the plan gets for enrolling these people, and the costs of each member.

$$\pi(q) = \sum_i n_i(q) \left[r_i - \sum_s m_{is}(q_s) \right] \tag{4}$$

where r_i is the risk-adjusted revenue the plan receives for individual i. The plan will choose a vector of shadow prices to maximize expected profit, Eq. (4). Defining $M_i = \sum_s m_{is}(q_s)$ to be total spending on a person, profit per person is $\pi_i = r_i - M_i$. Assuming that individuals share the same elasticity of demand for any service (allowing common elasticities to differ across services),[5] the profit maximizing condition for q_s, $s = 1, 2, \ldots, S$, becomes (see FGM):

$$q_s = \frac{\sum_i n_i m_{is}}{\sum_i \phi_i' m_{is} \pi_i}. \tag{5}$$

2.4. *The Efficiency Criterion*

The health plan allocates resources efficiently when it acts so as to equalize the degree of rationing across all S service areas. This is (second-best) efficient in the sense that the value of a dollar of health care spending is equalized across all possible uses. Formally, this requires $q_s = q$, for all s, where q is some constant characterizing the overall degree of rationing. When $q = 1$, a first-best efficiency is achieved. When $q > 1$, second-best efficiency is achieved but the overall budget for health is 'too small,' and when $q < 1$, it is 'too big.'

---

[5]Note that the fact that all individuals share the same elasticity of demand for a certain service does not imply that their demand curves are identical.

There is, however, no particular reason to expect profit maximization represented by Eq. (5) to lead to the same shadow price for each service s, unless the risk adjustment system is able to equalize the relative incentives to supply each service.

3. OPTIMAL RISK ADJUSTMENT

In the analysis of plan behavior just discussed, the risk adjustment formula was taken as given. We now consider how to structure the risk adjustment formula to induce the plan to provide services at the (second-best) efficient quality. A risk adjustment formula that achieves this goal will be referred to as *optimal risk adjustment*.

The analysis carried out here is very much in the spirit of the standard principal-agent literature. In that literature, the principal constructs an incentive scheme so that the agent, acting in its own interest, will behave according to the principal's goals. In what follows the regulator (the principal) sets a risk adjustment formula (an incentive scheme) to induce the profit maximizing plan (the agent) to provide the efficient quality (the regulator's goal).

We have in mind a situation where there are several identical health plans. Thus, Eq. (5) above describes the profit maximizing behavior of each of the health plans in equilibrium (taking the behavior of the other plans as given).

In a symmetric equilibrium, each individual has the same probability of being in the plan, so $n_i = n$. Assume that ϕ_i is uniform and the same for all i. Then, we can simplify Eq. (5) to say that second-best efficiency requires that for each s, Eq. (6) holds.

$$\frac{\sum_i m_{is}}{\sum_i m_{is} r_i - \sum_i m_{is} M_i} = \lambda, \tag{6}$$

for some $\lambda > 0$.

Equation (6) can be rewritten as

$$\frac{\text{cov}(m_s, r) - \text{cov}(m_s, M)}{\bar{m}_s} = \left(\bar{M} - \bar{r} + \frac{1}{\lambda} \right) \tag{7}$$

where covariances are defined as

$$\text{cov}(m_s, r) = \frac{1}{N} \sum_i (m_{is} - \bar{m}_s)(r_i - \bar{r})$$

and

$$\text{cov}(m_s, M) = \frac{1}{N} \sum_i (m_{is} - \bar{m}_s)(M_i - \bar{M}),$$

with

$$\frac{1}{N} \sum_i m_{is} \equiv \bar{m}_s, \bar{M} \equiv \frac{1}{N} \sum_i M_i, \quad \text{and} \quad \bar{r} \equiv \frac{1}{N} \sum_i r_i.$$

Eq. (7) embodies the main result of this paper. To equalize incentives to ration all services, the covariance of the risk adjuster with the use of every service must track the covariance of total predicted costs with the service's use. Intuitively, the optimal risk adjustment formula must have the property that by spending on a service, the cost consequences to a plan (from serving the demands of new members) relates to the revenue consequences (from the premiums they bring in) in the same way across all services. When this set of conditions holds, the plan has an incentive to ration all services with the same stringency.

It is worthwhile to contrast the conditions represented by Eq. (7) for the optimal way to set premiums to the usual approach based on statistical fit. Conventional risk adjustment seeks to bring per person premiums as close as possible to per person costs. The first contrast to be made is that we have S conditions characterizing optimal risk adjustment rather than one criterion based on fit. If a plan chooses the quality of S services, it is necessary to address the conditions for efficiency for each service, so more than one criterion seems evidently necessary. Second, the statistical criterion of fit of premiums, r, to costs, M, is replaced by criteria represented by covariances that lead profit maximization decisions of health plans to be identical with conditions for efficiency. When the extra revenue brought in by spending on service s (captured by the covariance between m_s and r) is in the same relation to the extra total costs incurred by spending on service s (captured by the covariance between m_s and M) for all services, profit-maximization is efficient.

We are now ready to consider how to use a risk adjustment formula to set premiums r in order to satisfy conditions for optimal risk adjustment. Suppose that a set of J risk adjusters (variables) is available to use in a risk adjustment formula. Call this set $X = (X_1, \ldots, X_J)$. The variable x_{ij} represents the value of the adjuster j for person i (x_{ij} could be the age or gender or health status of individual i). r_i is the risk-adjusted premium payment made on behalf of person i. A risk adjusted premium can be written as

$$r_i = X_i\beta \tag{8}$$

where β is a vector of weights on the risk adjuster variables. As can be seen from Eq. (8), for a given set of risk adjuster variables, the issue of designing a risk adjustment formula is a matter of setting the right weights β. Rather than using a regression, we find the β's as solutions to optimality conditions.

Using Eq. (8), each of the S equations in Eq. (7) can be written as

$$\frac{\sum_j \beta_j \text{cov}(m_s, x_j) - \text{cov}(m_s, M)}{\bar{m}_s} = \bar{M} - \bar{r} + \frac{1}{\lambda} \tag{9}$$

Note that Eq. (9) is linear in the coefficients of the risk adjusters β_j. The RHS of Eq. (9) is the same for all S equations.

It is interesting to note what Eq. (9) implies for the relationship between the covariance of the x's with expected costs on a service and the β's. If the $\text{cov}(m_s, x)$ is small, in order to equalize this to a target covariance, the β's must be larger.[6]

Solving for $\bar{M} - r + 1/\lambda$, we are left with $S - 1$ linear restrictions on the β_j's. Each of these restrictions takes the form of Eq. (10). In addition, a given budget b in the form of an average risk adjusted premium yields another linear restriction. We define *optimal risk adjustment* to be the weights $\beta_1, \ldots, \beta_J$ that satisfy the set of $S - 1$ equations (10), and the budget constraint in Eq. (11). We label any set of β's satisfying these s conditions β_j°.

$$\frac{\sum_j \beta_j^\circ \text{cov}(m_s, x_j) - \text{cov}(m_s, M)}{\bar{m}_s} = \frac{\sum_j \beta_j^\circ \text{cov}(m_s, x_j) - \text{cov}(m_s, M)}{\bar{m}_s}$$

$$s = 1, \ldots, S - 1 \tag{10}$$

$$\frac{1}{N} \sum_j \sum_i \beta_j^\circ x_{ij} \equiv \sum_j \beta_j^\circ \bar{x}_j = b \tag{11}$$

The system of Eqs. (10) and (11) will have at least one solution if a rank condition is satisfied, here, if $J > S$. We have assumed that the plan makes

---

[6]This is a generalization of a finding of Glazer and McGuire (2000), where it was shown that with one signal (risk adjuster variable), as the informativeness of the signal deteriorates, the weight on the signal increases in the optimal risk adjustment formula.

S independent rationing decisions, and there are J risk adjusters, none of which is a linear combination of the others. It is unclear what should be said about the magnitude of S, the number of rationing decisions made by a plan. On the one hand, a plan offers a very large number of different services. But on the other hand, from the standpoint of what management may practically pay attention to, there may be many fewer decision variables. For purposes of management, services might be grouped in just a few categories: rationing may be done for example at the level of primary care, pediatrics, mental health, cardiac care, and so on, leading to perhaps 10–20 groups. (There are 19 Major Diagnostic Categories, MDCs, for instance, that underlie the DRG system). As for the number of risk adjusters, J, this number could be very large. Consider age and gender alone. While only two 'variables' there are many potential degrees of freedom in age and gender. Medicare exploits these by creating age-gender cells. In a population ranged in age from say 1–65, a payer might feasibly create ten age $\times$ two gender cells for 20 mutually exclusive variables to use for risk adjustment. Adding zone of residence and eligibility status (among working people: employee, spouse, other dependent), geometrically enlarges J. Furthermore, diagnoses from prior health care use have been grouped into scores of categories in recently developed diagnosis-based classification systems (Ellis *et al.*, 1996; Weiner *et al.*, 1996). It thus seems quite safe to proceed on the assumption that the number of risk adjuster variables, J, exceeds the number of decisions made by management, S.

4. MINIMUM VARIANCE OPTIMAL RISK ADJUSTMENT (MVORA)

For a given per person budget b and a set X of risk adjusters, *Minimum Variance Optimal Risk Adjustment* (MVORA) is a vector of risk adjustment weights $\beta^* = (\beta_1^*, \ldots, \beta_J^*)$ that solves the following (constrained minimization) problem:

$$\underset{\beta_1,\ldots,\beta_J}{\text{Minimize}} \frac{1}{N} \sum_i \left(M_i - \sum_j \beta_j x_{ij} \right)^2 \tag{12}$$

$$\text{s.t.} \sum_j \beta_j \left[\frac{\text{cov}(m_s, x_j)}{\bar{m}_s} - \frac{\text{cov}(m_S, x_j)}{\bar{m}_S} \right] = \frac{\text{cov}(m_s, M)}{\bar{m}_s} - \frac{\text{cov}(m_S, M)}{\bar{m}_S}$$

$$s = 1, \ldots, S - 1 \tag{13}$$

and

$$\sum_j \beta_j \bar{x}_j = b \tag{14}$$

The set of $S - 1$ equations in Eq. (13) is a rewriting of the $S - 1$ equations in Eq. (10).

MVORA contends with both problems caused by adverse selection. The constraints guarantee the risk adjustment formula is optimal, in the sense that no quality distortion will take place. Minimizing the sum of the square of the deviations addresses problems that may arise when payments deviate from costs at the individual level.

The literature on conventional risk adjustment does not contain a formal statement of why conventional risk adjustment is the solution to an adverse selection problem in the market for health plans. No one, so far as we know, has supplied the argument for why the economic loss associated with a deviance between the risk adjusted payment and the predicted cost should go up according to the square of the difference. In this section, we follow the existing risk adjustment literature and simply presume that a better statistical fit of predicted to actual costs, as measured by an R^2 statistic, advances the cause of dealing with the selection problem related to individual access.

Before we go on to discuss the solution for MVORA, it may be worthwhile to present conventional risk adjustment in the context of our model. Conventional risk adjustment derives weights from the solution to an ordinary least squares regression of M on X.[7] Thus, conventional risk adjustment is, in fact, the solution to Eq. (12) without the constraints in Eq. (13) and is given by:

$$\beta^c = (X'X)^{-1}X'M$$

---

[7] A simple regression of M on X ignores the distributional characteristics of M. For many observations, $M = 0$ (no health care spending). Furthermore, among the positive observations, M is skewed to the right. Most of the empirical literature studying the effect of economic factors on health care use has employed a two-part model originally developed for the RAND Health Insurance Experiment (Duan *et al.*, 1983). In the first part, a use–no use equation is estimated with a logit or a probit regression. In the second part, an OLS regression is performed on a transformation (square root, log) of the dependent variable for the observations with positive spending. See Manning (1998) and Mullahy (1998) for recent discussion. The risk adjustment literature relies primarily on one-part linear regressions. The main rationale appears to be a desire for simplicity in the risk adjustment formula.

The conventional risk adjustment formula is therefore,

$$r_i^c = X_i \beta^c$$

We can express the set of S linear constraints in Eq. (13) in matrix form as $A\beta = C$, where A is an $S \times J$ matrix with elements

$$a_{sj} = \begin{cases} \dfrac{\text{cov}(m_s, x_j)}{\bar{m}_s} - \dfrac{\text{cov}(m_S, x_j)}{\bar{m}_S} & s = 1, \ldots, S-1 \\ \bar{x}_j & s = S \end{cases}$$

β is a $J \times 1$ vector of weights on the adjuster variables and C is an $S \times 1$ vector of constants with element

$$C_s = \begin{cases} \dfrac{\text{cov}(m_s, M)}{\bar{m}_s} - \dfrac{\text{cov}(m_S, M)}{\bar{m}_S} & s = 1, \ldots, S-1 \\ b & s = S \end{cases}$$

Note that the solution for MVORA described above is the estimated coefficients from a regression of M on X (i.e. as in conventional risk adjustment), constrained by the S linear restrictions in Eqs. (13) and (14) (Theil, 1961). Thus, we can write MVORA as

$$\beta^* = \beta^c + (X'X)^{-1} A' [A(X'X)^{-1} A']^{-1} (C - A\beta^c) \tag{15}$$

One can see that if the constraints in Eq. (13) are binding, MVORA will be different than conventional risk adjusters. One special case in which the constraints do not bind is when conventional risk adjustment is 'perfect' in the sense of completely capturing the variance in health care costs. In this case, $\sum_j \beta_j x_j = M$, and conditions (13) are exactly satisfied. Except in this extreme case, the constraints (13) will be binding and MVORA will differ from conventional. We can also observe that adding a new risk adjuster variable x_j will improve the regulator's ability to minimize Eq. (12). Adding a new risk adjuster with at least some correlation with some element of cost gives the regulator another instrument and must do at least as well in minimizing Eq. (12).

As the presentation of MVORA makes clear, the risk adjustment formula we propose depends on plan profit maximization. Strictly speaking, MVORA is the minimum variance risk adjustment formula that sustains the efficient expenditure decisions by plans as profit maximization. The question arises as to how to figure MVORA when expenditures are simply 'data' from some pattern of service expenditures generated by some other process, for example a fee-for-service system in which there is no health plan paid by capitation, and in which profit maximization by a health plan plays no role.[8] Any change in the payment system, for example, introduction of a risk-adjusted capitated system, will change incentives and change the pattern of services. A MVORA system can be calculated with first and second moment information from the data from the FFS system, but then introduction of the payment system would change the use patterns. It seems likely that a recalculation of the MVORA formula with the shift in use patterns, and perhaps a further recalculation, etc., would lead towards optimal service patterns, but such a question of the dynamic adjustments to risk adjustment is not formally confronted here. We are making only a weaker claim, that if the health plan is providing the efficient level of services while profit maximizing, MVORA will keep it there. (The conventional risk adjustment scheme would move the plan away from optimality).

5. AN EXAMPLE: CONVENTIONAL RISK ADJUSTMENT AND MVORA

Like conventional risk adjustment, MVORA can be found by using regression techniques in data. In this section we calculate conventional risk adjustment and MVORA in a very simple empirical example, to illustrate how MVORA works, and to show how it differs from conventional in the way premiums are figured.

Suppose data on per person spending comes from the following simple environment. There are two services a and d. The population is divided into three age groups, age 1, age 2 and age 3. The proportion of the population in age j, is α_j. Age is the only available risk adjuster. For each individual i, $x_{ij} = 1$ if the individual is in age j, and $x_{ij} = 0$ otherwise.

If an individual needs service a, the dollar value of services he will receive is m_a, regardless of his age group, and if an individual needs service d the dollar value of services he will receive is m_d, regardless of his age group. The proportion of individuals who need service a is the same in all three age groups and normalized to 1 and the proportion of individuals who need service d in age j is γ_j, $j = 1,2,3$.

In figuring MVORA, the information assumption we make in this example is the following. There are two types of people, the healthy and

---

[8]Medicare's risk adjustment system to pay HMOs is, for example, calibrated on data from the FFS sector.

the sick, differentiated by their use of service d. The healthy do not need d at all, the sick always need d. We assume that people know their type with certainty. That is, healthy people can accurately forecast that they will use m_a of service a and none of service d, and the sick type accurately forecast that they will use m_a of service a and m_d of service d. So, γ_j is the share of the sick types in age group j.

The age categories will be correlated with type so long as the γ_j differs for each age category. Age will thus have value as a risk adjuster. Conventional risk adjustment will be unable to fully solve the quality problem since under conventional risk adjustment private information remains about type and a health plan would want to 'underprovide' service d and 'overprovide' service a to attempt to attract the healthy within each age category. MVORA fixes this problem.

The calculations below are simplified because the age categories are $(0,1)$ and the anticipated use of m_d by the healthy type is zero. This allows us to avoid explicit summations over types in the covariance terms below.

Let r_j^c denote the conventionally risk adjusted premium paid for an individual in group j, then:

$$r_j^c = m_a + \gamma_j m_d \qquad (16)$$

Conventional risk adjustment simply pays for each individual the average cost of an individual in the age group the person belongs to.

Moving to optimal risk adjustment, we need to define some covariances for this example. One should first notice that since all individuals in all age groups use the same level of service a,

$$\operatorname{cov}(m_a, x_j) = 0, \quad \text{for } j = 1, 2, 3 \qquad (17)$$

and

$$\operatorname{cov}(m_a, M) = 0, \qquad (18)$$

where M denotes the total dollar value of services the individual receives.

As for service d, under our assumptions:

$$\operatorname{cov}(m_d, x_j) = \alpha_j (\bar{m}_{dj} - \bar{m}_d) \quad \text{for } j = 1, 2, 3 \qquad (19)$$

where:

$$\bar{m}_{dj} = \gamma_j m_d \qquad (20)$$

is the average dollar value of services d used by an individual in age j, and

$$\bar{m}_d = \sum_{j=1}^{3} \alpha_j \bar{m}_{dj} \tag{21}$$

is the population average use of service d.

Furthermore, since m_a is the same for all individuals, we get that:

$$\text{cov}(m_d, M) = \text{var}(m_d) \tag{22}$$

In order to calculate the optimally risk adjusted premium we assume that the plan breaks even namely,

$$b = m_a + \bar{m}_d \tag{23}$$

where b is the budget per person.

Note that under the conventionally risk adjusted premium above the plan also breaks even, so the comparison between the two payments schemes will be on an equal basis.

Plugging Eqs. (17)–(23) into Eqs. (10) and (11) we obtain that optimal risk adjustment is a triple $(\beta_1^o, \beta_2^o, \beta_3^o)$ that solves the following two equations:

$$\sum_{j=1}^{3} \beta_j^o \alpha_j (\bar{m}_{dj} - \bar{m}_d) - \text{Var}(m_d) = 0 \tag{24}$$

and

$$\sum_{j=1}^{3} \beta_j^o \alpha_j = m_a + \bar{m}_d \tag{25}$$

The MVORA is the triple $(\beta_1^*, \beta_2^*, \beta_3^*)$ that solves

$$\text{Min}_{\beta_1, \beta_2, \beta_3} \sum_{j=1}^{3} \alpha_j \left[\gamma_j (m_a + m_d - \beta_j)^2 + (1 - \gamma_j)(m_a - \beta_j)^2 \right] \tag{26}$$

s.t. Eqs. (24) and (25).

Table 1 presents a special case of the example above. The first column in Table 1 specifies the three age groups, the second specifies α, the proportion of each group in the population, the third column specifies γ, sickness d's probability, the fourth column specifies m_a, the dollar value of service a, the fifth column specifies m_d, the dollar value of service d. The last two columns compare r^c, the conventional risk adjustment premium, with r^*, the MVORA premium, for each age group.

Table 1. An example of Conventional and Minimum Variance Optimal Risk Adjustment

Age group	α	γ	m_a	m_d	r^c	r^*
1	0.6	0.05	150	200	160	5.28
2	0.2	0.2	150	200	190	325.37
3	0.2	0.3	150	200	210	538.77

As can be seen from the table, the conventional and MVORA premiums are quite different. For the relatively healthy age group 1 (the 'young') MVORA pays much less than conventional risk adjustment whereas for the other two age groups it pays much more. As is well-known, since age is an imperfect indicator of type, a conventionally risk adjusted premium will leave a health plan with some incentives to attract the healthy types (those that would use only service a) within each age group. The conventional premiums would therefore induce a plan to 'oversupply' treatment for service a and 'undersupply' treatment for service d. MVORA premiums counteract this incentive. By undersupplying service d, the plan would tend to discourage relatively more of the age 3 people. By paying more for the age 3 group, MVORA gives the plan a strong incentive to keep them. Indeed, MVORA figures the risk-adjusted weights so that the incentive to supply both service a and d is just balanced to efficiently allocate a fixed budget. The marked disparity between the conventional risk adjustment and MVORA is a consequence of the extreme assumption we make about private information. If individuals could not perfectly forecast their health care use, MVORA would be closer to conventional.

One can also return to Eq. (5) above to examine shadow prices if plans were paid by conventional risk adjustment. In our extreme example, the situation would be disastrous for service d. Since everyone who has positive spending on service d is a loser (negative π), the denominator of Eq. (5) is so small it is negative! Essentially, a plan has an incentive with conventional risk adjustment to reduce service d to as low a level as possible.

6. UNCERTAINTY AND ASYMMETRIC INFORMATION

The analysis so far has assumed that both the plan and the individual know with certainty the spending in dollars on each of the health care services that will be used by the individual, m_{is}. We shall now extend our model to the more realistic case where both the individual and the plan only hold some beliefs about the future health care needs of the individual, and these beliefs may not be the same. We will see that the two crucial elements in the analysis here are the plan's beliefs about each individual i's expected use of each service s, which we denote by $\tilde{m}_{is}$, and the plan's beliefs about individual i's beliefs of how much of the services he is expected to use, denoted by $\hat{m}_{is}$.

In Appendix A, we analyze plans' behavior in this case and show that the profit maximizing shadow prices are given by:

$$q_s = \frac{\sum_i n_i \tilde{m}_{is}}{\sum_i \phi_i' \hat{m}_{is}(r_i - \tilde{M}_i)}. \tag{5'}$$

A plan's expected profit for an individual is the product of the probability the person joins the plan times the profit or loss once he is a member. The probability that he joins depends on what the person believes he will receive in terms of services in the plan. The profit once he is enrolled depends on revenue and use in the plan. It is the plan's expectations about these two elements that will govern plan behavior in rationing care. Note that with respect to the decision to join a plan, the plan must form beliefs about what the consumers' expect. This is $\hat{m}$. Once in the plan, and from the point of view of the plan, what consumers expect is no longer relevant — what matters is what the plan expects a person to use. This is $\tilde{m}$. The placement of $\hat{m}$ and $\tilde{m}$ in Eq. (5′) reflects these considerations. See Appendix A for derivation.

Now MVORA can be redefined to be the solution to the following problem:

$$\operatorname*{Minimize}_{\beta_1,\ldots,\beta_J} \frac{1}{N} \sum_i \left(\tilde{M}_i - \sum_j \beta_j x_{ij} \right)^2 \tag{12'}$$

$$\text{s.t.} \sum_j \beta_j \left[\frac{\operatorname{cov}(\hat{m}_s, x_j)}{\bar{m}_s} - \frac{\operatorname{cov}(\hat{m}_S, x_j)}{\bar{m}_S} \right] = \frac{\operatorname{cov}(\hat{m}_s, \tilde{M})}{\bar{m}_s} - \frac{\operatorname{cov}(\hat{m}_S, \tilde{M})}{\bar{m}_S}$$

$$s = 1, \ldots, S-1 \tag{13'}$$

and

$$\sum_j \beta_j \bar{x}_j = b \tag{14'}$$

The objective function in Eq. (12′) is a modification of Eq. (12) to take into consideration a *plan's beliefs* about its expected loss (profit) on each individual. Condition (12′) is meant to capture the problem of individual access. As such, it is plan's expectations about what persons will cost in the plan that govern plans' decisions about access. We believe it is reasonable to suppose that if $\tilde{M}_i$ differs from r_i, access problems may emerge. Therefore, minimization of the sum of the squares of the deviations of r_i from a plan's expectations of costs, $\tilde{M}_i$, is a reasonable criterion. The constraint (13′) comes from Eq. (5′) in a way similar to the way we have obtained Eq. (13) from Eq. (5).

The solution for MVORA described above is the estimated coefficients from a regression of $\tilde{M}$ on X, constrained by the S linear restrictions. Thus, we can write MVORA as

$$\beta^* = \tilde{\beta} + (X'X)^{-1}A'[A(X'X)^{-1}A']^{-1}(C - A\tilde{\beta}) \qquad (15')$$

where, $\tilde{\beta} = (X'X)^{-1}X'\tilde{M}$, and A is an $S \times J$ matrix with elements

$$a_{sj} = \begin{cases} \dfrac{\text{cov}(m_s, x_j)}{\bar{m}_s} - \dfrac{\text{cov}(m_S, x_j)}{\bar{m}_S} & s = 1, \ldots, S-1 \\ \bar{x}_j & s = S \end{cases}$$

β is a $J \times 1$ vector of weights on the adjuster variables and C is an $S \times 1$ vector of constants with element

$$C_s = \begin{cases} \dfrac{\text{cov}(m_s, M)}{\bar{m}_s} - \dfrac{\text{cov}(m_S, M)}{\bar{m}_S} & s = 1, \ldots, S-1 \\ b & s = S \end{cases}$$

In the case of uncertainty and asymmetric information the conventional risk adjusters will be different than MVORA for two reasons. First, even if the constraints (13′) were not binding, the solution to MVORA will be $\tilde{\beta}$ and not β^c. Second, if the constraints are binding, the solution will be given by the constraints and will not come from an unconstrained regression.

7. DISCUSSION

The quality of health care offered by competing managed health care plans is the foremost concern of health policy in the U.S. and many other countries. Many elements of quality cannot be controlled by regulation, leaving open the opportunity for plans to manipulate the quality they offer in an effort to achieve a profitable mix of enrollees. Another policy concern is that plans may take actions to discriminate against particular individuals. The method of risk adjustment proposed here contends with both the quality and the access problem in an empirically implementable way. Conditions for optimal risk adjustment can be derived from the means and covariances among risk adjuster variables and elements of health care spending. A statistical fit criterion can then readily be applied to select among the weights satisfying conditions for efficient quality.

Application of our methodology requires that the distribution of health care spending in a population be available at the level of the service, not just in total. The concept of a service represents the level of aggregation at which management of a health plan makes decisions about resource allocation. In most health care claims data sets, information on the diagnosis, location of services (office, hospital, etc.), procedure conducted, and specialty or type of provider is typically included on the claim. Information is certainly available to classify health care encounters into the 'services' called for in our paper; the issue is, however, how all this data should be used to do so. This requires new work on 'classification' of health care use from the point of view of resource management. Theoretical work can consider the implications of using 'too fine' or 'too coarse' methods of aggregation for purposes of deriving conditions for optimal risk adjustment.

Our method also calls for information about expected health care costs, specifically, plans' expectations about the consumers' costs, and plans beliefs about consumers' expectations. While this may seem a dismaying prospect, in this respect we are no worse off than conventional risk adjustment. Careful discussions about the goals of conventional risk adjustment have recognized for some time that the objective of conventional risk adjustment is to explain 'predictable costs,' yet it is actual costs that we see in the regressions deriving recommended weights. The same fallback of using the distribution of actual spending as opposed to expected spending is available to our method as well.

Another way to look at the issue is as a topic for research. Health plans make the decisions about resource allocation and access on the basis of expectations. Regulators attempting to counter the adverse consequences of these decisions would benefit by knowing how plans make decisions and based on what information. The saliency of plans' expectations to the policy issues related to quality and access makes this a very important topic for empirical research.

ACKNOWLEDGEMENTS

This paper was written while McGuire was at Boston University. Research support from grants R01 MH59254 from the National Institute of Mental Health and P01 HS10803 from the Agency for Health Research and Quality are gratefully acknowledged. We are grateful to Margarita Alegria, Ana Balsa, Zhun Cao, David Cutler, Randy Ellis, Richard Frank, Alberto Holly, Mathias Kifmann, Kevin Lang, Joseph Newhouse, Mark Satterthwaite, Manuel Trajtenberg, and Alan Zaslavsky for comments on an earlier draft. Remaining errors are the authors' responsibility.

APPENDIX A. PROFIT MAXIMIZATION WITH UNCERTAINTY AND ASYMMETRIC INFORMATION

Let T denote the set of possible health states of each individual and let t denote an element in T. Let $v_t = \{v_{t1}(m_{t1}), v_{t2}(m_{t2}), \ldots, v_{ts}(m_{ts})\}$ denote the vector of S valuation functions for the S services, if an individual's health state is realized to be t. We assume that for each t and s, $v_{ts}(\cdot)$ satisfies the properties discussed earlier.

Let $\check{x}$ be some random variable, the value of which depends on the state t, and let k be a distribution function defined over T. Let $E_k[\check{x}]$ denote the expected value of $\check{x}$ with respect to the distribution k.

The order of moves is as follows: at the first stage, the plan chooses its level of shadow prices $q = (q_1, q_2, \ldots, q_S)$. When choosing q, the plan is uncertain about each individual i's health state t, and it holds prior beliefs about it, denoted by (the distribution over T) g_i. At the second stage, individuals observe the plan's level of shadow prices and decide whether or not to join. At this stage, the individual is uncertain about his true health state t and he holds some prior beliefs about it. Let f_i be a distribution function over T which denotes the *plan's beliefs about individual i's beliefs* about his health state t. Thus, both g_i and f_i are plans' beliefs, the first is the plan's beliefs about individual i's health state and the second is its beliefs about what the individual thinks his health state to be.

At the third stage, when services are provided, the individual's 'true' health state is already known. Hence, for a given shadow price q_s and a valuation function v_{ts}, the plan's expenditures on this individual in service s will be $m_{ts}(q_s)$, given by:

$$v'_{ts}(m_{ts}(q_s)) = q_s.$$

Let $v_t(q) = \sum_s v_{ts}(m_{ts}(q_s))$.

Let $\bar{u}_t$ denote the individual's utility if his health state is t and he chooses the alternative plan. The plan's assigned probability that the individual will join is given by (we drop momentarily the subscript i from the analysis):

$$n_f(q) = 1 - \phi(E_f[\bar{u}_t - \check{v}_t])$$

The plan's expected profit on the individual is

$$\pi_{fg}(q) = n_f(q) \left(r - E_g \left[\sum_s \check{m}_{ts}(q_s) \right] \right).$$

Differentiating with respect to $q_{s'}$ yields

$$\frac{d\pi_{fg}(q)}{dq_{s'}} = \phi' E_f[\check{v}'_{ts'}, \check{m}'_{ts'}] \left(r - E_g \left[\sum_s \check{m}_{ts}(q_s) \right] \right) - n_f E_g[\check{m}'_{ts'}]$$

Using $v'_{ts} = q_s$ and $m'_{ts} = (e_s m_{ts})/q_s$ for all t, where e_s is the elasticity of demand (common to all individuals) for service s (see FGM, 1999), the right-hand side becomes

$$e_{s'} \left(\phi' \hat{m}_{s'} (r - \bar{M}) - \frac{n_f \tilde{m}_{s'}}{q_{s'}} \right)$$

where $\hat{m}_{s'} = E_f[\check{m}_{ts'}]$ is the plan's belief about the individuals' prediction of the health resources he will consume, $\bar{m} = E_g[\check{m}_{ts'}]$ is the plan's prediction of its expenditure on the individual, and $\bar{M} = \sum_s \bar{m}_s$.

With a population of N individuals, the profit-maximizing q_s will therefore be (5') from the text.[9]

REFERENCES

Chapman, J.D., 1997. Biased Enrollment and Risk Adjustment for Health Plans, unpublished PhD dissertation, Harvard University.

Cutler, D., Zeckhauser, R., 2000. The anatomy of health insurance. In: Culyer, A., Newhouse, J. (Eds.), Handbook of Health Economics. North Holland.

Duan, N. *et al.*, 1983. A comparison of alternative models for the demand for medical care. *Journal of Economic and Business Statistics* 1, 115–126.

Ellis, R.P., Pope, G., Iezzoni, L. *et al.*, 1996. Diagnosis-based risk adjustment for medicare capitation payments. *Health Care Financing Review* 17(3), 101–128.

---

[9]Inducing a plan to supply services requires some profit. In the case of a perfect fit between a risk-adjusted payment r_i and $\bar{M}_i$, expected profit on each person would be zero. In this case, some fixed costs are necessary (as in any model of monopolistic competition).

Encinosa, W., 1999. The Economic Theory of Risk Adjusting Capitation Rates, Agency for Health Research and Quality, unpublished.

Enthoven, A.C., 1993. The history and principles of managed competition. *Health Affairs* 12 (Supplement), 24–48.

Frank, R., Glazer, J., McGuire, T., 2000. Measuring adverse selection in managed health care. *Journal of Health Economics* 19, 829–854.

Glazer, J., McGuire, T.G., 2000. Optimal risk adjustment of health insurance premiums: an application to managed care. *American Economic Review* 90(4), 1055–1071.

Keeler, E., Carter, G., Newhouse, J., 1998. A model of the impact of reimbursement schemes health plan choice. *Journal of Health Economics* 17(3), 297–320.

Keenan, P., Beeuwkes, B.M., McGuire, T., Newhouse, J., 2001. The prevalence of formal risk adjustment, Fall, Inquiry 38(3), 245–259.

Ma, C.-T.A., 1994. Health care payment systems: cost and quality incentives. *Journal of Economics and Management Strategy* 3(1), 93–112.

Manning, W.G., 1998. The logged dependent variable heteroskedasticity and the retransformation problem. *Journal of Health Economics* 17(3), 283–296.

Miller, R.H., Luft, H.S., 1997. Does managed care lead to better or worse quality of care? *Health Affairs* 16(5), 7–25.

Mullahy, J., 1998. Much ado about two: reconsidering retransformation and the two-part model in health econometrics. *Journal of Health Economics* 17(3), 247–282.

Neudeck, W., Podczeck, K., 1996. Adverse selection and regulation in health insurance markets. *Journal of Health Economics* 15, 387–408.

Newhouse, J., 1996. Reimbursing health plans and health providers: efficiency in production versus selection. *Journal of Economic Literature* 34, 1236–1263.

Rogerson, W., 1994. Choice of treatment incentives by a nonprofit hospital under prospective pricing. *Journal of Economics and Management Strategy* 3(1), 7–51.

Selden, T., 1999. Premium subsidies for health insurance: excessive coverage versus adverse selection. *Journal of Health Economics* 18, 709–725.

Shen, Y., Ellis, R.P., 2000. Cost Minimizing Risk Adjustment, unpublished, Boston University.

Theil, H., 1961. Economic Forecasts and Policy, 2nd Edition. North-Holland.

van deVen, W.P.M.M., Ellis, R.P., 2000. Risk adjustment in competitive health plan markets. In: Culyer, A.J., Newhouse, J.P. (Eds.), Handbook of Health Economics. North-Holland.

Weiner, J., Dobson, A., Maxwell, S. *et al.*, 1996. Risk adjusted capitation rates using ambulatory and inpatient diagnoses. *Health Care Financing Review* 17(3), 77–99.

Chapter 4

OPTIMAL QUALITY REPORTING IN MARKETS FOR HEALTH PLANS

Jacob Glazer[a,b] and Thomas G. McGuire[c,*]

[a] *Boston University, Boston, USA*
muse@hcp.med.harvard.edu

[b] *Tel Aviv University, Tel Aviv, Israel*

[c] *Harvard Medical School,*
Department of Health Care Policy, Boston, MA, USA

Received 1 November 2004; received in revised form 26 September 2005;
accepted 14 October 2005
Available online 13 December 2005

Quality reports about health plans and providers are becoming more prevalent in health care markets. This paper casts the decision about what information to report to consumers about health plans as a policy decision. In a market with adverse selection, complete information about quality leads to inefficient outcomes. In a Rothschild-Stiglitz model, we show that averaging quality information into a summary report can enforce pooling in health insurance, and by choice of the right weights in the averaged report, a payer or regulator can induce first-best quality choices. The optimal quality report is as powerful as optimal risk adjustment in correcting adverse selection inefficiencies.
©2005 Elsevier B.V. All rights reserved.

JEL classification: Ill; D82

Keywords: quality reports; health care; adverse selection

There is a general consensus that consumers know too little about the quality of health care services they buy, and improving what consumers know would make markets function better. Better-informed consumers may choose providers more appropriately. Furthermore, consumers and patients choosing on the basis of quality conveys incentives to providers to improve

---

*Corresponding author.

quality in the first place. These arguments motivate public regulators and business coalitions to discover and reveal characteristics of providers' quality of care.[1] There is, however, a glitch in the argument: markets in health care are subject to adverse selection-related inefficiencies even in the presence of complete information (Cutler and Zeckhauser, 2000; Van de Ven and Ellis, 2000). For example, consumers' knowledge about the quality of services they anticipate receiving at a health plan drives the plan to set quality suboptimally for services that will be used by enrollees whose expected costs exceed their expected revenue (Frank *et al.*, 2000). With consumers' information an essential element in the adverse selection causal chain, it is not self-evident that giving consumers more information will improve health care markets.[2]

This paper casts the decision of what information about quality to report to consumers as a policy instrument. We focus on markets for health plans, where in many cases a regulator supplies information to consumers about quality at the plans. For example, before choosing a plan, consumers in California can consult an annual report published by the state (Office of the Patient Advocate, 2003) containing plan ratings from a consumer survey and from medical record based indicators. More than 75 million people in the U.S. enroll in capitation-based health plans (Keenan *et al.*, 2001). These health plans provide a range of health care services, including obstetric care, mental health care, oncology, vision services and so on. Potential enrollees

---

[1] Public payers, like Medicare (Clancy and Scully, 2003), and private coalitions, like the Leapfrog Group (Berkmeyer *et al.*, 2000), are constructing quality reports intended to reward providers for improving quality. Medicare and the Federal Employees Health Benefit Plan (FEHBP), have made quality reports about plans or providers available to beneficiaries for some time, either as experiments or on a regular basis (Wedig and Tai-Seale, 2002).

[2] The economics literature outside of health care contains papers pointing out that in the presence of some other inefficiency, improving buyers' information need not improve the efficiency of a market equilibrium. Generally, the reason for this is that while more information may improve the quality of consumers' decisions, other parties to the exchange may behave differently when dealing with better-informed consumers, and their reactions might lead to a worse net efficiency effect of more information. For example, Schlee (1996) studies a market in which a monopolist sets price so as to equalize marginal cost and marginal revenue, but because information is imperfect, the marginal revenue reflects consumers' expectations about quality. With more information, consumers' expectations become more accurate, but may affect the shape of the marginal revenue function in ways that lead to a worse market outcome post better information (for related analyses in the general literature, see Hirshleifer, 1971; Mirman *et al.*, 1994; Glazer and McGuire, 2003).

choose a plan partly on the basis of what they anticipate will be the quality of services they receive in the plan.

Our main finding about reporting is intuitive and practical: by providing information only about the average quality of services in a health plan, rather than the quality of each of the elements of service a plan provides, a payer or regulator can give consumers helpful information but prevent a plan from setting quality of its services to try to attract a profitable mix of enrollees. The averaged report is powerful: the right weights for elements of quality in the averaged report induce a plan to produce the socially efficient quality of all services. This strong result emerges in a basic model of adverse selection where the efficient outcome is a pooling equilibrium and there are no heterogeneous tastes to be served among consumers. More complicated models of health insurance with plan heterogeneity (about which consumers would need to know) and some pricing related to risk might call for other information strategies.

Our general result, that social welfare in the case where consumers can only observe the average quality of each plan can be higher than social welfare in the case where consumers have full information about the quality of each of the services a plan offers, is somewhat surprising, especially under the assumption that consumers are rational. Consumers' rationality implies that even when they cannot observe the quality of each of the services a plan provides, and they can only observe the average quality of these services, in equilibrium, consumers do know the precise quality of each of these services. This property follows from the standard assumption that in equilibrium rational agents know the strategies of all other agents, which in our model implies that the consumers know the quality of the services each plan chooses. However, in both cases, the full information case and the case where consumers can only observe the average quality of each plan, individuals know the quality of each of the services each plans offers in equilibrium. The quality provided in the two cases will not be the same and the one offered in the latter case may be more efficient than the one offered in the first case. Thus, by revealing to consumers only the average quality of the different services a plan offers, a public regulator may be able to alter the quality of services offered by the plan without actually damaging what the consumers know about these qualities in equilibrium.

After a brief review of the policy context in Section 1, Section 2 modifies the model introduced by Rothschild and Stiglitz (1976), in order to demonstrate the inefficiencies due to adverse selection that may emerge in competitive insurance markets. Section 3 reviews the familiar result that if consumers can observe quality, the market equilibrium leads to inefficient quality profiles.[3] Section 4 changes what consumers observe to some "average" of the quality elements in a plan. We show in this case there is a unique pooling equilibrium associated with each weighted average quality report. Section 5 establishes that a payer or regulator can achieve the first-best quality profile by choice of the weights in the average report. Our analysis implies that regulation of quality reports can be a powerful tool for improving the efficiency of health insurance markets. Section 6 considers some extensions and reconsiders some of our assumptions. Section 7 contains some brief final comments.

1. QUALITY OF CARE AND ADVERSE SELECTION IN HEALTH CARE

Following a series of reports about the frequency of poor quality and the impact of poor quality on outcomes and costs, the quality of health care is attracting attention throughout the health care sector.[4] Some quality problems are simple "medical errors" in which decisions made, including those about choice of techniques or technologies, would be revised if management or physicians were aware of best practices (Institute of Medicine, 1999). Other quality problems are systemic and due to "standard operating procedures" that fail to make full use of information systems or embody sufficient checks on human error (Classen and Kildgridge, 2002; Institute of Medicine, 2001). The quality problems that could be addressed with reporting to consumers are different: plans do not always have the incentives to provide the socially efficient level of care (Galvin and Milstein, 2002), and altering incentives can, therefore, be part of the solution (Sage *et al.*, 2003). The most pervasive incentive problem in health care markets is the problem of adverse selection (Van de Ven and Ellis, 2000).

---

[3]The model set up is similar to that in Glazer and McGuire (2000), with the exception of our treatment of the premium paid to plans. Glazer and McGuire applied the model introduced by Rothschild and Stiglitz (1976) to illustrate the limitations of the conventional risk adjustment mechanisms and to demonstrate how risk adjustment weights should be structured in order to optimally address the quality distortion problems due to adverse selection incentives in managed care. In this paper there is no risk adjustment and a plan is paid the same for all enrollees.

[4]The March/April (2003) issue of *Health Affairs* contains a number of policy-related papers on health care quality. The Institute of Medicine has produced a number of important reports on quality, a recent one being IOM (2003).

The fundamental problem of adverse selection is that risk bearing plans have incentives to discourage enrollment by potential members whose expected revenue falls short of expected costs. It has been known for some time that in a population facing choice, persons joining managed care plans are less costly than those staying in fee-for-service (Hellinger, 1995), though by itself, this is not necessarily associated with an inefficiency (Pauly, 1985). Efficiency problems stem from actions a plan takes to discourage enrollment of the likely financial losers. In public and private health insurance in the U.S., provisions requiring "open enrollment" prohibit plans from excluding eligible enrollees. Instead, plans can discourage enrollment by costly potential enrollees by providing a low quality of care of the services these enrollees are likely to use. Incentives to distort an insurance plan to discourage demand from "bad risks" were integral to one of the first models of insurance markets (Rothschild and Stiglitz, 1976), and these same ideas have been applied to health insurance (Glazer and McGuire, 2000; Newhouse, 1996) where the practice has been termed "service-level selection." It is generally recognized that the "quality problem" in managed care plans varies by service, and that plans have the means and the motive to ration care more tightly for some services and less tightly for others (Luft and Miller, 1988; Newhouse, 2002).

An emerging empirical literature confirms the presence of service-level selection activities by health plans. Frank *et al.* (2000) derived the characteristics of services that would be subject to under and over provision in managed care, and found that the incentives to ration various services varied considerably. One of the consistent findings in this literature so far is that the incentive to tightly ration mental health care is particularly strong. Cao (2003) finds that aged Medicare beneficiaries joining managed care plans have psychiatric Part B costs 30% lower than persons not joining managed care, whereas for physician primary care services in Part B, those joining managed care plans have 4% higher costs. Medicare beneficiaries with mental health problems appear to anticipate lower quality of care in managed care plans (in comparison with people with problems handled by general medical services), and are thereby *more* deterred from joining the plans relative to the average beneficiary. Cao and McGuire (2003) found evidence for service-level selection in Medicare by examining how greater HMO enrollment affected the distribution of patters of service use among beneficiaries remaining in regular Medicare. Mello *et al.* (2002) found a differential pattern of selection in Medicare for Part A and Part B costs consistent with service-level selection.

The health services literature on quality reporting in health care contains mixed findings about how reports affect consumer and plan behavior. When asked hypothetical questions, consumers say that they value reported measures of quality, and would use them in plan choice (Edgman-Levitan and Cleary, 1996; Hibbard and Jewett, 1996). Some studies of the actual effect of distribution of report card information found no discernible effect on plan choice (Chernew and Scanlon, 1998; Farley et al., 2002), but other studies have found an effect (Beaulieu, 2002; Scanlon et al., 2002). Wedig and Tai-Seale (2002) exploit a natural experiment created by the timing of report card information for federal employees and find that the reports apparently increase consumers' willingness to choose lower priced plans when they have some credible information about quality. Chernew et al. (2004) find employers' decisions about offering plans are positively related to plans' performance scores. When effects of reporting have been found, they have not always been salutary, however. Publication of physician and hospital coronary artery bypass graft (CABG) mortality rates in New York and Pennsylvania induced providers to operate more on the less severely ill, and operate less on the more severely ill. Weighing the benefits and costs, Dranove et al. (2003) concluded the reports reduced social welfare.

2. THE MODEL

Suppose that there are two types of individuals, L and H, who can contract two illnesses, a and c. Illness a we call an acute illness and both types of people have the same probability of contracting this illness, $p_a > 0$. The two types are distinguished in their probability of contracting the chronic illness c. Let $p_i, i \in \{H, L\}$ denote the probability that a person of type i contracts illness c. Then, $p_H > p_L > 0$. The proportion of H types in the population is λ, $0 < \lambda < 1$. Let $p_c \equiv \lambda p_H + (1 - \lambda)p_L$ denote the (expected) probability that a randomly drawn person contracts the chronic illness. We assume that each individual knows her type.[5]

If a person (of either type) has illness $j, j \in \{a, c\}$, her utility from treatment will be increased by $V_j(q_j)$, where $q_j > 0$ denotes the "quality" of the services devoted to treat illness j, with $V_j' > 0$ and $V_j'' \leq 0$.[6]

---

[5] For more discussion of the assumptions in this section, see Glazer and McGuire (2000).
[6] The economic literature models quality in two ways: as a form of quantity rationing, as here and in Pauly and Ramsey (1999), or as a shadow price as in Keeler et al. (1998), or

Thus, we make the simplifying assumption that the benefits from treatment are independent of one another and the same to all individuals. If a person has both illnesses, her utility, if treated, will simply be increased by $V_a(q_a) + V_c(q_c)$.

Treatment services are provided by health plans. A health plan is characterized by a quality pair (q_a, q_c). Thus, if a person of type i, $i \in \{H, L\}$ joins a plan with a quality pair (q_a, q_c), her expected utility will increase by:

$$U_i(q_a, q_c) = p_a V_a(q_a) + p_i V_c(q_c) \tag{1}$$

All plans have the same cost function. A plan's cost of treating a person with illness j, $j \in \{a, c\}$ at a quality level q_j is $C_j(q_j)$, where $C'_j > 0, C''_j > 0$. Thus, if a person of type $i, i \in \{H, L\}$ joins a plan that offers a quality pair (q_a, q_c), the plan's costs are expected to increase by:

$$C_i(q_a, q_c) = p_a C_a(q_a) + p_i C_c(q_c) \tag{2}$$

In our model, each plan gets to choose its quality pair and the focus of our analysis is on the quality pairs that will be offered by the plans and purchased by the consumers in equilibrium. Before we study the market equilibrium, however, it is worthwhile to briefly discuss the socially efficient outcome. The *socially efficient* quality pair (q_a^*, q_c^*) equalizes marginal benefit of treatment to marginal cost, thus solving the following pair of equations:

$$V'_a(q_a^*) = C'_a(q_a^*)$$
$$V'_c(q_c^*) = C'_c(q_c^*) \tag{3}$$

High- and low-risk types have different probabilities of becoming ill, but once ill, receive the same utility from treatment. Thus, the efficient level of quality is independent of the probability of becoming ill and is the same for both types.

Assume that there are no copayments for use of services and that the premium paid to a plan (either by the consumers or by a payer) for each enrollee is exogenously set and is the same to all plans and for all individuals. Thus, we assume no price competition among plans and no

---

Frank *et al.* (2000). When consumers are identical in their demands given they are ill, and differ only in the probability of having an illness, the two approaches are equivalent.

risk adjustment.[7] More specifically, throughout the paper we assume that
the premium is set at r^*, where

$$r^* = p_a C_a(q_a^*) + p_c C_c(q_c^*) \tag{4}$$

Thus, the premium is set such that the plan is expected to break even
if it offers the socially efficient quality pair (q_a^*, q_c^*) and attracts randomly
drawn individuals from the entire population. Further assume that all
individuals must choose a plan and plans must accept every applicant.
Each individual can choose only one plan and each plan can offer only one
quality pair (q_a, q_c).

The order of moves in our model is as follows: first plans (simultaneously) choose their quality pair (q_a, q_c), then individuals choose plans on
the basis of whatever information they have about plans' quality and plans
collect a revenue of r^* per enrollee, finally each individual's health state
(whether she has illness a and/or c) is realized and plans pay the costs of
treatment.

We will study the competitive equilibrium in two situations, one where
individuals can fully observe each plan's quality pair when they choose a
plan and the other where individuals can only observe a weighted average
of the two dimensions of each plan's quality.

3. CONSUMERS CAN FULLY OBSERVE QUALITY

Assume that, before choosing a plan, individuals can fully observe the
quality profile (q_a, q_c) of each plan. Our definition of a competitive
equilibrium in this case is similar to that of Rothschild and Stiglitz (1976).
A *competitive equilibrium* in this market is a set of quality pairs such that,
when individuals choose a plan to maximize expected utility, (i) no quality
pair in the equilibrium set makes negative expected profit and (ii) there
is no quality pair outside the equilibrium set that if offered, will make a
positive profit.

The following proposition builds on Rothschild and Stiglitz (1976) and
Glazer and McGuire (2000).

Proposition 1. *Suppose that individuals can observe the quality pair
of each plan. If λ (the proportion of the H types in the population) is*

---

[7]The role of risk adjustment as an alternative mechanism to address problems of adverse
selection is discussed in Section 6.

sufficiently large, then a competitive equilibrium exists and is characterized
by two quality pairs.[8] *H types choose a plan that offers the quality pair:*

$$\left(q_a^{\mathrm{H}}, q_c^{\mathrm{H}}\right) = \operatorname{argmax} U_{\mathrm{H}}(q_a, q_c)$$

$$\text{s.t. } C_{\mathrm{H}}(q_a, q_c) = r^*$$

and L types choose a plan that offers the quality pair:

$$\left(q_a^{\mathrm{L}}, q_c^{\mathrm{L}}\right) = \operatorname{argmax} U_{\mathrm{L}}(q_a, q_c)$$

$$\text{s.t. } C_{\mathrm{L}}(q_a, q_c) = r^*$$

$$\text{and} \quad U_{\mathrm{L}}(q_a, q_c) = U_{\mathrm{H}}\left(q_a^{\mathrm{H}}, q_c^{\mathrm{H}}\right)$$

The proof of the proposition above is well established (see Glazer and
McGuire, 2000). The reason that the socially efficient quality pair (q_a^*, q_c^*)
cannot be an equilibrium pair is that if all plans offer this quality profile,
each (single) plan will have an incentive to deviate to a different pair, say
(q_a', q_c') with a better acute care (i.e., $(q_a' > q_a^*)$) and a worse chronic care
(i.e., $(q_c' < q_c^*)$), attracting only the L types and making a strictly positive
profit. The equilibrium in the full information case is described in Fig. 1.
The curves r_i^*, $i = \mathrm{H}, \mathrm{L}$ represent all plans, i.e., pairs of (q_a, q_c) that break

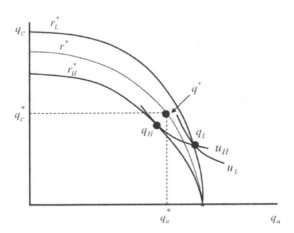

Figure 1. Equilibrium when quality is observable.

---

[8]The exact condition is that λ should be sufficiently large so that $U_{\mathrm{L}}(q_a^{\mathrm{L}}, q_c^{\mathrm{L}}) \geq U_{\mathrm{L}}(q_a, q_c)$
for every (q_a, q_c) for which $p_a C_a(q_a) + p_c C_c(q_c) = r^*$.

even if the plan attracts only individuals of type i, when the premium is r^*. The points denoted by $q_i, i = $ H or L, depict the plan chosen by type i in equilibrium, i.e., $q_i = (q_a^i, q_c^i)$. Curves $u_i, i = $ H, L, represent type i's indifference curves that go through the point q_i. The curve r^* represents all plans that break even if the plan attracts a random sample of the population, and the point q^* depicts the socially efficient levels of quality. We can see, therefore, that in a market with full information and no risk adjustment, plans will not offer the socially efficient quality profile in equilibrium.[9]

In what follows we study the case where consumers cannot observe any of the quality elements composing the good and the only information they can rely on is the average quality of these elements. One could, of course, allow for many other information configurations. If, for example, in our model consumers could not observe one of the two elements of the product's quality and could perfectly observe the other, each plan would set the "unobserved" element of quality at its lowest feasible level and the level of the other element at its highest level so that it breaks even given the premium and given that it attracts a random sample of the population. If both elements of quality were unobservable by consumers, all plans would have set both of them at their lowest feasible level. The case analyzed below is the one we believe is the most interesting as it demonstrates the potential "power" of quality indices as regulatory instruments.

4. INDIVIDUALS CAN ONLY OBSERVE AVERAGE QUALITY

In many markets, including in health care, individuals must chose complicated products or services on the basis of quality summaries without being able to observe all of the quality elements composing the good. For a given quality pair (q_a, q_c) chosen by a plan and $0 < a < 1$, let

$$\bar{q}_a = \alpha q_a + (1 - \alpha) q_c \tag{5}$$

be the (weighted) average quality of this plan. Assume that individuals cannot observe (q_a, q_c) but they can observe $\bar{q}_\alpha$ of each plan. That is,

---

[9]The reason for inefficiency of equilibrium is that plans cannot change different premiums to the two types. This could be because plans cannot observe type, or, because regulation requires equal premiums.

individuals cannot observe the quality of each of the services a plan offers, but they can observe some summary indicator of the plan's quality profile.

The fact that individuals can only observe the "average" quality of each plan, and not the quality of each service a plan offers, will affect the market equilibrium. The profitability of any quality pair (q_a, q_c) depends on individuals' beliefs about the quality of each service, given that they can only observe the average quality of the two services. In order to analyze competitive equilibrium in the market where individuals only observe average quality of each plan, one therefore needs to generalize the earlier competitive equilibrium concept to incorporate individuals' beliefs about quality in the definition of equilibrium. We apply the following definition (which is in the spirit of Perfect Bayesian and Sequential equilibria).

A *competitive equilibrium* is a set of quality pairs offered by plans and a set of individuals' belief functions that specify for each individual her beliefs about the quality pair of each plan, for every possible average quality $\bar{q}_a$ of that plan,[10] such that: (i) each plan maximizes its profit given all the other pairs offered and given individuals' beliefs, (ii) each individual chooses a plan that offers her the highest expected utility given her information and given her beliefs, (iii) there is no quality pair outside the equilibrium set that if offered will make a positive profit and (iv) in equilibrium, individuals' beliefs are confirmed.

The following lemma will be important for our further analysis of this case.

Lemma 1. *Assume some* α, $0 < \alpha < 1$, *and suppose that all individuals can only observe the average quality* $\bar{q}_\alpha$ *of each plan. If, in equilibrium, a plan offers the quality pair* (q'_a, q'_c) *and a share* λ', $0 \leq \lambda' \leq 1$, *of the individuals that join this plan are of type H, then it must be that*

$$\frac{p_a C'_a(q'_a)}{\alpha} = \frac{p'_c C'_c(q'_c)}{1 - \alpha} \tag{6}$$

where

$$p'_c = \lambda' p_\text{H} + (1 - \lambda') p_\text{L}. \tag{7}$$

---

[10]Formally, the assumption is that for each consumer k there is a belief function B_k : $R_+ \times \to R_+ \times R_+$, such that for every average quality $\bar{q}_\alpha$, the function specifies beliefs about a plan's quality profile (q_a, q_c) given that average quality. In order to simplify the analysis, we assume that a consumer's beliefs depend only on the plan's average quality and not on the plan's identity or the average quality of the other plans.

Proof.   Notice that Eq. (6) above is derived from the first-order conditions for the following problem:

$$\min_{(q_a, q_c)} \quad p_a C_a(q_a) + P'_c C_c(q_c)$$

$$\text{s.t.} \quad \alpha q_a + (1 - \alpha) q_c = \bar{q}'_\alpha$$

where $\bar{q}'_\alpha = \alpha q'_a + (1 - \alpha) q'_c$. Thus, if (q'_a, q'_c) does not satisfy (6), the plan can offer another quality pair (q''_α, q''_C), say, with the same average quality as (q'_a, q'_c) but lower (expected) costs per enrollee. If the plan deviates to this (new) quality pair its profit will be higher since its revenue will not change (individuals see the same average quality, and therefore, do not change their beliefs about the plan's quality pair) but its costs will be lower.   □

The intuition for this result is quite simple and very general. Since individuals can only observe the average quality of all the services a plan offers, the plan has no incentive to provide a quality profile that yields the same average as another quality but costs more. Condition (6) above will be later referred to as the incentive compatible (IC) condition.

For a given α, $0 < \alpha < 1$, the curve $\text{IC}(\alpha, \lambda)$, in Fig. 2, represents all quality profiles that satisfy the IC condition for the (pooling) case where $\lambda' = \lambda$, i.e., the case where the plan attracts a random sample of the population. Increasing the weight that the averaging formula assigns to service a by increasing α shifts to the right the set of quality pairs that the plan may offer in equilibrium. The curve r^* in that figure depicts all quality profiles that satisfy the zero profit (pooling)

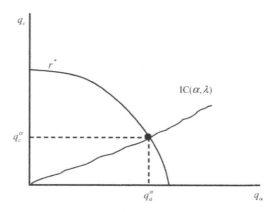

Figure 2.   The equilibrium quality profile in the averaged information case.

condition:

$$p_aC_a(q_a) + p_cC_c(q_c) = r^*$$

As the following proposition shows, the quality pair that is located at the intersection of these two curves, denoted by (q_a^α, q_c^α), is the unique quality pair offered by the plans in the competitive equilibrium in the case where individuals can only observe the average quality of each plan.

Proposition 2. *Assume some* $\alpha, 0 < \alpha < 1$. *Suppose that all individuals can only observe the average quality* $\bar{q}_\alpha$ *of each plan. A unique competitive equilibrium exists. In equilibrium all plans offer the same quality pair* (q_a^α, q_c^α) *characterized by:*

$$\frac{p_aC_a'(q_a^\alpha)}{\alpha} = \frac{p_cC_c'(q_c^\alpha)}{1-\alpha} \tag{8}$$

and

$$p_aC_a(q_a^\alpha) + p_cC_c(q_c^\alpha) = r^* \tag{9}$$

Proof. Assume some $\alpha, 0 < \alpha < 1$ and let

$$\bar{q}_\alpha^* = \alpha q_a^\alpha + (1-\alpha)q_c^\alpha \tag{10}$$

be the average quality (that all individuals observe) of a plan that offers the quality pair (q_a^α, q_c^α).

In order to show that (q_a^α, q_c^α) is an equilibrium, assume that (all) individuals' beliefs are such that for every average quality $(\bar{q}_\alpha)$ they observe, and for every plan, individuals believe that the plan has chosen the quality profile that yields $\bar{q}_\alpha$ and that satisfies the IC condition, with $\lambda' = \lambda$. Thus, individuals believe that among all quality profiles that yield a particular average quality, the plan offers the one located on the curve IC(α, λ) in Fig. 2. Given these beliefs, one can see that if all plans offer the quality pair (q_a^α, q_c^α), individuals beliefs will be confirmed.

In order to show that all plans offering (q_a^α, q_c^α) is an equilibrium, it remains to be shown that no plan can offer another quality profile and make a strictly positive profit. Suppose that some plans (at least one) offer the quality pair (q_a^α, q_c^α) and one plan offers a different quality pair (q_a', q_c') with average quality $\bar{q}_\alpha'$. If $\bar{q}_\alpha' = \bar{q}_\alpha^*$ individuals will believe that the plan's quality pair is (q_a^α, q_c^α), the plan will attract a random sample of the population and will lose money since its costs must be higher than the costs of producing

(q_a^α, q_c^α). If $\bar{q}'_\alpha > \bar{q}^*_\alpha$ all individuals will choose this (new) plan believing that its quality pair is on the curve $\text{IC}(\alpha, \lambda)$ in Fig. 2 but to the right of (q_a^α, q_c^α). In this case the plan will lose money since any quality pair with an average quality higher than $\bar{q}^*_\alpha$, that attracts all individuals, must be above the zero profit pooling curve r^*, as it is at least as expensive as the quality pair that yields this same average quality and satisfies the IC condition. If $\bar{q}'_\alpha < \bar{q}^*_\alpha$ then all individuals will believe that $q'_a < q_a^\alpha$ and $q'_c < q_a^\alpha$ and none of them will choose this (new) plan.

In order to show that (q_a^α, q_c^α) is the unique equilibrium, notice first that there cannot be any other (pooling) equilibrium in which each plan attracts a random sample of the population. Suppose, therefore, that there exists an equilibrium in which one plan offers the quality pair (q'_a, q'_c) and λ' of its individuals are of the type H, $0 \le \lambda' \le 1$, and another plan offers the quality pair (q''_a, q''_c) and λ'' of its individuals are of type H, $0 \le \lambda'' \le 1$, with $\lambda'' > \lambda'$. Since at least some type L's choose (q'_a, q'_c), individuals of type L (weakly) prefer the quality pair (q'_a, q'_c) over the quality pair (q''_a, q''_c). Since the indifference curves in our utility functions satisfy the single-crossing property, the H type individuals will strictly prefer the quality pair (q'_a, q'_c) over (q''_a, q''_c) which contradicts the initial assumption that $\lambda' < \lambda''$. These same arguments can be easily applied to the case where type L strictly prefers (q'_a, q'_c) over (q''_a, q''_a). □

5. CHOOSING A FORM OF REPORT

Although quality ratings are available to individuals in many markets, health care has the special feature that some of these ratings are done by payers, such as when the Federal Employee Health Benefit Program or the federal Medicare program rates HMOs. Private insurers also rate the medical groups and hospitals they offer as choices to their enrollees. This section addresses the question of how to choose the weights in an averaged quality report, a function that could be assumed by a public regulator, such as a state agency, or by a payer. We will refer here to a "payer" with both payers and public regulators in mind. We conduct this analysis under the strong assumption that the firm is unable to reveal information about quality to consumers and consumers cannot find out about quality on their own. The consequences of relaxing this assumption are considered in the next section.

In the full information case, if equilibrium exists it never yields the socially optimal quality profile. As the following corollary to Proposition 2

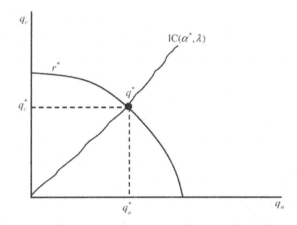

Figure 3.   Market equilibrium with optimal averaged report.

shows, an averaged quality report can move the market equilibrium to the efficient quality profile.

Corollary 1. *Suppose that all individuals can only observe the average quality of each plan and $\alpha = \alpha^*$, where α^* is given by:*

$$\frac{p_a C_a'(q_a^*)}{\alpha^*} = \frac{p_c C_c'(q_c^*)}{1 - \alpha^*}, \tag{11}$$

then all plans offer the socially efficient quality pair (q_c^*, q_c^*) in the competitive equilibrium. Figure 3 shows this equilibrium.

Corollary 1 has two significant implications. The first is that social welfare (measured by the expected utility of a randomly drawn individual) can be higher in equilibrium where individuals can only observe the average quality of each plan than in equilibrium where individuals have full information about plans' quality.

The second implication of Corollary 1 has to do with policy about information disclosure. Suppose that when choosing a health plan, individuals cannot observe the quality profile of health plans and the only information they can rely on is the information provided to them by a payer or other agency acting on their behalf. Assume that the payer can fully observe each plan's quality profile. Corollary 1 says that to maximize social surplus, the payer will not reveal all information to individuals but only the weighted average quality of each plan, where the weights come from (11).

How should weights be chosen for an averaged quality report? Equation (11) relates the relative weights for two services, α and $1 - \alpha$, to characteristics of two services a and c. Equation (11) could be rewritten as follows:

$$\frac{\alpha^*}{1 - \alpha^*} = \frac{p_a C'_a(q^*_a)}{p_c C'_c(q^*_c)} \tag{11'}$$

The relative weights on quality of services a and c depend on the probabilities of the two illnesses and the marginal costs of quality at the efficient quality. The quality weights are like relative prices equal to marginal cost at the efficient level of production.

Equation (11') tells us how to use the α and $1 - \alpha$ weights to induce a desired quality mix. Suppose it was determined with some initial setting of the weights that the quality of chronic care was too low in relation to acute care. To induce plans to put more emphasis on quality of chronic care, the payer or regulator then reduces α and increases $1 - \alpha$, increasing the relative importance of chronic care in the averaged report. For the cost-minimizing condition (11') to remain true, the plan must decrease q_a and increase q_c.

6. EXTENSIONS AND RECONSIDERATION OF ASSUMPTIONS

6.1. *Extension: More than Two Services*

A natural question is whether the averaged report on quality can succeed in inducing a plan to provide efficient quality if there are more than two dimensions of quality. Although we do not provide a formal analysis, the averaged quality report mechanism generalizes readily to the case of more than two services. With only an averaged quality available to individuals, it remains true that the market equilibrium must be a pooling equilibrium. With many dimensions of quality, producing the reported average at the minimum cost (Lemma 1) continues to imply a unique set of quality choices that are a function of the weights on the averaged quality and the premium. Thus, in competitive (zero profit) equilibrium plans will produce the highest averaged quality given the fixed premium for a random sample of enrollees, and the quality of the various dimensions will be determined by the cost minimization decision. By choosing the weights to compose the average, a payer can direct the IC condition to intersect the pooling quality zero profit surface at the point of the desired mix of qualities.

6.2. *Extension: Plans Attempt to Select Low-Risks with Other Mechanisms*

In our paper so far plans make decisions about the quality of services. There may be other plan design features a plan can use to attempt to attract low-risk enrollees, such as copayments, deductibles, or deciding about coverage for "optional" services, such as drugs or dental care. The first point to note about these mechanisms is that they are verifiable, and may therefore be easier to regulate directly (by mandating benefits). To the extent that they are not regulated and remain as tools for selection, the analysis we have done for service-level selection also applies to these mechanisms. In other words, if plans use insurance coverage (as was done in the original Rothschild–Stiglitz analysis) as a selection device, an averaged report of the type proposed here would address these inefficiencies as well.

We now reconsider some of our assumptions and how these might influence our conclusion about the usefulness of an averaged report. We group these into assumptions about mechanisms to achieve selection that an averaged report may not address, assumptions about strategies a regulator could use to combat selection, and assumptions about information.

6.3. *Person-specific Mechanisms to Select Enrollees*

A health plan can take actions to target individual enrollees or potential enrollees. For example, a plan might simply deny enrollment to an applicant it anticipates would be high cost. Or, in order to discourage a current enrollee from remaining in the plan, a plan could discriminate in the quality or the accessibility of the services it offers to that enrollee. Representatives of the plan might, as an example, make it more difficult for older people to schedule appointments quickly. Open enrollment and non discriminatory provisions of contracts between payers and health plans prohibit plans from attempting to select in these ways, which does not of course mean that plans never do these things. In a conference on risk adjustment, representatives of private employers regarded open enrollment provisions as being effective in preventing plans from denying enrollment from costly employees and families (Glazer and McGuire, 2001). It should be noted, however, that the averaged quality report does not alter a plan's incentives to select in this way. This is in contrast to risk adjustment, which, by bringing revenue associated with an enrollee closer to expected cost, does mitigate these incentives.

6.4. *Other Mechanisms to Deal with Adverse Selection*

There are several mechanisms regulators can use to deal with plans' incentives to select profitable enrollees. If the quality of a service is not only observable but also verifiable a regulator or a payer can make quality part of the contract. The regulator, for example, may set up standards for treating chronically ill patients and reward those plans that meet these standards. The main problem with this type of mechanism, however, is that in many cases, the quality of care is not easy to verify and even if it is, putting it in the contract could make the contract very complicated. Furthermore, making quality of care part of the contract might create a whole set of new incentives not always in the direction desired by the regulator. Plans might select enrollees or perform procedures in a way that will boost their quality score.

Another mechanism to address adverses election is risk adjustment. If plans are paid more (less) for patients that are expected to cost more (less), their incentives to select enrollees are reduced. However, it is hardly ever the case that risk adjustment can completely eliminate the adverse selection problem. As long as individuals have some information about their future health care needs, that the payer cannot use as part of its risk adjusted payment scheme, incentives to select enrollees on the basis of this information will remain.

A third mechanism to lessen plans' incentives to select enrollees is cost sharing between the payer and the plan. Cost sharing can take different forms but the idea common to all of them is that the plan does not bear the full marginal health care costs of its enrollees and in particular of the most expensive ones. However, as long as the plan is held responsible for some if these costs, the incentives to select the more profitable ones still remain.

It seems, therefore, that even though there are other mechanisms to address incentives to select enrollees, none of them is powerful enough to eliminate concerns about adverse selection. Ultimately, a payer or regulator can make a choice among these approaches, and our work can be viewed as adding another tool to the set of things available to address selection.

6.5. *Consumer Behavior and Information*

Our analysis above calls attention to the crucial role of consumer beliefs in market equilibrium with imperfect information. We make the standard assumption that individuals can anticipate how a plan would choose qualities to produce a reported average. The literature on the effect of quality reports implies that individuals may simply be not very good at processing reports (Hibbard *et al.*, 2000). The advantage of an averaged report from the standpoint of ease of understanding is a distinct point from the one we identify in this paper. Study of how consumers understand reports will be necessary in order to draw conclusions for the best form and information to be contained in the reports.

Another key assumption in our model is that individuals rely exclusively on information from the regulator to learn about quality. Other routes for learning may undermine a regulator's control of what individuals know: first, consumers may themselves have experience or may undertake some search for information; second, plans may have an incentive to reveal information in addition to that which is required by a regulator. Incorporating these features is likely to put restrictions on what a regulator is able to achieve.

In health insurance markets, an employer plays the role of a consumer by contracting with the plan or plans employees may choose among. An employer might want to know all elements of quality of plans, but still, in terms of what is provided to employees, would want the report that minimizes inefficiencies due to adverse selection.

This paper starts with a set of quality measures available to a regulator and asks what weights should be used. One could take another step back and ask what information should be collected on the basis of cost, accuracy, or other factors. We have sought to point out some of the benefits of use of information for purposes of addressing adverse selection that should be weighed along with these cost considerations.

7. DISCUSSION

In many sectors of the economy, quality reports integrate into market functioning in positive ways. Consumer demand for quality reports supports publication of private rating services, such as *Consumer Reports*, that contribute to market evaluation of quality. Quick acceptance of new ratings by consumers is not, however, to be expected. Years elapsed, for example, between the introduction of *U.S. News and World Report* magazine's rating of colleges and the emergence of the powerful effects (plus and minus) these ratings now have on patterns of college admissions and other practices (Avery *et al.*, 2003). In spite of mixed results in the literature to date, quality reporting remains a plausible low-cost strategy for making improvement in the quality of health care services.

Managed care plans paid by capitation are prevalent in California for both commercial employer-based health insurance and public insurance for the elderly and poor, and reports about health plan and provider group quality are also highly developed in California. The state makes available summary ratings based on 1–3 "stars" in four categories of quality (e.g., "care for staying healthy," "care for getting better") that are based on underlying more detailed clinical data (Office of the Patient Advocate, 2003).[11] Our analysis could be viewed as applying to a market such as California where the state is structuring the information available to consumers and employees.

Casting quality reports as a policy instrument turns up an important and simple conclusion: an averaged quality report can remedy adverse selection incentives in markets for health plans. The reasoning is straightforward. Averaging quality across its many dimensions and reporting only the average enforces pooling in health insurance. Choosing the weights in the average to reflect relative marginal benefits at the efficient quality mix ensures health plans allocate resources to elements of quality in the right way.

The power of quality reporting to correct selection-related incentives seems not to have been appreciated previously. For purposes of comparison, as we have shown here, in the canonical model of health insurance markets, an averaged quality report matches the performance of optimal risk adjustment.

ACKNOWLEDGEMENTS

Research support from the National Institute of Mental Health (R01 MH 59254, and R34 MH071242) and the Agency for Healthcare Research and Quality (P01 HS10803) is gratefully acknowledged.

REFERENCES

Avery, C., Fairbanks, A., Zeckhauser, R., 2003. The Early Admissions Game: Joining the Elite. Harvard University Press, Cambridge, MA.

Beaulieu, N.D., 2002. Quality information and consumer health plan choices. *Journal of Health Economics* 21, 43–63.

---

[11]See also, *California Health Care Performance Results Report on Quality*, a publication of a collaborative coordinated by the Pacific Business Group on Health (2003).

Berkmeyer, J.D., *et al.*, 2000. Leapfrog Safety Standards: The Potential Benefits of Universal Adoption. Leapfrog Group, Washington.

Cao, Z., 2003. Comparing Pre-HMO Enrollment Costs between Stayers and Switchers: Medicare Evidence of Service-Level Selection. Boston University.

Cao, Z., McGuire, T.G., 2003. Service-level selection by HMOs in Medicare. *Journal of Health Economics* 22(1), 89–116.

Chernew, M., Gowrisankaram, G., McLaughin, C., Gibson, T., 2004. Quality and employer's choice of health plans. *Journal of Health Economics* 23(3), 471–492.

Chernew, M., Scanlon, D., 1998. Health plan report cards and insurance choice. *Inquiry* 35, 9–22.

Clancy, C.M., Scully, T., 2003. A call to excellence: how the Federal Government's health agencies are responding to the call for improved patient safety and accountability in medicine. *Health Affairs* 22(2), 113–115.

Classen, D., Kildgridge, P., 2002. The roles and responsibility of physicians to improve patient safety within healthcare delivery systems. *Academic Medicine* 77(10), 963–972.

Cutler, D., Zeckhauser, R., 2000. The Anatomy of Health Insurance. In Culyer and Newhouse (eds.) *Handbook of Health Economics*, North-Holland, Amsterdam.

Dranove, D., Kessler, D., McClellan, M., Satterthwaite, M., 2003. Is more information better? The effects of 'Report Cards' on health care providers. *Journal of Political Economy* 111 (3), 555–588.

Edgman-Levitan, S., Cleary, P.D., 1996. What information do consumers want and need? *Health Affairs* 15, 42–56.

Farley, D.O., Short, P., Elliot, M.N., Kanouse, D.E., Brown, J.A., Hays, R.D., 2002. Effects of CAHPS health plan performance information on plan choices by New Jersey medicaid beneficiaries. *Health Services Research* 37(4), 985–1007.

Frank, R.G., Glazer, J., McGuire, T.G., 2000. Measuring adverse selection in managed health care. *Journal of Health Economics* 19 (November), 829–854.

Galvin, R., Milstein, A., 2002. Large employers' new strategies in health care. *The New England Journal of Medicine* 347(12), 939–942.

Glazer, J., McGuire, T.G., 2000. Optimal risk adjustment of health insurance premiums: an application to managed care. *American Economic Review* 90(4), 1055–1071.

Glazer, J., McGuire, T.G., 2001. Private employers don't need formal risk adjustment. *Inquiry* 38(3), 242–244.

Glazer, J., McGuire, T.G. What should consumers be told about product quality? Unpublished, 2003.

Hellinger, F., 1995. Selection bias in HMOs and PPOs. *Inquiry* 32, 135–142.

Hibbard, J., Jewett, J., 1996. What type of quality information do consumers want in a health care report card? *Medical Care Research and Review* 53, 28–47.

Hibbard, Judith, H., Harris-Kojetin, L., Mullin, P., Lubalin, J.S., Garfinkel, S.A., 2000. Increasing the impact of health plan report cards by addressing consumer concerns. *Health Affairs* 19(5), 138–143.

Hirshleifer, J., 1971. The private and social value of information and the reward to inventive activity. *American Economic Review* 61, 561–574.

Institute of Medicine. Crossing the Quality Chasm. National Academy Press, Washington, DC, 2001.

Institute of Medicine. To Err is Human. National Academy Press, Washington, DC, 1999.

Keeler, E.B., Newhouse, J.P., Carter, G., 1998. A model of the impact of reimbursement schemes on health plan choice. *Journal of Health Economics* 17(3), 297–320.

Keenan, P.S., Beeuwkes Buntin, M.J., McGuire, T.G., Newhouse, J.P., 2001. The prevalence of formal risk adjustment. *Inquiry* 38(3), 245–259.

Luft, H.S., Miller, R.H., 1988. Patient selection and competitive health system. *Health Affairs* 7(3), 97–112.

Mello, M.M., Stearn, S.C., Norton, E.C., 2002. Do Medicare HMOs still reduce health services use after controlling for selection bias? *Health Economics* 20(11), 323–340.

Mirman, L., Samuelson, L., Schlee, E., 1994. Strategic information manipulation in duopolies. *Journal of Economic Theory* 62, 363–384.

Newhouse, J.P., 2002. Pricing the Priceless: A Health Care Conundrum. MIT Press, Cambridge, MA.

Newhouse, J.P., 1996. Reimbursing health plans and health providers: selection versus efficiency in production. *Journal of Economic Literature* 34(3), 1236–1263.

Office of the Patient Advocate. California's Quality of Care Report Card 2003–2004. The State of California, 2003.

Pacific Business Group on Health. California Health Care Performance Results: Report on Quality, http://www.cchri.org/ reports/CCHRI_2003.pdf, 2003.

Pauly, M.V., 1985. What is Adverse about Adverse Selection? JAI Press.

Pauly, M.V., Ramsey, S.D., 1999. Would you like suspenders to go with that belt? An analysis of optimal combinations of cost sharing and managed care. *Journal of Health Economics* 18(4), 443–458.

Rothschild, M., Stiglitz, J., 1976. Equilibrium in competitive insurance markets: an essay in the economics of imperfect information. *Quarterly Journal of Economics* 90, 629–649.

Sage, W.M., Hyman, D.A., Greenberg, W., 2003. Why competition law matters to health care quality. *Health Affairs* 22(2), 31–44.

Scanlon, D., Chernew, M., McLaughlin, C., Solon, G., 2002. The impact of health plan report cards on managed care enrollment. *Journal of Health Economics* 21(1), 19–41.

Schlee, E., 1996. The value of information about product quality. RAND Journal of Economics 27 (Winter (9)), 803–815.

Van de Ven, W.P., Ellis, R.P., 2000. Risk Adjustment in Competitive Health Plan Markets. In Culyer and Newhouse (eds.) *Handbook of Health Economics*, North Holland.

Wedig, G.J., Tai-Seale, M., 2002. The effect of report cards on consumer choice in the health insurance market. *Journal of Health Economics* 21(6), 1031–1048.

Chapter 5

USING GLOBAL RATINGS OF HEALTH PLANS TO IMPROVE THE QUALITY OF HEALTH CARE

Jacob Glazer

Tel Aviv University, Israel
Boston University, United States

Thomas G. McGuire*

Harvard Medical School, United States
mcguire@hcp.med.harvard.edu

Zhun Cao

Center for Multicultural Mental Health Services Research,
Cambridge Health Alliance, United States

Alan Zaslavsky

Harvard Medical School, United States

Received 14 August 2007
Received in revised form 21 February 2008
Accepted 5 May 2008
Available online 14 May 2008

Global ratings, such as those based on consumer satisfaction, are a commonly used form of report on the performance of health plans and providers. A simple averaging of the global rating by plan members leads to a problem: it gives a plan greater incentives to improve services used by low-cost members than services used by high-cost members. This paper presents a formal model of consumer formation of global ratings and the incentives these rating convey to plans. We use this model to characterize weights on consumer respondents to correct the incentive problem. We implement our proposed solution using data from the Consumer Assessments of Health Care Providers and Systems (CAHPS) and the Medicare Current Beneficiary Survey (MCBS).

---

*Corresponding author. at: Department of Health Care Policy, Harvard Medical School, 180 Longwood Avenue, Boston, MA 02115, United States. Tel.: +1-617-432-3565; fax: +1-617-432-2905.

Our correction is low-cost, easily implemented on an on-going basis, and insensitive to assumptions about why health plans care about quality ratings.

JEL classification: I11, C21

Keywords: quality reporting; health care quality

1. INTRODUCTION

When choosing a health plan, consumers have ready access to formal reports about plan coverage, price, indicators of quality of care at the plan, and ratings of consumer satisfaction with services the plan offers. One important component of these reports, consumer satisfaction, is often reported in a summary rating. For example, the widely used Consumer Assessments of Healthcare Providers and Systems (CAHPS®) survey asks:

"Using any number from 0 to 10, where 0 is the worst health plan possible and 10 is the best health plan possible, what number would you use to rate your plan?"

Following Hays *et al.* (1999), we will refer to ratings derived from questions such as these as "global" ratings. Global ratings of this form are commonly asked and reported in other surveys of plans and hospitals.

Quality reports can improve health care markets in two ways, by giving consumers information so they can choose a plan that best meets their needs and by conveying incentives to plans to improve their rating to attract more enrollees. In this paper we are concerned with the second function of quality reporting; specifically, the incentives conveyed to a plan to provide high quality by a global rating report. We show that a simple averaging of global ratings of plan members weighting each member equally, the current practice in quality reporting, gives a plan incentives to improve some services more than others. After characterizing the problem, we propose a simple way to fix it, and illustrate how this can be done with recent CAHPS survey data on Medicare beneficiaries. The solution we propose is straightforward and readily implementable on an ongoing basis.

If all patients had the same needs and the rating scale of "worst possible" to "best possible" could be interpreted as equivalent to "no healthcare benefit provided" to "all possible benefit provided", then a system that reports averaged ratings would convey incentives to provide services to all patients equally. However, when some patients have greater healthcare needs (and potential benefits of care) than others, but all report on the same scale, points on the scale no longer represent the same amount of benefit for different patients. Instead the benefit to less needy patients is overvalued (since a small potential benefit is stretched across the entire scale) while the benefit to needier patients is undervalued (since a large potential benefit is compressed into the same scale). A health plan attempting to maximize its reported ratings then has an incentive to undertreat needier patients and overtreat less needy patients. However, this distortion of the scale can be corrected by weighting reports by patients proportionally to their potential benefit from healthcare; this unequal weighting has the same effect as expanding the scale for the needier patients. We approximate the potential benefit for a patient by the mean spending for a patient with similar health-related characteristics in fee-for-service (FFS) Medicare (as estimated with data from the Medicare Current Beneficiary Survey) and then apply these weights to determine their impact on comparisons of ratings of health plans.

Section 2 illustrates the incentive problem with a simple numerical example. It also includes a review of the literature on the impact of quality reports and the formation of "global ratings". Following this review, Section 3 presents a model of global ratings that describes the incentive problem and its solution. Section 4 shows how our correction based on weighting responses by expected costs can be done with CAHPS health plan data for Medicare in 2004. The section also uses Medicare data to quantify the distorted incentives introduced by a global rating. Section 5 summarizes the main point of the paper and identifies some next steps for research.

2. BACKGROUND

2.1. *A Numerical Illustration*

The following example illustrates the problem and the nature of the potential solution. A health plan has two enrollees, A and B. Person A uses just service S1 whereas Person B uses both S2 and S3. In a baseline situation depicted in Table 1, the plan spends 5 on each of the three services. Enrollees rate quality of each service they use just in proportion to cost and rate a plan in proportion to the average rating they give to each service they use. So Person A's global rating is 5 as is Person B's. The averaged global rating for the two enrollees is thus also 5, shown in the last column of the table. The health plan considers improving the quality of either S1 or S2. Raising spending on S1 to 10 raises the rating of Person A to 10 yielding an averaged global rating of 7.5. Raising spending on S2 to 10 raises the global rating of Person B only to 7.5 because B also uses S3 and

Table 1. Quality choices, averaged ratings and costs at a health plan

	Person A			Person B				Averaged global rating
	S1		Global rating	S2		S3		Global rating	
	Cost	Quality		Cost	Quality	Cost	Quality		
Baseline	5	5	5	5	5	5	5	5	5
Improve S1	10	10	10	5	5	5	5	5	7.5
Improve S2	5	5	5	10	10	5	5	7.5	6.25

yields an average global rating of only 6.25. (The same calculation would go through for raising quality of S3.) Thus, the plan gets more rating per dollar by spending on S1, the service used by the lower-cost enrollee. Balanced incentives to raise quality across services S1 and S2 would be restored if the averaged global rating weighted Person B's response twice Person A's response. The appropriate relative weight comes from the relative spending at baseline.

2.2. *Quality Reports and Health Plan Markets*

Research on health plan quality reports has focused on whether reports about quality affect consumers' (or employers') choice of health plan. At least some consumers are prepared to spend time assimilating information in the reports and choose a plan on the basis of the information provided (Farley *et al.*, 2002). Jin and Sorensen (2006) find evidence that consumers appreciate and respond to quality in markets for health plans without quality reporting, and in addition, that formal quality reports from the National Committee on Quality Assurance (NCQA) contain information that also affects plan choice. Papers studying introduction of quality reports to federal employees (Wedig and Tai-Seale, 2002), Medicare beneficiaries (Dafny and Dranove, 2004), and private employees (Chernew *et al.*, 2004; Beaulieu, 2002; Scanlon *et al.*, 2002) find that reports affect choice. Employers may also change their offerings in response to quality reports (Chernew *et al.*, 2004). The magnitudes of these effects are small, though. One recent paper studied the health plan market around Minneapolis, St. Paul, MN, and found no measurable effect of quality information and plan switching (Abraham *et al.*, 2006). These papers do not study the importance of different types of information contained in quality reports. One paper suggests that consumers favor global satisfaction over reports of technical quality of care (Schultz *et al.*, 2001).

Quality reports are intended to induce plans (or providers) to improve the quality of care. Employing the invisible hand's "pay-for-performance", quality reports that make demand for a plan more responsive to the plan's choice of quality can lead, in market equilibrium, to a higher overall level of health plan performance. This potential impact of quality reports has not been studied in health plan markets, though it has been investigated in connection with hospital quality reports, with findings that suggest hospitals are alert to the selection-related incentives (Dranove *et al.*, 2003).

A quality report could also motivate a plan or provider through an internal concern for organizational/professional prestige. In other words, even if in their market choices consumers ignored a report, managers of a health plan might seek a high rating for their own professional satisfaction. The arguments we make below about incentive problems/solutions with global ratings go through if global ratings motivate plans for this reason as well as for reasons related to demand response by consumers.

2.3. *Consumer Formation of Global Ratings*

The relationship between plan features controlled by the plan (e.g., waiting time for an appointment, technical quality of care) and the global rating conferred by members governs the incentives a plan faces to maximize a score on a global rating. If consumer ratings are not sensitive to some dimension of plan performance, the plan gets no reward in terms of ratings for improvement. Cognitive psychologists have studied how individuals formulate responses to various types of questions asked in health-related surveys, such as the mental processes employed to recall numbers of health care visits or the nature of comparisons undertaken for a person to decide if their overall health is "excellent, good, fair or poor" (Fienberg *et al.*, 1985). As far as we know, there is no consensus in this literature about how global ratings are formed, but drawing on related studies, we anticipate (1) variation in the cognitive process leading to a rating, (2) anchoring of endpoints based on personal or indirect experience of associates, and (3) salience of more recent, unusual events. These general patterns do not unfortunately offer specific guidance in terms of a theoretical model of how enrollees score plans in a global rating question.

CAHPS and other global ratings have been widely collected for a number of years, and a number of studies have investigated empirically the factors that contribute to higher or lower CAHPS scores. On average, enrollees tend to rate plans very highly (Tai-Seale, 2004). In one study of elderly and CAHPS, more than half the respondents gave their overall health care (using a CAHPS question) a perfect 10; only about 15% of respondents rated their care less than an 8 (Chang *et al.*, 2006). Beyond this, characteristics of enrollees are associated with scoring. Older enrollees score plans higher, and sicker enrollees score plans lower (Zaslavsky *et al.*, 2001). Racial/ethnic minorities tend to give plans a higher CAHPS global rating score (Lurie *et al.*, 2003; Zaslavsky *et al.*, 2000a). It is not easy to interpret these results because it may be hard to separate whether different people tend to score the same events differently, or whether within the same plan, different people have different experiences (Zaslavsky *et al.*, 2001; Zaslavsky and Cleary, 2002). Furthermore, the effect of respondent characteristics on ratings can vary across plans (Zaslavsky *et al.*, 2000b).

A number of papers have been interested in how technical measures of the quality of care relate to global consumer ratings. Studies have found either weak (Schneider *et al.*, 2001) or no (Chang *et al.*, 2006) relationship between technical quality and consumer rating. Chang *et al.* (2006) did find that better patient-provider communication was associated with higher global ratings.

3. INCENTIVES CREATED BY GLOBAL RATING

Based on the literature on managed care plans, this section develops a model of the incentives for plan quality created by a global rating system. This will allow us to characterize in general terms the incentive problems created when global ratings are simply averaged over all enrollees, and then go on to propose a simple solution to the incentive problem.

3.1. *A Managed Care Plan Rationing Services*

The model presented here incorporates health plan quality reports into the model of plan behavior in managed care proposed by Frank *et al.* (2000). Consider a health plan with N members indexed by i. The health plan offers S services. Let m_{is} denote the amount the plan will spend on providing service s to member i, and let: $m_i = \{m_{i1}, m_{i2}, \ldots, m_{iS}\}$. The value of the benefits member i gets from the plan is assumed to be

$$v_i(m_i) = \sum_s v_{is}(m_{is}) \tag{1}$$

where $v_{is}(\ )$ is the member's valuation of spending on service s, measured in dollars, and where $v'_{is} > 0$, $v''_{is} < 0$. The v_i is the sum of the member's valuations of services offered by the plan.

The plan rations the amount of health care a patient receives. Here, we adopt the shadow-price approach to modelling rationing in managed care.[1] The patient must "need" or benefit from services above a certain threshold in order to qualify for receipt of services. Let q_s be the service-specific shadow price the plan sets determining access to care for service s. Then, a patient with a benefit function for service s of $v_{is}()$ will receive a quantity of services m_{is} determined by

$$v'_{is}(m_{is}) = q_s \qquad (2)$$

Let the amount of spending determined by the equation above be denoted by $m_{is}(q_s)$. Note that (2) is simply a demand function, relating the quantity of services to the (shadow) price in a managed care plan. Let $q = \{q_1, q_2, \ldots, q_S\}$ be a vector of shadow prices the plan chooses and $m_i(q) = \{m_{i1}(q_1), m_{i2}(q_2), \ldots, m_{iS}(q_S)\}$ be the vector of spending member i receives.

Rationing by (2) implies that within a service, plan funds are allocated efficiently across members. Fully efficient rationing requires further that funds be allocated efficiently across all services. This is achieved by equality of each q_s. The (second-best) efficient q_s can be found by maximizing the sum of member benefits $v_i(m_i)$ subject to a plan budget fixed by capitation payments. We designate the shadow price that solves this constrained maximization as q^0. We now investigate the incentives a global rating system creates for a plan to choose a vector, q, rationing services its members receive and compare it to the efficient rationing q^0.

3.2. *Member Ratings*

Plan's choice of shadow prices to ration care will in general differ from the optimal (second-best) shadow prices. In order to characterize plan choices we begin by considering how members rate plans in response to plan rationing. We assume members have a conception of the maximum utility they might attain in a plan and a conception of the minimum utility they might attain. (Indeed, the CAHPS global rating question explicitly asks a respondent to consider a "10" to mean "the best plan possible" and

---

[1] For discussion of the shadow price approach to rationing in managed care see Frank *et al.* (2000), or Keeler *et al.* (1998). The alternative is a quantity rationing approach. See Pauly and Ramsey (1999).

J. Glazer et al.

a "0" to mean the "worst plan possible".) A member's rating of a plan
is then determined by the actual utility a member receives in relation to
the maximum and minimum utility. We regard the maximum utility to be
the utility attained when rationing is at its most generous, giving members
services up to the point of zero marginal benefit and corresponding to the
case when $qs = 0$, all s. Thus,

$$v_i^{\max} = \sum_s v_{is}(m_{is}(0)) \tag{3}$$

Minimum utility is the utility attained when rationing is at the least
generous, which we arbitrarily define to be when $q_s = 1$.[2] Thus,

$$v_i^{\min} = \sum_s v_{is}(m_{is}(1)) \tag{4}$$

Assume that each individual is asked to rate the plan on the interval
between 0 and 1 with the interpretation that the higher is the individual's
rating of the plan the more satisfied she is with that plan. Let r_i denote
individual i's rating of the plan and let v_i denote individual i's utility at
that plan. If we assume that r_i is strictly increasing in v_i, and it assigns
a rating of 0 to $v_i^{\min}$ and a rating of 1 to $v_i^{\max}$, then any such r_i can be
approximated by

$$r_i = \frac{v_i - v_i^{\min}}{v_i^{\max} - v_i^{\min}} \tag{5}$$

The rating function above captures some of the important elements
that seem to affect how people actually form their ratings. Members have
a conception of the maximum benefit they might attain in a plan and a
conception of the minimum benefit they might attain. A member's rating
of a plan is determined by the actual benefit a member receives in relation
to the maximum and minimum utility. Hereafter, we will call $v_i^{\max} - v_i^{\min}$
the "potential benefit" of individual i. A feature of the rating function
above, that will be very important later on, is that two individuals with
the same (dollar value of) benefits will rate the plan differently if their
potential benefit is different.

---

[2]Values $q = 0$ and $q = 1$ have special properties in the model above but these are not
important here. We picked these two values to simplify the presentation. $q_{\min}$ and $q_{\max}$
would have worked just as well.

Thus, for any q with elements between 0 and 1, we can rewrite the member's rating:

$$r_i(q) = \frac{\sum_s v_{is}(m_{is}(q_s)) - v_i^{\min}}{v_i^{\max} - v_i^{\min}} \tag{6}$$

The overall rating of the plan is then given by

$$R(q) = \frac{1}{\sum_i w_i} \sum_i w_i r_i(q) \tag{7}$$

where w_i is a weight assigned to individual i.

3.3. *Plan Rationing to Maximize Rating and Profit*

Here we consider how a plan would choose to ration services in the presence of a global rating system, assumed to be the only information available to the consumer choosing a plan. The natural starting point for such an analysis would be an expression for the profit gained by the health plan as a function of the global rating. Our problem is simplified by recognizing that the global rating in profit maximization is produced efficiently (a form of cost minimization). Suppose R^* is the global rating that maximizes profits. Since R^* is all that is known about the plan by consumers, enrollment and revenue at the plan (which may depend on risk adjustment) are a function of R^*. Fixing R^*, revenues are not otherwise a function of the vector of q_s the plan chooses to attain this R^*. Thus, profit maximization also implies that the plan would seek to attain the rating R^* at the minimum cost.

An equivalent approach to minimizing cost of attaining a certain R^* is to study the dual problem, maximizing global rating subject to a budget. We study the plan's choice of rationing when it seeks to maximize $R(q)$ subject to a fixed spending on services which we call M:

$$\sum_i \sum_s m_{is}(q_s) = M \tag{8}$$

By the first-order conditions and (8) we get that the plan's choice of rationing q^* to maximize rating is given by the solution to the following system of equations:

$$\left[\frac{\sum_i (w_i m'_{i1}(q_1))/(v_i^{\max} - v_i^{\min})}{\sum_i m'_{i1}(q1)} \right] q_1^*$$
$$= \left[\frac{\sum_i (w_i m'_{is}(q_s))/(v_i^{\max} - v_i^{\min})}{\sum_i m'_{is}(q_s)} \right] q_s^*, \quad s = 2, \ldots, S \tag{9}$$

and the budget constraint, (8).

Stemming from the literature on risk-adjustment and incentives related to adverse selection, a number of papers have stressed that plans have a motive to ration differentially by service, and either measure these incentives empirically (Frank *et al.*, 2000; Ellis and McGuire, 2007), or assess their consequences in terms of patterns of enrollment (Cao and McGuire, 2003) or services (Mello *et al.*, 2002). If existing risk adjustment systems tend to underpay for the sick and overpay for the healthy, plans have an incentive, similar to the one studied here, to underprovide services used by the sick in relation to those used by the healthy. Keenan *et al.* (2007) study CAHPS data from Medicare and find consumer ratings of health plans consistent with this hypothesis. Sicker consumers at plans paid by capitation rate the quality of care they receive and the quality of their doctor lower in relation to traditional Medicare than do healthier consumers. Our analysis implies that global rating exacerbates the incentives to undersupply services used by the sicker more costly enrollees.

Note that the incentives associated with the plan's choices of rationing in (9) are, however, distinct from the incentives associated with adverse selection usually studied in the literature on managed care plan rationing. With a single global rating being all consumers know about a plan, all enrollees prefer a higher to a lower ranking. Without further assumptions (that we are not making here), the level of the global ranking itself is not a selection device. The incentives studied here are those stemming from cost-minimization with respect to production of a global rating.

3.4. *Optimal Weighting*

Recall that the (budget constrained) socially efficient rationing rule is given by $q_s = q_1$ for $s = 2, \ldots, S$ and the budget constraint (8). Equation (9) above will enable us to identify the conditions under which the rating formula induces the plan to provide the socially efficient quality profile

$$w_i^* = k(v_i^{\max} - v_i^{\min}) \tag{10}$$

for every i and for some $k > 0$. From Eq. (9) above one can see that if $w_i = w_i^*$ for every i, then $q^* = q^0$. If the weight assigned to each individual, w_i, is set in (the same) proportion to her potential benefit, the rating procedure induces the plan to provide the socially efficient quality. Hereafter, we refer to w_i^* from (10) as the optimal weight.

In order to say something more about the optimal weights, consider the potential benefit $v_i^{\max} - v_i^{\min}$. For each service s and individual i, let

$\Delta m_{is} = m_{is}(0) - m_{is}(1)$, the extra spending on service s individual i enjoys in the most generous rationing compared to the least generous. As a linear approximation, the change in the utility of spending to member i on service s as the shadow price falls from 1 to 0 is the area of a triangle with base Δm_{is} and height of 1. The potential benefit is the sum of the areas of these triangles, one for each service:

$$v_i^{\max} - v_i^{\min} = \frac{1}{2} \sum_s \Delta m_{is}$$

Making a "demand response" assumption that $((\Delta m_{is})/(m_{is}(0)) = \delta$, for all i and for all s,[3]

$$v_i^{\max} - v_i^{\min} = \frac{1}{2}\delta M_i \tag{11}$$

where $M_i = \sum_s m_{is}(0)$, the total spending of person i with rationing at lowest level $q_s = 0$ for all s.

Our conception of "potential benefit" in (11) resting behind individuals' ratings of health plans is shown graphically in Fig. 1. The figure depicts

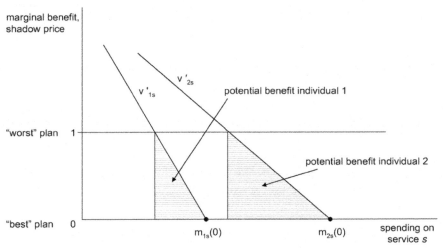

Figure 1.   The "Potential Benefit" in health plans among enrollees with different demands.

---

[3]This is essentially that the arc elasticity of demand is the same across services.

marginal benefits for one service, s, for two individuals, 1 and 2. Individual 1 receives fewer benefits from service s and individual 2 receives more. The "worst" conceivable health plan rations with a shadow price of 1 and the best plan rations at zero. The key assumptions we have made about utility are that the benefits from each service can be added to get the total; the reduction in spending from an increase in rationing is proportional to spending at a shadow price of zero, and the slope of the marginal benefit function is constant. These assumptions imply that for these two individuals, the difference in utility (measured in dollars) at the worst and the best plans are the shaded triangular areas. These areas are proportional to spending with the shadow price of zero,[4] and along with the additivity of benefits assumption allow us to express potential benefit as in (11).

Using this definition of potential benefit, and in particular Eqs. (10) and (11), we get that:

$$w_i^* = kM_i \qquad (12)$$

for any $k > 0$. Thus, if the rating function assigns to each individual i a weight proportional to her total spending at $q_s = 0$ for all s, the plan will maximize its rating at the socially efficient quality level. Note that with the equality of demand response assumption for all i and s, the optimal weight is proportional to spending for any $q_s = q$, not just $q_s = 0$, $s = 1, \ldots, S$.

Another feature of the optimal weight deserves note. Plans choose quality levels, so, to be precise, M_i is the *plan's expectation* about individual i's spending at $q_s = 0$.[5] (The optimal weighting equalizes plan incentives to increase the ratings of all members as the plan sees it through its expectations about members' relative spending.) Recognizing that optimal weights are based on plan's expectations about spending, not actual spending, implies that we should use a predictive model of individual spending rather than actual person-by-person numbers. Our cell-based predictions are described below in Section 4.2.

---

[4]This is true, as we noted above, for any two shadow prices corresponding to best and worst.

[5]For more discussion of the role of plan expectations in characterizing plan incentives, see Glazer and McGuire (2002).

3.5. *Conventional Rating and Incentives to Distort Quality*

In practice, global rating mechanisms simply average all scores. Our analysis can demonstrate the distortion in incentives created by such a mechanism. Assume that $w_i = 1$ for all i, then Eq. (9) becomes

$$\left[\frac{\sum_i (m'_{i1}(q_1))/(v_i^{\max} - v_i^{\min})}{\sum_i m'_{i1}(q_1)}\right] q_1^*$$

$$= \left[\frac{\sum_i (m'_{is}(q_s))/(v_i^{\max} - v_i^{\min})}{\sum_i m'_{is}(q_s)}\right] q_s^*, \quad s = 2,\ldots,S \qquad (13)$$

Noting that $m'_{is}(q) = \delta m_{is}(0)$ and $v_i^{\max} - v_i^{\min} = (1/2)\delta M_i$ we can rewrite (13) as

$$\frac{q_1^*}{\bar{m}_1(0)} \sum_i \frac{m_{i1}(0)}{M_i} = \frac{q_s^*}{\bar{m}_s(0)} \sum_i \frac{m_{is}(0)}{M_i}, \quad s = 2,\ldots,S \qquad (13')$$

where $\bar{m}_s(0) \equiv (1/N) \sum_i m_{is}(0)$.

In general, the q^* satisfying (13') and (8) will not be the same as the efficient q^0 described above. From (13'), we can see that the factor determining how the q's will be set in relation to some numeraire, say q_1, is how m_{is} relates to M_i. This is the correlation across members of spending on service s with total spending. Services with a high positive correlation with total spending will have a low value of the summation term in (13') and will be associated with a high q, i.e., more strict rationing. A positive correlation between m_{is} and M_i derives from m_{is} being relatively large. A service with high levels of spending on average will be more correlated with total spending for the definitional reason that total spending is the sum of its components. Furthermore, a positive correlation can come about because some services are associated with need for health care across a range of illnesses. For example, if depression is a common comorbidity for many chronic (and expensive to treat) illnesses such as heart disease and cancer, mental health services will tend to be positively correlated with total spending.

The incentive to distort quality of services by strict rationing comes about because it is cheaper to "produce" high quality ratings by investing in some services in comparison to others. A service that tends to be used by members who use many services (a high correlation between m_{is} and M_i) will have any investment in the service diluted by the fact that members using a lot of care are influenced by other factors in ratings. Conversely, investment in a service used by members who make little use of the plan will tend to yield a higher return.

3.6. *Reporting More Than One Global Rating*

One might naturally ask how our analysis would change if each plan reported more than one global rating. Before considering this, note that within our model, the optimal global rating achieves the efficient choice of rationing. Unless we change the model in some way, there is nothing to be gained by more than one report. Also, within the model presented so far, we know there is something to be lost. If there were to be a report about each service corresponding to the full-information allocation, incentives for adverse selection would be created and the plan choice of rationing would in general be inefficient. Plausible changes in the model could be made introducing heterogeneity among potential enrollees that would likely alter the conclusion that a single global rating is optimal. In this section, we make some preliminary comments about potential extensions to our analysis recognizing heterogeneity among potential enrollees.

The simplest form of heterogeneity would be if there were two plans that differ according to an observable characteristic (location), and enrollees were heterogeneous in their valuation of this characteristic. If this heterogeneity in taste were distributed independently of service demands, our single global rating system (now of each plan) would likely remain optimal. If, however, consumers' valuation of location is correlated with some service demands, there may be some value in separate reports on location-related and location-unrelated service quality. Some incentives for adverse selection could be introduced (depending on the form of risk adjusted payments) in exchange for a better sorting of consumers between the two plans.

Another direction for extension which is more complicated, but which we think is more interesting, is to suppose that the $v(m)$ function describing consumer valuation of services is composed of two parts: a component related to medical need that the plan sees and rations according to, and a component related to preferences that the plan averages over for all the enrollees in the plan. The purpose of the need/preference distinction would be to capture, for example, different willingness to pay for medical services that high and low-income consumers might have that would tend to be disregarded by providers at managed care plans. Managed care providers, for example, might be willing to spend the same amount of time counseling a high or low-income patient about the risk/benefit tradeoff associated with a surgical procedure. This amount of time would be decided at the plan level in response to the average preferences of enrollees. This average might be "too little" counseling for a high-income patient who would be willing to pay for more but cannot given the plans' rationing systems. Other characteristics of consumers (gender, age or even health status itself) might also condition preferences for health care.

Variation in preferences of this form creates a place for more than one type of health plan in terms of the level of rationing, and potentially the premium if the costs of the rationing plans vary as well. An efficient reporting system is called upon to achieve the efficient rationing at each (say, two) plans, and, sort consumers efficiently between the plans. In this case, there may be reason to have more than one global report, perhaps by groups of consumers. The decision about group-specific reports would require evaluation of a tradeoff between preference satisfaction and unwelcome incentives associated with adverse selection. However, that is resolved, we believe the weighting we propose here will be part of the efficient reporting policy.

4. APPLICATION TO CAHPS IN MEDICARE

This section applies the ideas from Section 3 to the largest system for global rating of health plans in the U.S., the CAHPS surveys, used nationally for Medicare managed care plans for almost 10 years (Goldstein *et al.*, 2001). CAHPS is intended to measure the aspects of care consumers can best report on, and which also correlate with clinical measures of quality (Cleary and Edgman-Levitan, 1997; Schneider *et al.*, 2001). CAHPS has been the basis of many studies in health services investigating the determinants of what consumers value in plans and in how consumer valuation affects plan choice.[6] CAHPS surveys do not include expenditures, however, and cannot therefore be a source of data on the weights required to modify the averaging for global ratings. We use the Medicare Current Beneficiary Survey (MCBS) to supplement CAHPS with expenditure data. The MCBS is also a national survey collected annually containing publicly available information on a sample of Medicare beneficiaries.

---

[6]The Agency for Healthcare Quality and Research maintains a website devoted to CAHPS containing information about CAHPS surveys and published and unpublished research material. See http://www.cahps.ahrq.gov.

Our primary purpose in this section is to show that our idea contained in (12) for weighting consumer plan ratings can be implemented readily. As a secondary purpose, we apply Eq. (13') to our data to check for the degree of distortion of rationing incentives introduced by a global rating system that weights each consumer equally.

4.1. *Data on Plan Ratings*

Data are from the 2004 Medicare CAHPS Survey conducted by CMS. We exclude those who disenrolled during the year, were 64 or younger, enrollees in private fee-for-service plans, and those with missing data on any item used to match with the MCBS. After these exclusions, a maximum of 113,807 respondents in 169 plans remain in the data. In this analysis, we report on two CAHPS global rating items that summarize benficiary-assessed quality and discriminate well among plans, the rating of the plan and the rating of the care received. Both are reported on a 0–10 scale with 10 being best.

The mean scores of health plans on these items are adjusted for beneficiary characteristics that are not under the direct control of the plan, are associated with ratings and have distributions that differ across plans. The standard Medicare CAHPS adjustment model includes age, education, self-reported general and mental health status, the Medicaid dual eligible flag, flags for proxy assistance with or completion of the form by a proxy respondent, and interactions of health status and age with region (Zaslavsky *et al.*, 2001). Note that this adjustment corrects for predictable differences in plan mean ratings due to the distributions of member characteristics, but does not alter the relative weight given to responses from members with different characteristics.

MCBS data used in this analysis are taken from the 1996,1997,1999 and 2000 Cost and Use Files. The MCBS is a continuous, multipurpose survey of a representative national sample of the Medicare population, and therefore can be an ongoing source of expenditure weights for CAHPS. In addition to survey questions, such as self-assessed health status, the MCBS contains information about health plan coverage, and for beneficiaries in traditional fee-for-service Medicare, merged claims from Medicare Part A (hospital care) and Part B (Medical Providers). Respondents are surveyed for up to 3 years and then replaced. We restrict our sample to those beneficiaries in traditional Medicare aged 65 or older, living in the 50 States, alive during the year of survey, without ESRD and enrolled in both Part A and B.

Table 2. CAHPS and MCBS

Respondent characteristics	CAHPS (%)	MCBS (%)
Age		
65-69	20.4	18.3
70-74	28.3	28.0
75-79	23.9	23.7
80-84	16.6	16.3
85+	10.8	13.6
Gender		
Male	40.9	40.3
Female	59.2	59.7
General health status (GHS)		
Excellent	7.5	14.9
Very good	24.4	28.0
Good	38.9	33.0
Fair	24.1	17.9
Poor	5.0	6.3
Smoking status		
Non-smoker	48.7	42.6
Smoker	51.3	57.4

Sources: 2004 Medicare Managed Care CAHPS Survey, $N = 113{,}807$. MCBS 1996,1997,1999, 2000, $N = 27{,}467$.

Aggregated over all 4 years there are 27,467 person-year observations in the sample.

Table 2 contains descriptive information about the respondents from the two data sources on the variables we used to match expenditures to survey responses. The age and gender distributions in CAHPS and MCBS are very similar. The MCBS traditional Medicare sample appears to be slightly healthier overall than the CAHPS sample with more respondents reporting their health as "excellent", or "very good". The MCBS also contains fewer smokers. The four age categories, two genders, five general health status categories and two smoker categories yield the 100 cells used in this analysis for purposes of weighting.

4.2. *Deriving Expenditure Weights*

The optimal weight from (12) is proportional to a member's spending in a plan. Managed care plans generally do not have these data, let alone supply them to Medicare on a regular and timely basis. Instead, we use data from Medicare beneficiaries in traditional FFS Medicare, not in managed care plans, to derive relative weights. FFS Medicare data have the advantage that resource use can be assumed to be driven by beneficiary demand and not affected by plans' decisions about management. It is known that overall spending in Medicare managed care plans is lower than in regular Medicare (Brown *et al.*, 1993), that higher cost beneficiaries are more likely to be in regular Medicare (Hellinger, 1995), and that higher costs among beneficiaries in regular Medicare are not uniform across service types (Cao and McGuire, 2003). Though patterns of fee-for-service relative spending differ from those shown in managed care plans, it is not clear what this implies for any bias in relative total spending by cell. The optimal weight need only be proportional to spending, so an overall shrinkage in total spending in managed care plans may not materially alter the desired weights.

The optimal weight is the plan's expected spending for an individual based on their characteristics. We develop and apply a simple cell-based prediction for each person in the CAHPS data. Since we figure spending from one data set, the MCBS, and seek to weight member ratings in another, CAHPS, we can merge estimated spending with CAHPS responses based only on variables common to the two data sets. The common variables we use are age (five categories), gender, self-rated health status (E, VG, G, F, P) and lifetime smoker (Y/N). In total, we have 100 cells and therefore 100 different expenditure weights that we merge with the CAHPS surveys. All of these variables are highly predictive of health care use.

We used the average of the total payment amount, including amount paid by all payers and out-of-pocket payment by the beneficiaries, as a basis for expenditure weights. The overall average spending was \$5,359 for all years together. The average spending in each cell is listed in Appendix A. The mean spending differs quite a bit across the cells (implying substantially different weights) and the cell means move in reasonable patterns. For example, among aged 65–69 year old female non-smokers, the averages by self-rated health status are – E: \$1,415, VG: \$2,246, G: \$3,266, F: \$6,917, P: \$10,938. The 100 cell means capture 6.7% of the variance in total expenditure. This compares to the approximately 10% of the variance explained by the Diagnostic Cost Group (DCG) system adopted by Medicare for managed care plan payment that uses demographic, geographic and detailed diagnostic information (van de Ven and Ellis, 2000).

4.3. *Results: CAHPS Weighting*

Table 3 shows means and standard deviations ratings of care and plan before our weighting, and statistics on the same of ratings after weighting

Table 3. Care and plan ratings, medicare CAHPS 2004 original (unweighted) and weighted

	Original		Weighted	
	Mean	S.D.	Mean	S.D.
Care rating	8.85	0.23	8.75	0.26
Plan rating	8.43	0.40	8.34	0.43

The N for care rating is 83,260, and for plan rating is 109,656.

by predicted spending per respondent. Not all respondents answered both questions accounting for the different N's by rating. In the case of both care and plan ratings, the weighted ratings fell slightly, indicating that respondents with higher predicted costs tend to rate plans less highly. In addition, the standard deviation of the plan ratings increased slightly. The original and weighted ratings at the plan level are highly correlated, with Pearson correlation coefficients of .966 and .986 for the care and plan ratings, respectively.

We converted the original and weighted ratings into z-scores for each plan to see how much weighting changed plan rankings. The difference in the z-score between the original and weighted ratings captures the magnitude of the shift due to the weighting. For example, a difference in the z-score of $+.5$ after the weighting indicates that the plan shifted up .5 of a standard deviation of plan means in the ratings due to the weighting. The mean absolute difference in the z-scores for care rating was .20 and for plan rating was .14. To get a sense of the importance of a .20 standard deviation shift, when evaluated at the mean, .20 corresponds to an increase of 8.0 percentile rankings (i.e., the mean change shifts a plan above or below 8.0% of the other plans). At one standard deviation above the mean, a .20 shift moves a plan 5.0 percentile points. A .14 shift, the mean absolute difference in plan rating due to the weighting, corresponds to a 5.6 percentile shift at the mean and a 3.4 percentile shift at one standard deviation above the mean.

The main purpose of this section was to demonstrate that application of optimal weights could be done readily. We had no expectation about how much of a difference the optimal weighting would make in plan rankings. The increase in the spread of scores is probably a good thing since there is such tight clustering at the high end in member's scores in general. The difference in the ranking of plans appears to be noticeable, but slight.

4.4. *Results: Incentives in Unweighted Global Ratings*

As a secondary empirical analysis, we used the MCBS data, categorized by service, to investigate the incentives for a plan to ration services to maximize an unweighted global rating score. We were interested in whether the shadow prices implied by (13) differed by service; a higher shadow price implying more strict rationing. Differences in shadow prices across services means a plan has incentives created by global ratings to ration some services more strictly than others.

It is not clear how services should be grouped for purposes of studying plan incentives to ration. Conceptually, one would want to group services by the tools available to ration. For example, a plan might decide about the extent and quality of its network of contracting radiologists, making this a category of services subject to incentives. If all non-primary care specialists were contracted for together, the unit of analysis should be more aggregated.[7] Here we choose a high and a low level of aggregation to investigate incentives created by unweighted global rating. Note that the optimal weights can be figured without knowing how "services" should be defined for purposes of rationing.

Our first, more aggregated analysis distinguishes only three services: Inpatient hospital care (Part A), Outpatient hospital care (Part A) and Medical provider (primarily physician) care (Part B). Applying the formula contained in (13), the shadow prices for these three aggregated services are Inpatient hospital (.56), Outpatient hospital (.27) and Medical providers (.30), indicating that the incentives are to ration inpatient hospital care about twice as strictly as outpatient hospital and medical provider care. This is not surprising, as use of inpatient care is likely to be more highly correlated with total spending.

We next studied services at a disaggregated level. Any Part A or Part B service for which average spending exceeded $100 per year was treated as a separate category. An "Other Part A" and "Other Part B" category was the sum of the spending in all the categories less than $100 each. We also separated mental health spending in Parts A and B because that service has been found to be subject to incentives to underprovide in other analyses (e.g., Cao and McGuire, 2003; Ellis and McGuire, 2007). The results are contained in Table 4. Most inpatient hospital shadow prices

---

[7]See Glazer and McGuire (2002) for more discussion of the designation of a "Service" in the context of optimal risk adjustment analysis.

Table 4.   **Shadow prices for selected inpatient and outpatient services**

	Shadow price
Inpatient services	
Diseases and disorders of the nervous system	0.52
Diseases and disorders of the respiratory system	0.50
Diseases and disorders of the circulatory system	0.62
Diseases and disorders of the digestive system	0.53
Diseases and disorders of the musculoskeletal system and connective tissue	0.51
Mental diseases and disorders, substance use	0.52
Factors influencing health status and other contacts with health services	0.91
All other inpatient hospital care	0.52
Medical provider services	
Primary care services	0.24
Cardiology	0.36
Ophtho and optometry	0.22
Orthopedic surgery	0.31
Psychiatry	0.29
Radiology	0.30
Urology	0.37
Laboratory	0.24
Oncology	0.87
All other medical provider care	0.31
Outpatient hospital service	0.27

Source: Author's analysis of MCBS data.

by more detailed service are around .5–.6. Most medical provider services are around .2–.3. Notably, however, oncology has a very high shadow price of .87, and the medical specialties with the next highest shadow prices are urology (.37) and cardiology (.36). Higher spending by enrollees who make use of these specialties creates an incentive to ration them more strictly than other physician care.

The incentive to selectively supply services due to global ratings is analogous to adverse selection incentives stemming from capitation payments to plans. If a plan is rewarded by revenue weighted equally for all enrollees (i.e., capitation without risk adjustment), the plan has incentives to provide high quality of care for services used by low-cost enrollees and incentives to provide low quality of care to services used by high-cost enrollees (Frank *et al.*, 2000). Analogously, if the plan is rewarded by global ratings weighted equally for all enrollees, the plan has incentives to provide high quality of care for services used by low-cost enrollees, this time because improving care for people who don't use much care is cheaper than improving care for enrollees who use a lot of care. To continue with the analogy, risk adjusting capitation payments can address service-level adverse selection problems, and as we have shown, weighting global ratings by expected expenditures solves the adverse selection problem associated with global ratings.

Other research has characterized incentives created by capitated payments to ration at the service level in Medicare managed care. Mello *et al.* (2002) find evidence for stricter rationing of Part A than Part B in Medicare. Cao and McGuire (2003) and Ellis and McGuire (2007) use a national 5% sample of beneficiaries and more disaggregated categories. Pulmonary disease, oncological services and inpatient psychiatric care are among the services found by Ellis and McGuire (2007) to be subject to underprovision because of incentives in capitated payments.

5. CONCLUSIONS AND DIRECTIONS FOR FUTURE RESEARCH

Global ratings are common in quality reports on plans and providers, and have the advantage that they are easy to collect and understand. As we show here, if global ratings of a plan are a simple average of the ratings of the members, a plan's incentives to improve quality are inadvertently distorted towards services used by low-cost members and against those used by high-cost members. Such a distortion is particularly worrisome because it would reinforce distortions caused by imperfect risk adjustment working against the same set of services (Frank *et al.*, 2000). Fortunately, there is an easy intuitive fix for this problem with global ratings. Weighting responses by expected expenditures, giving more say in the global rating to enrollees who cost more, eliminates the distortion and restores balance in incentives to improve quality. This prescription is effective even without knowing what the right way to classify "services" is within a health plan and without knowing whether a plan is motivated by the desire to attract consumers or simply a professional concern with high ratings. Using MCBS weights in CAHPS has a very low cost. The weights are computed in a one-time operation from publicly available data (See Appendix A) and can be used repeatedly to weight responses.

Global or summary ratings have another, related advantage in dealing with adverse selection. Global measures can either be derived from direct questions ("Overall, how would you rate your plan?") or constructed by weighting dimensions of plan or provider performance collected separately into a summary measure (Shahian *et al.*, 2001). A summary or global measure reinforces pooling in health insurance markets. Everyone, no matter what their pattern of service demand, prefers a higher to lower rated plan. This tendency toward pooling is in contrast to rating systems that report on components of plan services (e.g., mental health care, pediatric care, diabetes care) that can contribute to separation according to demand for primary versus some forms of chronic care (for example). Furthermore, by choosing weights to put on elements of plan or provider performance, a regulator can construct a summary measure to counter adverse selection incentives that may arise from other forces, such as competition between plans in a capitated payment environment (Glazer and McGuire, 2006). Overall, a well-constructed global measure of health plan performance is a promising basis for plan quality reporting.

When global ratings are based on "consumer satisfaction" or some other enrollee-reported subjective measure of performance, interpretation of the rating by either plan administrators or potential enrollees depends on an understanding of how consumers decide to rate a plan high or low. In the course of developing our argument here, we made assumptions about how consumers decide on a rating, the key ones being that it costs more to "move" the rating of a person who uses more services in a plan, and that ratings are related to quality of the services a persons uses. While these assumptions seem reasonable on their face, they are certainly open to question. In any case, study of the quantitative relationship between what a plan does in terms of quality (in many dimensions) and how consumers rate a plan are warranted. This is useful information to plan administrators who must work to improve their plan, consumers who must decide what plan to join, and regulators and payers who must set the terms on which these choices are made.

ACKNOWLEDGMENTS

This research was supported by grant R34 MH071242 from the National Institute of Mental Health and the Henry Crown Institute of Business Research (Glazer). Zaslavsky's work was supported by contract number # 500-95-007 from the Centers for Medicare and Medicaid Services (CMS). Cao's work was supported by grant R03 MH71602 from the National Institute for Mental Health. We thank Amy Heller and Elizabeth Goldstein at CMS and the CAHPS project team at Westat for their work that developed the CAHPS datasets used here. We are grateful to Paul Cleary,

Richard Frank and Joseph Newhouse for helpful discussion and comments on an earlier draft. Opinions in the paper are the authors' own.

APPENDIX A. CROSSTAB OF TOTAL EXPENDITURE ON AGE, GENDER, HEALTH STATUS, SMOKING STATUS

				Total expenditure	
Agecat	Female	Genhealth	Smoke.lt	Mean	S.E.
65–69	Male	Excellent	Non-smoker	908.11	136.93
65–69	Male	Excellent	Smoker	2341.95	380.47
65–69	Male	Very good	Non-smoker	2373.50	641.78
65–69	Male	Very good	Smoker	2759.77	266.90
65–69	Male	Good	Non-smoker	3635.23	622.07
65–69	Male	Good	Smoker	5160.92	543.27
65–69	Male	Fair	Non-smoker	4110.74	1284.16
65–69	Male	Fair	Smoker	8500.75	1137.83
65–69	Male	Poor	Non-smoker	12557.54	4240.11
65–69	Male	Poor	Smoker	16823.99	3640.15
65–69	Female	Excellent	Non-smoker	1415.21	163.49
65–69	Female	Excellent	Smoker	1835.39	390.66
65–69	Female	Very good	Non-smoker	2246.16	263.35
65–69	Female	Very good	Smoker	2159.98	196.42
65–69	Female	Good	Non-smoker	3265.90	327.01
65–69	Female	Good	Smoker	4673.40	480.71
65–69	Female	Fair	Non-smoker	6916.72	857.02
65–69	Female	Fair	Smoker	8168.95	754.69
65–69	Female	Poor	Non-smoker	10938.31	2425.01
65–69	Female	Poor	Smoker	14843.89	1574.41
70–74	Male	Excellent	Non-smoker	1498.31	226.30
70–74	Male	Excellent	Smoker	2782.09	315.91
70–74	Male	Very good	Non-smoker	2669.73	504.27
70–74	Male	Very good	Smoker	4145.65	292.72
70–74	Male	Good	Non-smoker	4432.63	537.58

(*Continued*)

Appendix A   (*Continued*)

Agecat	Female	Genhealth	Smoke.lt	Total expenditure	
				Mean	S.E.
70–74	Male	Good	Smoker	5328.99	365.68
70–74	Male	Fair	Non-smoker	8850.01	2305.78
70–74	Male	Fair	Smoker	7580.99	562.08
70–74	Male	Poor	Non-smoker	15624.68	4271.11
70–74	Male	Poor	Smoker	18245.22	2435.61
70–74	Female	Excellent	Non-smoker	2004.73	311.76
70–74	Female	Excellent	Smoker	2673.07	309.49
70–74	Female	Very good	Non-smoker	2809.16	218.95
70–74	Female	Very good	Smoker	2860.03	209.69
70–74	Female	Good	Non-smoker	4561.33	347.41
70–74	Female	Good	Smoker	5720.15	514.65
70–74	Female	Fair	Non-smoker	6956.66	528.49
70–74	Female	Fair	Smoker	8282.56	774.92
70–74	Female	Poor	Non-smoker	10896.33	1665.65
70–74	Female	Poor	Smoker	15454.93	1876.04
75–79	Male	Excellent	Non-smoker	2842.41	646.07
75–79	Male	Excellent	Smoker	3166.11	336.91
75–79	Male	Very good	Non-smoker	4379.71	584.86
75–79	Male	Very good	Smoker	4137.61	300.21
75–79	Male	Good	Non-smoker	5689.90	603.32
75–79	Male	Good	Smoker	5918.69	412.92
75–79	Male	Fair	Non-smoker	7834.88	1238.15
75–79	Male	Fair	Smoker	9384.35	866.68
75–79	Male	Poor	Non-smoker	11729.17	3594.97
75–79	Male	Poor	Smoker	16246.19	2271.39
75–79	Female	Excellent	Non-smoker	2258.61	289.87
75–79	Female	Excellent	Smoker	2963.89	405.18
75–79	Female	Very good	Non-smoker	3201.48	184.62
75–79	Female	Very good	Smoker	4006.53	331.07
75–79	Female	Good	Non-smoker	4872.26	298.09
75–79	Female	Good	Smoker	5141.31	331.07
75–79	Female	Fair	Non-smoker	7914.13	675.25

(*Continued*)

J. Glazer et al.

Appendix A   (*Continued*)

Agecat	Female	Genhealth	Smoke.lt	Total expenditure	
				Mean	S.E.
75–79	Female	Fair	Smoker	7997.21	695.41
75–79	Female	Poor	Non-smoker	11570.12	1345.49
75–79	Female	Poor	Smoker	13807.11	1874.69
80–84	Male	Excellent	Non-smoker	3419.91	543.35
80–84	Male	Excellent	Smoker	4001.81	446.21
80–84	Male	Very good	Non-smoker	3520.34	413.85
80–84	Male	Very good	Smoker	5345.29	619.01
80–84	Male	Good	Non-smoker	5950.74	655.50
80–84	Male	Good	Smoker	6726.35	429.46
80–84	Male	Fair	Non-smoker	7957.58	888.35
80–84	Male	Fair	Smoker	8820.60	640.69
80–84	Male	Poor	Non-smoker	16718.25	3117.36
80–84	Male	Poor	Smoker	16678.33	1674.73
80–84	Female	Excellent	Non-smoker	2638.37	333.08
80–84	Female	Excellent	Smoker	3127.23	360.47
80–84	Female	Very good	Non-smoker	3880.60	278.25
80–84	Female	Very good	Smoker	4222.59	534.94
80–84	Female	Good	Non-smoker	5140.77	274.33
80–84	Female	Good	Smoker	5909.91	409.80
80–84	Female	Fair	Non-smoker	7248.82	487.26
80–84	Female	Fair	Smoker	6703.35	504.41
80–84	Female	Poor	Non-smoker	10843.34	1083.41
80–84	Female	Poor	Smoker	11855.63	1693.49
85+	Male	Excellent	Non-smoker	3651.95	762.52
85+	Male	Excellent	Smoker	3937.71	536.31
85+	Male	Very good	Non-smoker	4897.20	624.99
85+	Male	Very good	Smoker	5378.70	593.23
85+	Male	Good	Non-smoker	4644.57	513.41
85+	Male	Good	Smoker	6618.48	514.69
85+	Male	Fair	Non-smoker	6689.37	877.09
85+	Male	Fair	Smoker	7835.95	682.15
85+	Male	Poor	Non-smoker	9526.57	1925.70

(*Continued*)

Appendix A   (*Continued*)

| Agecat | Female | Genhealth | Smoke.lt | Total expenditure | |
				Mean	S.E.
85+	Male	Poor	Smoker	10861.96	1434.27
85+	Female	Excellent	Non-smoker	3312.23	291.47
85+	Female	Excellent	Smoker	3420.80	418.71
85+	Female	Very good	Non-smoker	3750.47	208.44
85+	Female	Very good	Smoker	4847.81	548.21
85+	Female	Good	Non-smoker	5443.77	254.87
85+	Female	Good	Smoker	5621.96	554.12
85+	Female	Fair	Non-smoker	6288.66	437.47
85+	Female	Fair	Smoker	8535.99	825.29
85+	Female	Poor	Non-smoker	8899.71	710.13
85+	Female	Poor	Smoker	9955.20	1403.42

Source: Medicare Current Beneficiary Survey (1996-2000). The statistics are calculated by authors.

REFERENCES

Abraham, J.M., Feldman, R., Carlin, C., Christianson, J., 2006. The effect of quality information on consumer health plan switching: evidence from the Buyers Health Care Action Group. *Journal of Health Economics* 25, 762–781.

Beaulieu, N.D., 2002. Quality information and consumer health plan choices. *Journal of Health Economics* 21(1), 43–63.

Brown, R., Bergeron, J.W., Clement, D.G., 1993. Do health maintenance organizations work for medicare? *Health Care Financing Review* 15, 7–24.

Cao, Z., McGuire, T.G., 2003. Service-level selection by HMOs in medicare. *Journal of Health Economics* 22, 915–931.

Chang, J.T., Hays, R.D., Shekelle, P.G., MacLean, C.H., 2006. Patients' global ratings of their health care are not associated with the technical quality of their care. *Annals of Internal Medicine* 144, 665–672.

Chernew, M.E., Gowrisnkaran, G., McLaughlin, C., Gibson, T., 2004. Quality and employers choice of health plans. *Journal of Health Economics* 23, 471–492.

Cleary, P.D., Edgman-Levitan, S., 1997. Health care quality: incorporating consumer perspectives. *Journal of the American Medical Association* 278(19), 1608–1612.

Dafny, L., Dranove, D., 2004. Do report cards tell people anything they don't already know? The case of medicare HMOs, NBER Working Paper, #1142.

Dranove, D., Kessler, D., McClellan, M., Satterthwaite, M., 2003. Is more information better? The effects of'report cards' on health care providers. *Journal of Political Economy* 111(3), 555–588.

Ellis, R.P., McGuire, T.G., 2007. Predictability and predictiveness in health care spending. *Journal of Health Economics* 26(1), 25–48.

Farley, D.O., Short, 2002. Effect of CAHPS performance information on health plan choices by Iowa Medicaid beneficiaries. *Medical Care Research and Review* 59(3), 319–336.

Fienberg, S.E., Loftus, E.F., Tanur, J.M., 1985. Cognitive aspects of health survey methodology: an overview. The Milbank Memorial Fund Quarterly. *Health and Society* 63(3), 547–564.

Frank, R., Glazer, J., McGuire, T.G., 2000. Measuring adverse selection in managed health care. *Journal of Health Economics* 19, 829–854.

Glazer, J., McGuire, T.G., 2002. Setting health plan premiums to ensure efficient quality in health care: minimum variance optimal risk adjustment. *Journal of Public Economics* 84, 153–173.

Glazer, J., McGuire, T.G., 2006. Optimal quality reporting in markets for health plans. *Journal of Health Economics* 25(2), 295–310.

Goldstein, E., Cleary, P.D., Langwell, K.M., 2001. Medicare managed care CAHPS: a tool for performance improvement. *Health Care Financing Review* 22(3), 101–107.

Hays, R.D., Shaul, J.A., Williams, V.S.L., 1999. Psychometric properties of the CAHPS 1.0 survey measures. *Medical Care* 37(3), MS22–MS31.

Hellinger, F., 1995. Selection bias in HMOs and PPOs: a review of the evidence. *Inquiry* 32, 135–142.

Jin, G.Z., Sorensen, A.T., 2006. Information and consumer choice: the value of publicized health plan ratings. *Journal of Health Economics* 25(2), 248–275.

Keeler, E.B., Newhouse, J.P., Carter, G., 1998. A model of the impact of reimbursement schemes on health plan choice. *Journal of Health Economics* 17(3), 297–320.

Keenan, P.S., Elliot, M.N., Cleary, P.D., Zaslavsky, A.M., Landon, B.E., 2007. Quality assessments by sick and health beneficiaries in traditional medicare and medicare managed care, unpublished.

Lurie, N., Zhan, C., Sangl, J., Bierman, A.S., Sekscenski, E.S., 2003. Variation in racial and ethnic differences in consumer assessments of health care. *The American Journal of Managed Care* 9(7), 502–509.

Mello, M.M., Stearns, S.C., Norton, E.C., 2002. Do medicare HMOs still reduce health services use after controlling for selection bias? *Health Economics* 11, 323–340.

Pauly, M.V., Ramsey, S.D., 1999. Would you like suspenders to go with that belt? An analysis of optimal combinations of cost sharing and managed care. *Journal of Health Economics* 18(4), 443–458.

Scanlon, D.P., Chernew, M.E., McLaughlin, Solon, G., 2002. The impact of health plan report cards on managed care enrollment. *Journal of Health Economics* 21(1), 19–41.

Schneider, E.C., Zaslavsky, A.M., Landon, B., Lied, T., Sheingold, S., Cleary, P.D., 2001. National quality monitoring of medicare health plans: The relationship between enrollees' reports and the quality of clinical care. *Medical Care* 39(12), 1313–1325.

Schultz, J., 2001. Do employees use report cards to assess health care provider systems? *Health Services Research* 36(3), 509–530.

Shahian, D.M., Normand, S.L., Torchiana, D.F., Lewis, S.M., Pastore, J.O., Kuntz, R.E., Dreyer, P.I., 2001. Cardiac surgery report cards: comprehensive review and statistical critique. *Annals of Thoracic Surgery* 76(6), 2155–2168.

Tai-Seale, M., 2004. Does consumer satisfaction information matter? Evidence on member retention in FEHBP plans. *Medical Care Research Review* 61, 171–186.

van de Ven, W.P.M.M., Ellis, R.P., 2000. Risk adjustment in competitive health plan markets. In: Culyer, A.J., Newhouse, J.P. (Eds.), *Handbook of Health Economics*. Elsevier, North Holland.

Wedig, G.J., Tai-Seale, M., 2002. The effect of report cards on consumer choice in the health insurance market. *Journal of Health Economics* 21(6), 1031–1048.

Zaslavsky, A.M., Hochheimer, J.N., Schneider, E.D., Cleary, P.D., 2000a. Impact of sociodemographic case mix on the HEDIS measures of health plan quality. *Medical Care* 38(10), 981–992.

Zaslavsky, A.M., Zaborski, L.B., Cleary, P.D., 2000b. Does the effect of respondent characteristics on consumer assessments vary across health plans? *Medical Care Research and Review* 57(3), 379–394.

Zaslavsky, A.M., Zaborski, L.B., Ding, L., Shaul, J.A., 2001. Adjusting performance measures to ensure equitable plan comparisons. *Health Care Financing Review* 22(3), 109–126.

Zaslavsky, A.M., Cleary, P.D., 2002. Dimensions of plan performance for sick and healthy members on the consumer assessments of health plans study 2.0 survey. *Medical Care* 40(10), 951–964.

Chapter 6

GOLD AND SILVER HEALTH PLANS: ACCOMMODATING DEMAND HETEROGENEITY IN MANAGED COMPETITION

Jacob Glazer[a,b] and Thomas G. McGuire[c,*]

[a] *Tel Aviv University, Israel*

[b] *Boston University, United States*

[c] *Harvard Medical School, Department of Health Care Policy, Boston, MA, United states*
mcguire@hcp.med.harvard.edu

Received 10 December 2009
Received in revised form 9 November 2010
Accepted 31 May 2011
Available online 28 June 2011

New regulation of health insurance markets creates multiple levels of health plans, with designations like "Gold" and "Silver." The underlying rationale for the heavy-metal approach to insurance regulation is that heterogeneity in demand for health care is not only due to health status (sick demand more than the healthy) but also to other, "taste" related factors (rich demand more than the poor). This paper models managed competition with demand heterogeneity to consider plan payment and enrollee premium policies in relation to efficiency (net consumer benefit) and fairness (the European concept of "solidarity"). Specifically, this paper studies how to implement a "Silver" and "Gold" health plan efficiently and fairly in a managed competition context. We show that there are sharp tradeoffs between efficiency and fairness. When health plans cannot or may not (because of regulation) base premiums on any factors affecting demand, enrollees do not choose the efficient plan. When taste (e.g., income) can be used as a basis of payment, a simple tax can achieve both efficiency and fairness. When only health status (and not taste) can be used as a basis of payment, health status-based taxes and subsidies are required and efficiency can only be achieved with a modified version of fairness we refer to as "weak solidarity." An overriding conclusion is that the

---

*Corresponding author.

regulation of premiums for both the basic and the higher level plans is necessary for efficiency.

JEL classification: 110, 114, 118

Keywords: health economics; managed competition; health insurance

1. INTRODUCTION

In economic terms, an individual's utility from medical treatment generally depends on her health status (e.g., her general medical condition, the illness she suffers from, and the severity of this illness) as well as other factors such as her income, education and tastes which affect utility and demand for most goods and services. Respecting individual preferences calls for taking into account both sets of factors in deciding her best treatment. However, particularly in managed care environments, supply-side factors and rationing rules also affect care provided. The clinician treating this patient may not weigh all of the factors affecting her utility equally. Either because of professional inclination or unfamiliarity with patient preferences, clinicians may be more responsive to the individual's health status than to other "taste" factors affecting her utility. An immediate consequence of this simple observation is that individuals in a health plan will receive similar treatment if their health status is the same, even if their benefits from the services are not. Social efficiency will not generally be served by such uniform treatment, and welfare could be improved if individuals with greater "taste" for health services were in different plans than those with lower taste.

In the U.S., pursuit of public policy objectives of extending coverage and controlling costs brings health insurance more under public control, and consequently, accommodating demand heterogeneity becomes an issue for regulation rather than simply being "left to the market." One public policy response to demand heterogeneity creates "Gold," "Silver" and possibly other heavy-metal plans representing levels of coverage and generosity. The publicly created health insurance market in Massachusetts designates Platinum, Gold and Silver Plans, and national health care reform calls for Platinum, Gold, Silver and Bronze. The design of efficient and equitable health policy in this policy context is the focus of this paper. We carry out the analysis when two types of health plans can efficiently serve tastes, a basic plan which we term "Silver" and a more generous plan which we term "Gold."

This paper studies how to efficiently and fairly implement a "Silver" and "Gold" health insurance plan within a policy context of managed competition. In managed competition, private plans compete for enrollees subject to regulation of premiums and benefits (Enthoven, 1980). Managed competition characterizes health policy in many countries, including Germany, Israel, Netherlands, Switzerland, the U.S. and other countries where regulated private plans compete in a market for enrollees. Our "Silver Plan" covers a basic bundle of health care services. The "Gold Plan" offers better coverage/higher quality of care, but is more expensive. For efficiency, we want groups with a higher willingness to pay for health care to be in the Gold Plan. For fairness, we want the sick and the healthy to pay the same for plan membership in both plans. As far as we know, the literature does not contain a description of an enrollee premium-plan payment policy that achieves these two objectives.

After a literature review in Section 2, Section 3 describes our model in which consumers differ in two dimensions, health status and "taste" for health care, and are served by competing managed health care plans. A Regulator pays plans and may levy plan-specific taxes. Plans compete on services and premiums. We lay out explicit criteria for what we mean by efficiency and fairness. Efficiency is based on maximizing net consumer benefit. Fairness is based on the solidarity principle that the sick should pay the same as the healthy for health insurance. Section 4 considers the case in which both health status and "taste" are available as a basis of payment. The natural interpretation of "taste" in this case is "income," a taste-related individual characteristic that can be used to condition premiums or as basis for taxation. We show that incremental cost pricing of individual premiums is efficient but unfair, and that average cost premiums are fair but not efficient. By use of a new policy with an income-based tax on plan membership the Regulator can achieve both an efficient and fair allocation.

Many factors affecting demand (e.g., subjective valuation of health) cannot be used as a basis for either Regulator payment to plans or premiums charged to enrollees. Section 5 considers regulation when taste cannot be used as a basis for payment. We show that no payment policy leads to both efficiency and fairness. When we weaken the solidarity principle to be that the sick pay no more for health insurance than the healthy, efficiency and fairness can be achieved. We describe the tax and premium policy that achieves efficiency and "weak solidarity" in this context. Section 6 concludes the paper and comments on applications of our analysis to payment systems built around the idea of managed competition.

2. LITERATURE REVIEW

From the beginning, proponents of managed competition recognized the problem of serving heterogeneous demands in a health insurance market in which a Regulator specifies a basic plan, and allows competition on price and quality (Diamond, 1992; Enthoven, 1980). Heterogeneity in demand stems from differences in health status and heterogeneity associated with "taste" factors. Health status heterogeneity is addressed by risk-adjustment of the payments made to health plans.[1] Taste heterogeneity raises distinct issues and comes about when, for example, higher-income groups are willing to pay for higher quality care than is provided in the basic plan. "Taste adjustment" of plan payments would not attain efficiency if clinicians in a plan failed to allocate resources in response to tastes.[2]

Researchers have characterized premium policies that achieve either efficiency or fairness, but not both. One way to accommodate diverse tastes with a Silver and Gold Plan sets the premium for the Silver Plan at the same level for all. Then, the Regulator charges each person the incremental cost they would incur in the Gold over the Silver Plan, and lets them choose the plan they want (Keeler *et al.*, 1998). This premium policy efficiently sorts individuals among the plans, but by charging more for the sick, violates principles of equity.

Entohoven and Kronick (1989) and others argue that managed competition accommodates tastes by allowing Gold Plans to both upgrade services over a Silver Plan and also charge a higher premium to pay for the upgrade. The idea, as expressed by Pizer *et al.* (2003), is that "Beneficiaries who highly value certain benefits can search for a plan that offers those benefits and pay the marginal premium that corresponds to their choice." This policy is fair in the sense that everyone pays the same for plan membership, but it fails to efficiently sort consumers between plans. If the premium

---

[1] A large literature in health economics studies how to pay plans so as to induce them to accept enrollees across risk groups and to provide services efficiently. For reviews, see Newhouse (2002) and Van de Ven and Ellis (2000). In managed competition the public sector collects the revenues and repackages it as risk-adjusted payments before sending it to plans. Importantly, decision makers within the health plans, i.e., clinicians, must be willing to allocate funds according to health status, a reasonable if oftentimes implicit assumption. Demand heterogeneity can also stem from factors clinicians may be less responsive to in resource allocation decisions, a point we call attention to in this paper.
[2] It would also likely be unacceptable politically to collectively finance a plan payment system that paid more for groups with higher taste for health care.

for the Gold Plan is average (not marginal) incremental cost, low-cost consumers will be inefficiently discouraged and high-cost consumers will be inefficiently encouraged to join the Gold.[3]

As far as we know there has not been much research in economics addressing the issues of efficiency and equity in markets where consumers' demand is driven by both tastes and need. One exception is Bundorf *et al.* (2009), who show in a theoretical analysis that uniform pricing will generally not lead patients to efficiently sort themselves across plans. We also obtain this result in the context of our model and use it as a benchmark for the analysis that follows. The second and larger part of their paper estimates the efficiency loss due to inefficient pricing. Our paper differs from Bundorf *et al.* (2009) in several important aspects. First, we study explicitly the market equilibrium that will emerge under different regulatory regimes. Second and more important, our concern is not only with efficiency but also with fairness. In fact, one of our main objectives is to demonstrate the tension between efficiency and fairness that emerges in markets where consumers differ not only in their needs but also in their tastes, and to propose a mechanism to address this tension.[4] Third, we propose several regulatory policies that can be applied to implement both an efficient and fair allocation, under various assumptions about the tools available to the regulatory agency.

In order to characterize premium and plan payment policies that achieve efficiency and fairness, we analyze payment policy within an explicit model of managed competition. Surprising in light of its popularity as a basis for national policy, the managed competition paradigm — competing managed care plans subject to regulation of benefits and premiums serving

---

[3] In very special circumstances a single Gold Plan premium can sort consumers efficiently between two plans (see Feldman and Dowd (1982), Ellis and McGuire (1987) or Cutler and Reber (1998) for such models) but in general as we explain in more detail below, a single premium either set by the market or by a Regulator does not lead to efficient sorting between two plan types. Bundorf *et al.* (2009) points out the special assumption in these models.

Miller (2005) considers optimal sorting in a different context, an employer setting an incremental premium employees must pay for a more generous plan. Miller points out that the employer may be able to set the payment (which in this context goes back to the employer) to extract some of the additional surplus sicker workers get from employer-based health insurance.

[4] Smart (2000) considers insurance against a financial loss when consumers differ in probability of loss and in risk aversion. This form of demand heterogeneity also interferes with efficiency of markets when firms cannot price risk separately to the different risk groups.

a diverse population — has not been formally modeled in the literature. Models of competitive health insurance markets drawing on Rothschild and Stiglitz (1976) show how a Regulator should set risk adjusted payments (e.g., Glazer and McGuire, 2000) or regulate quality (Encinosa, 2001) in the presence of heterogeneity in health status, but not heterogeneity in taste. Analysis in papers incorporating "taste" of some form is conducted with two plans (or sectors) and disregard conditions of competitive equilibrium that come into play in managed competition.[5] Other papers model heterogeneity as "distance" between two plans.[6] To study regulation of payment policy in managed competition, we first construct a working model of managed competition with demand heterogeneity. Plans set premiums and benefits (subject to regulation). Consumers choose plans. Our purpose is to describe what the Regulator must do to ensure the market outcome is efficient and fair.

3. CONSUMERS AND GOLD AND SILVER MANAGED CARE PLANS

Before we present the mechanics of our model, we call attention to the concepts of efficiency and fairness which play an important role in our analysis. By efficiency we mean the conventional utility maximization. The point to stress is that in our paper utility is affected by "taste" as well as "need," and we regard both factors as equally legitimate when it comes to efficiency. Other approaches to health policy focus on need and implicitly assume that the same treatment is efficient for the entire population. If this were so, there is no efficiency rationale for Silver and Gold health plans. We are interested, in this paper, in a context in which the diversity among the population in taste for health care is regarded as a valid concern for social policy.

　　Fairness also matters for policy towards the social merit good, health insurance. In health policy, fairness is about health status (the sick should not pay more than the healthy) as well as ability to pay (the rich should pay more than the poor). In this paper, we base our concept of fairness on the European "solidarity principle" which dictates that

---

[5]Feldman and Dowd (1982), Ellis and McGuire (1987), Keeler *et al.* (1998) and Cutler and Reber(1998).
[6]Encinosa and Sappington (1997), Jack (2006) and Olivella and Vera-Hernandez (2007). Travel costs confer some market power on the two competing plans.

individuals in poor health should pay the same for health insurance as those in good health.[7] Principles of solidarity have been made most explicit in policy discussions in Germany.[8] As Stock *et al.* (2006) explain, the guiding principle of Germany's Social Health Insurance is solidarity: "Services are rendered according to medical need." Furthermore, "[Financing] implies cross-subsidization from low to high risks, [and] from high-income to low-income earners..." Concern for fairness motivates regulation of health insurance premiums in the U.S. as well, prohibiting or limiting discrimination by health status.[9] These strictures limit how well premiums charged to enrollees can match persons with health plans serving their preferences.

3.1. *Consumers and Efficient Health Care*

Four types of consumers differ by health status and a taste factor that we refer to for now as "income." Later, in Section 5, we will use the more general term "taste" when the factor differentiating types is unavailable for use in payment policy. Consumers can be healthy (h) or sick (s), and poor (p) or rich (r). Type is unchanging and there is an equal number of each type. We define $v_{ij}(x)$ to be the benefit of health spending x to a consumer with health status $i, i = h, s$, and income $j, j = p, r$, where $v'_{ij} > 0$ and $v''_{ij} < 0$. Based on the discussion above, the efficient level of care for each

---

[7]For a review of the application of solidarity principles in the context of competing health plans, see Van de Ven and Ellis (2000). Sass (1995) is a European philosophical perspective on solidarity. Stone (1993), in a U.S. context, contrasts solidarity principles with ideals of actuarial fairness in the organization and pricing of health insurance.

[8]In a recent interview, the then Minister of Health in Germany, Ulla Schmidt, put it this way: "My overarching personal goal as Minister of Health has been to preserve for Germany's health system the principle of social solidarity, by which we mean that everyone in Germany should have guaranteed access to state-of-the-art medical care and contribute to the financing of this guarantee on the basis of the household's ability to pay." Cheng and Reinhardt (2008, p. 205).

[9]Federal non-discrimination policies towards health insurance premiums are described in GAO (2003). Regulations are administered by the IRS, govern ERISA plans and prohibit discrimination in premiums charged and in premium contributions by employees according to health status. The Kaiser Family Foundation (2009) lists ten states that restrict use of health status in setting premiums in the individual health insurance market (often limiting the differential that can be charged by health status), and eight states that have some form of community rating regulation. This prohibition of discrimination on the basis of health status could also be cast as an efficiency issue: in a socially efficient policy, individuals would be protected from risk of changing health status.

type is where $v'_{ij}(x^*_{ij}) = 1$. To simplify some of the discussion we further assume that $v'_{hj}(x) = v'_{sj}(kx)$, $k > 1$ for every $x, j = p, r$. [10]

3.2. *Plans' Rationing Rule*

Clinicians in the plan ration care. The literature contains two rationing rules, one in which clinicians set quantity or a maximum quantity (Baumgardner, 1991; Pauly and Ramsey, 1999) and the other in which clinicians ration according to a shadow price, equating the value of care at the margin across users within a plan (Frank et al., 2000). Notably in these papers, the clinician's view of a patient's benefit from health care is identical to the patient's own view. We call attention to this assumption because in the current paper we allow taste to matter for the patient but not for the clinician.

We assume that benefits due to "health factors" matter to patients and doctors — patients because it is their health, and doctors because they are professionally trained to respond to health needs of patients. We assume, in contrast, benefits due to non-health factors matter to the patient but not to the doctor. What we have in mind is this: a rich person may have higher willingness to pay for health care than a poor person, but from the doctor's point of view, care to a rich person is no more valuable than care to a poor person. Provider rationing practices matter in managed care plans, the subject of this analysis. The assumption that patient taste does not affect provider decisions about resource allocation is obviously an extreme one. Our point — and all that matters for our results — is that rationing decisions are less responsive to taste than to health status.

Putting this in terms of our model, we make the following assumption about clinician rationing. The budget for health care in a plan is allocated among individuals so as to equalize clinicians' assessment of the marginal benefit from care to a shadow price: $v'_{ip}(x) = \lambda$, $i = h, s$. It is as if clinicians "see" only two benefit functions $v_{hp}(x)$ and $v_{sp}(x)$, and they disregard the

---

[10] Higher demand for care among those with greater "taste" for health care could stem from two basic factors, ability to pay and preferences. The high and low-taste groups could have the same utility function, but if one group had more income, it would have higher demand than the low-income group. Alternatively, groups might have the same income but have different utility functions. In this paper, we do not distinguish between these two possibilities. In either case, economic efficiency calls for serving higher demand. Interpretation of equity could be affected by whether higher demand originates from ability to pay or from utility.

elevated benefit the rich have over the poor. The shadow price, λ, exhausts the budget clinicians have to spend on their patients. The assumption we have made above that $v'_h(x) = v'_s(kx)$ implies that $x_s/x_h = k$ in a plan. In other words, rationing by a shadow price implies the sick will get a proportion $(k > 1)$ more than the healthy in a plan, regardless of their income.

An obvious consequence of this assumption is that the healthy rich and healthy poor would be allocated the same health care in a plan, as would the sick rich and sick poor. Therefore, since $x^*_{ir} > x^*_{ip}$, it will not be efficient to put the rich and the poor in the same health plan. Note, however, that if the healthy and sick from the same income group were in the same health plan, clinician rationing by a shadow price could achieve the efficient health care for both the healthy and sick so long as the budget to spend is enough to pay for the efficient level of care. We can thus foresee that for efficiency the healthy and sick poor should be in the Silver Plan and the healthy and sick rich in the Gold Plan.

3.3. *Regulation*

Our main goal in this paper is to study whether and how the Regulator can induce plans to provide the efficient levels of care and individuals to sort themselves efficiently across plans without violating the criteria for fairness. Our leading assumption is that the levels of care provided by the health plans cannot be directly monitored (i.e., payments cannot be based on x_{ij}) and the Regulator must apply other mechanisms to induce plans to provide the efficient care. The "Regulator's Policy" consists of health status risk-adjusted payments (made by the Regulator) to plans, denoted by $\pi_i, i = h, s$, and taxes (paid by the individuals to the Regulator) which may depend on the individual's type and the plan she chooses, denoted by $t^m_{ij}, i = h, s, j = p, r$ and $m = G, S$. After the Regulator announces its policy, plans choose their policy. A "plan's policy" consists of the levels of services they will provide, denoted by $x = (x_h, x_s)$, and the premium individuals pay (directly to the plan) if they join the plan, denoted by $y = (y_{hp}, y_{hr}, y_{sp}, y_{sr})$. Given the Regulator's Policy and the plans' policy, individuals choose the plan that maximizes their net benefit. More formally, we have in mind the following four-stage model:

Stage 1: The Regulator announces its tax and risk adjustment policies (t, π) In addition, the Regulator may impose some restrictions on the plans' premiums.

Stage 2: Each plan announces its policy (y, x) which consists of the premium individuals pay if they join the plan and the level of service the plan provides. Each plan's services consists of a pair (x_h, x_s) such that $x_s = kx_h$, $k > 1$.

Stage 3: Individuals choose plans and plans must accept everyone. Individuals pay taxes to the Regulator and premiums to the plans according to the plan they have chosen. The Regulator pays plans the risk adjusted payments.

Stage 4: Plans provide services.

It is important to notice here that even though the Regulator's Policy cannot be conditioned on the level of services the plans offer, it can be conditioned on the premiums the plans charge. Given the Regulator's Policy in Stage 1, a *competitive equilibrium,* in Stage 2, is a profile of plans' policies such that, given that each individual chooses the plan that maximizes her utility, each plan makes zero profit and no plan can offer another policy that will make a strictly positive profit.

3.4. *Fair Payment Policies*

Each of the four types will be required to pay premiums and possibly taxes upon joining the Gold and Silver Plans. The distinction between premiums and taxes is that premiums are payments made to the plan that the plan can use for services, whereas taxes are paid to the government. Regulator payments to plans are assumed to be financed by distributionally acceptable taxes.[11]

We say a payment policy is fair if the payments (health plan-related premiums and taxes) a sick person must make for the Gold Plan are equal to the payments a healthy person must make. The sick and healthy must also pay the same for the Silver Plan. Furthermore, for fairness we require that payments a low taste (poor) person must make for each plan be no

---

[11]This could be, for example, a payroll tax shared by employer and employee, as in Germany (Stock *et al.*, 2006). We disregard any efficiency consequences of tax finance in terms of distorting employment or other decisions. Taxes and subsidies in this analysis are aimed at correcting prices facing persons with different demands making choice of health plans. One can always add or subtract a constant tax or subsidy from every person to compensate for any fiscal imbalance between taxes collected and subsidies paid, in order to make the consumer tax-subsidy portion of health plan financing "budget neutral." In this case, there are no implications of alternative premium policies studied here for the efficiency of taxation in the rest of the economy.

more than the payments made by a high taste (rich) person.[12] A payment policy that meets these conditions will be said to satisfy "strong solidarity." Later we relax the health condition to an inequality (sick pay no more than the healthy at each plan) and refer to this as "weak solidarity."

Note that our definition of fairness applies to premiums for both the Gold and the Silver Plan. One could argue alternatively that fairness is about the basic plan (or Silver Plan) and there is no equity issue associated with sicker people paying more than the healthy for a health plan upgrade. If a Gold Plan is relevant for just a small group in the upper end of the income distribution, this alternative position has merit. If, however, as is increasingly the case, a society's basic plan is just that, large segments of the population, not just the elite, will be efficiently served by more generous coverage. In this case, fairness in Gold Plan premiums matters too.

3.5. *Silver and Gold Plans Providing Efficient Care*

In order to illustrate our main insights we analyze premium and payment policies in the context of an example where $v_{ij}(x_{ij}) = \gamma_{ij}(x{ij})^{(1/2)}$, $\gamma_{hp} = 2$, $\gamma_{hr} = 3$, $\gamma_{sp} = 4$, and $\gamma_{sr} = 6$. In this section we use this example to describe the efficient care for the rich and the poor and the efficient allocation of types across plans. With these utility functions the efficient levels of care are given by $x_{ij}^* = \gamma_{ij}^2/4$, $i = h$, s, $j = p, r$. As we have discussed above, since providers in each health plan do not distinguish between rich and poor individuals, one plan cannot provide the efficient levels of care for all types. Thus, in order for the rich types and the poor types to obtain their respective efficient level of care, two different plans must be offered, one (the "Silver Plan") that provides the efficient levels of care for the healthy poor and the sick poor, and the other (the "Gold Plan") that provides the efficient levels of care for the healthy rich and the sick rich. Notice, however, that in principle, a poor individual could choose to join the Gold Plan (in which case she would get the same level of care as the healthy rich if she is a healthy poor type and the same level of care as the sick rich if she is a sick poor type). Similarly, a rich individual could choose to join the Silver Plan and obtain the level of care as if she where a poor type.

---

[12]Even though this last fairness condition is readily satisfied, we prefer to state it as part of our definition as it is usually understood to be part of what is meant by solidarity.

Table 1. Benefits and costs in Silver and Gold Plans at efficient levels of care.

	Healthy benefit	Cost	Sick benefit	Cost
Silver Plan				
Poor	2	1	8	4
Rich	3	1	12	4
Gold Plan				
Poor	3	2.25	12	9
Rich	4.5	2.25	18	9

Table 1 assumes utility is for type i, j, $v_{ij} = \gamma_{ij}(x_{ij})^{(1/2)}$, with $\gamma_{hp} = 2$, $\gamma_{hr} = 3$, $\gamma_{sp} = 4$, and $\gamma_{sr} = 6$.

Table 1 describes the benefits and costs, for each of the four types, in a Silver or Gold Plan. (Appendix A contains the analog of Table 1 for the more general case.) The Silver Plan provides the efficient level of care for the poor, and the Gold Plan provides the efficient level of care for the rich. Note that, reflecting our assumption about rationing in managed care, the healthy poor and the healthy rich would get the same care in the Silver Plan (spending of 1). The rich benefit more from this care because of their higher γ in their benefit function. We explain briefly the origin of the numerical entries in Table 1. Consider first the Silver Plan, designed for the poor. The efficient care for the healthy poor is $x^*_{hp} = 1$, since $\gamma_{hp} = 2$. At this cost, the benefit received by a healthy poor individual is found by putting this x^* into the healthy poor benefit function $2(x)^{(1/2)} = 2$. A healthy rich person in the Silver Plan gets the same care as the healthy poor, but since the healthy rich person benefits more ($\gamma_{hr} = 3$), the benefit of the Silver Plan is 3 for this type. Efficient care for the sick poor $x^*_{sp} = 4$, and the entries for the sick rich and poor in the Silver Plan are found in a similar fashion. Entries in the Gold Plan are based on efficient spending for the healthy and sick rich, and then assigning the corresponding benefits to each of the poor and the rich at this spending level.

Note that the net social benefit (benefit minus cost) of the healthy and sick poor is higher in the Silver Plan and the net social benefit of the rich types is higher in the Gold Plan. Efficiency requires the poor to be in the Silver Plan and the rich to be in the Gold Plan. The budget for the Silver Plan is 5, the sum of the costs of efficient care for the poor healthy and poor sick $(1 + 4)$. It can be readily seen that with a budget of 5, clinicians would allocate 1 to the healthy and 4 to the sick, confirming that the Silver Plan could enroll both the healthy and sick poor efficiently. The Gold Plan can enroll both the rich sick and healthy, and with a budget of 11.25, the sum of costs of effective care for the rich healthy and rich sick provide the efficient care to both.

The policy problem of accommodating taste heterogeneity would be easily solved if providers allocated plan resources in response to taste as readily as they do in response to health status. In this case, there would be no need to have Gold and Silver Plans with higher and lower levels of funding. One plan, with demand-responsive providers, would fulfill efficiency. However, as long as there is some less response in rationing to taste than to health status, more than one type of plan is necessary for efficiency.

Note there is no demand-side cost sharing in any plan. Efficiency requires full coverage if health care need is uncertain. We are thus not concerned with financial risk aversion. We are also not concerned in this paper with moral hazard which would be roughly constant across all the premium policy options we consider.

4. IMPLEMENTATION WHEN BOTH HEALTH STATUS AND INCOME ARE AVAILABLE AS A BASIS OF PAYMENT

Suppose that both the individual's health status and her income (taste) are verifiable and, hence, can serve as a basis for taxes and payments. In the context of the example described in Table 1, we analyze three payment policies associated with different approaches to setting taxes and individual premiums. The health status risk-adjusted plan payments supporting these premium policies will also be described. The first two premium policies, incremental cost premiums and incremental average cost premiums, have been considered in the literature. We will show that these policies sacrifice fairness or efficiency. The third policy regulates Gold Plan premiums and introduces taxes to achieve both fairness and efficiency. Rather than offering formal propositions, we employ the example to make these points.

4.1. *Incremental Cost Premiums*

Under the incremental cost premium policy, the Regulator, in Stage 1, sets no taxes or subsidies and makes a risk-adjusted payment to any plan equal to the cost of providing the efficient care for the poor: $\pi_i = x_{ip}^*$; $i = s, h$. In our example, $\pi_s = 4, \pi_h = 1$. Furthermore, the Regulator sets no restrictions on plans' premium so that a premium could depend both on individual's health status and her income. In such a case, in Stage 2, two plans will be offered in equilibrium, Gold and Silver. The Silver plan will charge no premium and will provide the efficient level of care for the poor. The premium for the Gold Plan for each person will be: $y_{ij} = x^*_{ir} - x^*_{ip}$, $i = h, s, j = r, p$. (In our example, the incremental premiums are $y_{hp} = y_{hr} = 1.25$, $y_{sp} = y_{sr} = 5$.) The Gold Plan will provide the efficient levels of care for the rich. It is straightforward to see that this policy leads to efficiency. The poor are in the Silver Plan, the rich in the Gold Plan. Every person receives the first-best level of care and both plans break even.

Competition forces Silver and Gold Plans to spend their revenue. Silver Plans spend their budget, coming entirely from risk-adjusted plan payments, on efficient care for the sick and healthy poor. Gold Plans, paid by the Regulator and by individual premiums from the healthy rich and sick rich, have just enough to provide efficient care for the rich. Assuming a Gold Plan can price discriminate by health status, competition also forces Gold Plans to choose these premiums, since these are the premiums that when the money is spent on care, maximize the net benefit of the rich.

As shown earlier by Keeler *et al.* (1998), the incremental cost policy thus implements the efficient care with a Silver and Gold Plan as described in Table 1. The problem with this policy is that it violates our standard of fairness. The sick pay more, an incremental cost premium of 5, to join a Gold Plan than the healthy, an incremental cost premium of 1.25.

Result 4.1. *Regulatory policy allowing incremental cost premiums can implement an efficient Silver and Gold Plan, but, by charging more to the sick, violates fairness.*

4.2. *Incremental Average Cost Premiums*

In practice in managed competition, health plans are generally prohibited from charging higher premiums to individuals with worse health status. Consider next a policy in which a Regulator makes a health status risk-adjusted payment to plans, and plans are free to charge any premium, so long as it is the same to every enrollee. Thus, $\pi_i = x^*_{ip}$, $i = s, h$, as before; but now, $y_{ij} = y$, $i = h, s, j = p, r$, where the level of y is chosen independently by each plan. A key feature of the example in Table 1 is that the extra benefit to the healthy rich type from going to the Gold Plan is less than the extra benefit to the sick poor type. This implies that there is no premium for the Gold Plan that would attract the healthy rich and not the sick poor. For the Gold Plan to attract the healthy rich, it must be that $y \leq 1.5$, the difference between the healthy rich benefit in the Gold Plan and their benefit on the Silver Plan. For the Gold Plan not to attract the sick poor, it must be that $y \geq 4$, the difference between the sick poor benefit in the Gold Plan and their benefit in the Silver Plan. Obviously, no premium satisfies these two constraints, and therefore efficiency is not possible under this policy.

The condition in our example that the healthy rich are willing to pay less than the sick poor to join the Gold Plan is not restrictive. With continuous types, it will certainly be true that the healthiest among the rich would pay less to join a Gold Plan than the sickest among the poor. And with this, no premium sorts the two groups efficiently. Note that risk adjustment cannot fix this problem.

Result 4.2. *No payment policy with a single premium for all enrollees at the Gold Plan can implement the efficient care.*

Note that this result about any single premium failing to achieve efficiency applies to the particular form of single premium, the average cost premium. The result parallels the argument made by Bundorf *et al.* (2009).

This result leaves open the question of what an equilibrium would look like in the case of a single premium. As far as we know the managed competition equilibrium with taste heterogeneity has not previously been portrayed in the literature. We describe the equilibrium in our example here, which turns out, not surprisingly, to be an application of Rothschild and Stiglitz (1976).

Suppose that, in Stage 1, the Regulator announces no taxes or subsidies, and a risk adjustment policy paying a plan $\pi_i = x_{ip}^*$ for each individual whose health status is $i, i = h, s$. Further, assume that plans must charge the same premium to all enrollees. In equilibrium, two plans will be offered. One plan (the Silver Plan) will charge no premium and will offer the first-best levels of care for the poor (x_{hp}^*, x_{sp}^*). The other plan (the Gold Plan) will charge a premium of 5, the incremental cost for the sick rich, and will offer the first-best levels of care for the rich (x_{hr}^*, x_{sr}^*). The Gold Plan will attract only the sick-rich individuals whereas the Silver Plan will attract all other individuals, namely, the healthy-poor, the sick-poor and the healthy-rich. Notice that this equilibrium is inefficient since the healthy-rich individuals choose the Silver Plan instead of the Gold Plan, and hence, they do not receive their first best level of care. Appendix B demonstrates that this outcome is an equilibrium in the case of our example.

The two-plan equilibrium that emerges in our example is not the only possible form of equilibrium in managed competition with taste heterogeneity. It is also possible for equilibrium to be characterized by a Silver Plan serving the poor and two plans serving the rich. In a result reminiscent of a Rothschild-Stiglitz separating equilibrium, the sick rich would get efficient care in a plan they choose, and the healthy rich would be in a plan that maximizes their utility subject to separating from the sick rich. Note that this equilibrium is also inefficient as the healthy rich do not get efficient care.

4.3. Average Cost Premiums and Income-Based Taxes

We have shown in the previous two sections that the incremental cost premium policy is efficient but unfair and the average cost premium policy is fair but inefficient. In this section we describe a new policy that achieves both efficiency and fairness. The new policy involves several key elements. First, the Regulator sets the premium for the Silver *and* the Gold Plan (to prevent separation). Second, the premium for the Gold Plan is based on average cost so as to maintain fairness. Third, income-based taxes direct the rich and the poor to the Gold and Silver Plan respectively.

Specifically, consider a policy in which the Regulator sets the same risk-adjusted payment above, $\pi_i = x_{ip}^*; i = s, h$, and now offers a menu to the plans according to which they can choose for all their members a premium of 0 or a premium of the average of the incremental cost of the healthy and sick rich for care in the Gold Plan $y = (1.25 + 5)/2 = 3.125$. A plan that charges the premium $y = 0$ will be referred to as a Silver Plan, and a plan that charges $y = 3.125$ will be referred to as a Gold Plan. Note that premiums for Silver and Gold Plans are set by regulation, not by plans as in the first two cases. Furthermore, introduce taxes. Let $t_r = 1.625$ be a tax on the rich and a negative tax (subsidy) to the poor $t_p = -.875$ if and only if they join a plan that charges a premium of 0. The healthy rich only gain an incremental benefit of 1.5 in the Gold Plan. When they must pay a premium for Gold of 3.125, they must be taxed at least 1.625 to not prefer Silver. Similarly, the sick poor gain 4 in benefits joining Gold. At the premium of 3.125, they must be subsidized at least .875 to prefer Silver.

Another interpretation of this policy is as a means-tested premium subsidy for the Silver Plan. The poor would be subsidized to join the plan, and the rich would pay a positive premium to join. We refer to these as subsidies and taxes in this paper however since the money flow is between the Regulator and the individual rather than between the Plan and the individual (as in the case of premiums).

It can readily be shown that if the Regulator sets the risk- adjusted payment to plans equal to efficient care for the poor, limits premiums to the two values above, and sets the taxes as just described, the competitive equilibrium will lead to the efficient care provided by a Silver and Gold Plan. The Gold Plan charges a single premium of incremental average cost. The poor go to the Silver Plan, the rich to the Gold Plan. Furthermore, this outcome is fair. Healthy and sick of each income group face the same payments (premiums plus taxes) for membership in the plans. All the poor receive a subsidy in the Silver Plan.

The tax on the rich and subsidy to the poor for joining the Silver Plan keep the healthy rich from preferring the Silver Plan (when having to pay average incremental cost for the Gold Plan) and discourage the sick poor from the Gold Plan (when paying only the average incremental premium). Note that the poor receive the subsidy by staying in the Silver Plan, but the rich pay no taxes by electing the Gold Plan.

An important finding is that the Regulator must set the premiums for Gold Plans at the average incremental cost for the rich, rather than, as in the previous two cases, allowing Gold Plans to choose any combination of premium and services they wish. This prevents plans from setting a premium-service combination that separates the healthy from the sick leading to inefficient service for the healthy (a la Rothschild-Stiglitz). With the Gold Plan premium at the average incremental cost, the rich healthy subsidize the rich sick (as required by fairness).[13]

Result 4.3. *Regulated premiums for both plans and imposing taste (income) based taxes and subsidies to join the Silver Plan can achieve efficiency and strong solidarity.*

5. TASTE UNAVAILABLE AS A BASIS FOR PAYMENT POLICY

So far we have equated "taste" for health care with "income." Income is, however, only one of the non-health factors that affect willingness to pay for health care. Other factors such as subjective valuation of health, faith

---

[13]As long as risk adjustment can fully capture differences in health cost and risk, this result extends to a continuum of health types.

in technology, tolerance of side effects, etc., are less readily observable by Regulators (or plans). Even if they were observable, these other factors affecting demand may not be a suitable basis of discriminatory taxes and subsidies. For example, willingness to pay for health care varies by education; yet it is not acceptable to tax or subsidize based on years of schooling for purchase of health insurance. In this section, we consider the case in which taste is not available as a basis for payment policy. This may be due to unobservability or to inappropriateness as a basis for payment. In other words, we assume in this section that Regulator payments to health plans cannot be conditioned on taste; premiums plans charge individuals cannot be conditioned on taste; and finally, no taste-based subsidies or taxes are possible. However, health status and plan choice are observable and can be used as a basis for subsidies or taxes. In other words, the Regulator can choose t_s^S, t_h^S, t_s^G and t_h^G, a set of taxes on plans that can vary by health status. We maintain assumptions about how managed care and managed competition work. Clinicians allocate the budget at a plan according to a shadow-price rule in which "taste-related" differences in benefits are ignored. Competition forces plans to spend their budgets. Individuals choose plans to maximize their benefits. What can be done to implement efficient care in this case? Can it be done fairly? To answer these questions, we turn again to our example. Table 2 expresses the constraints on payments and premiums for low and high-taste individuals to choose the right plans and for those plans to provide the efficient care. Note that to avoid introducing new notation, the $j = p, r$ subscript is retained, but now p indicates low-taste and r indicates high-taste. Conditions for fairness as well as efficiency are included in the table. Imposing the conditions for efficiency and strong solidarity encounters a contradiction.

The first condition for efficiency is that health plans must be able to finance efficient care. Risk adjusted payments to the Silver Plan must sum to funds necessary to pay for efficient care for the low-taste, $x_{sp}^* + x_{hp}^*$ in the general case, or $4 + 1 = 5$ in our example. Note that these payments, π_s and π_h, just need to sum to 5, they need not be equal to 4 and 1 respectively. Furthermore, when the premium y is collected from enrollees in the Gold Plan, revenue to the plan must be enough to finance efficient care for the high-taste. Solidarity requires a single premium. We can solve for $y = 3.125$ in our example.

The next pair of conditions for efficiency ensure that the low-taste choose the Silver Plan. In general terms, the utility the low-taste sick person

Table 2. **Conditions for implementing efficient care and fairness when taste is unavailable as a basis of payment.**

Conditions for efficiency

General case	Table 1 example
Health plans can finance efficient care	
Silver: $\pi_s + \pi_h = x^*_{sp} + x^*_{hp}$	$\pi_s + \pi_h = 4 + 1 = 5$
Gold: $\pi_s + \pi_h + 2y = x^*_{sr} + x^*_{hr}$	$5 + 2y = 9 + 2.25$
	$y = 3.125$
Low-taste choose the Silver Plan	
Sick: $v_{sp}(x^*_{sr}) - y - t^G_s < v_{sp}(x^*_{sp}) - t^S_s$	$12 - 3.125 - t^G_s < 8 - t^S_s$
	or $8.75 < t^G_s - ts^S$
Healthy: $v_{hp}(x^*_{hr}) - y - t^G_h < v_{hp}(x^*_{hp}) - t^S_h$	$3 - t^G_h < 2 - t^S_h$
High-taste choose the Gold Plan	
Sick: $v_{sr}(x^*_{sr}) - y - t^G_s \geq v_{sr}(x^*_{sp}) - t^S_s$	$18 - 3.125 - t^G_s \geq 12 - t^S_s$
Healthy: $v_{hr}(x^*_{hr}) - y - t^G_h \geq v_{hr}(x^*_{hp}) - t^S_h$	$4.5 - 3.125 - t^G_h \geq 3 - t^S_h$
	or $-1.625 \geq t^G_h - t^S_h$

Conditions for fairness

Strong solidarity: Equal payments for sick and healthy $t^S_s = t^S_h$, $t^G_s = t^G_h$

Weak solidarity: $t^S_s \leq t^S_h$, $t^G_s \leq t^S_h$

would get in the Gold Plan (care designed for the high-taste less premium for Gold less any tax on the sick joining the Gold Plan) must be less than the utility the sick low-taste person would get in the Silver Plan (efficient care for the low-taste less any tax for the sick joining the Silver Plan). These general conditions are translated into our numerical example on the right-hand side of the table. The conditions put inequality constraints on the values of the taxes on the Gold and Silver Plans.

The final set of conditions for efficiency ensure that the high-taste people choose the Gold Plan. These are developed in the same way and also put a pair of numerical inequality constraints on the values of taxes on the Gold and Silver Plans.

We can now see the contradiction. Solidarity requires payments for the sick and low-taste to be the same for each health plan. Since the Silver Plan is free and the premium for the Gold Plan is the same for all, solidarity then also requires plan-based taxes to be the same for the sick and healthy: $t^S_s = t^S_h = t^S$ and $t^G_s = t^G_h = t^G$. For the low-taste sick to choose the Silver Plan, $t^G - t^S \geq 0.875$, but for the high-taste healthy to choose the Gold Plan, $t^G - t^S \leq -1.625$, a contradiction. In other words, there is no set of taxes on Silver and Gold Plans using only health status (and not taste)

that can implement the efficient level of care and satisfy our criteria for
fairness.

Result 5.1. *When taste cannot be used as a basis of payment, no feasible
Regulator's Policy achieves efficiency and strong solidarity.*[14]

Consider next what can be done if we modify the conditions for fairness
to what we refer to as "weak solidarity." By weak solidarity we mean that
the tax on the sick should be no more than (rather than equal to) the tax
on the healthy for joining a particular plan. In other words, weak solidarity
requires: $t_s^S \leq t_h^S$ and $t_s^G \leq t_h^G$. In our example, if we set $t_s^G = t_h^G = 0$,
conditions for efficiency imply $t_s^S = -0.875$ and $t_h^S = 1.625$, satisfying weak
solidarity.

More generally, one can see that the constraints in Table 2 imply that
if $v_{sp}(x_{sr}^*) - v_{sp}(x_{sp}^*) > v_{hr}(x_{hr}^*) - v_{hr}(x_{hp}^*)$, namely the incremental benefit
of the sick low-taste type from joining the Gold Plan is higher than the
incremental benefit of the healthy high-taste type from joining that plan,
then the conditions for efficiency imply that $t_h^S - t_s^S > t_h^G - t_s^G$ and, hence:
(*i*) strong solidarity (i.e., $t_h^G = t_s^G$ and $t_h^S = t_s^S$) cannot be achieved and
(*ii*) weak solidarity ($t_h^S \geq t_s^S, t_h^G \geq t_s^G$) implies that $t_h^S - t_s^S > t_h^G - t_s^G \geq 0$.
Thus, any increase in $t_h^G - t_s^G$ (i.e., a departure from strong solidarity in
the Gold Plan) will also require an increase in $t_h^G - t_s^S$ (i.e., an even greater
departure from strong solidarity in the Silver Plan). Therefore, to minimize
deviation from strong solidarity, the best a Regulator can do is $t_h^G = t_s^G$ and
$t_h^S \geq t_s^S$. Thus if, $v_{hp}(x_{hr}^*) - v_{hp}(x_{hp}^*) > v_{sr}(x_{sr}^*) - v_{sr}(x_{sp}^*)$, strict fairness
cannot be achieved and the best one can do is $t_h^S = t_s^S$ and $t_h^G \geq t_s^G$.[15]

In addition to the conditions about sorting of types among plans,
implementation must also consider conditions for profit maximization by
plans. For reasons similar to those discussed in Section 4.3, Regulatory
policy must set the menu of premiums health plans can charge to be
either 0 or the average incremental cost for efficient care for the rich in
the Gold Plan, 3.125.

Result 5.2. *When taste cannot be used as a basis of payment, Gold Plan
premium regulation along with a subsidy to the sick and a tax to the healthy
for joining the Silver Plan achieves efficiency and weak solidarity.*

---

[14]Notice that Result 4.2 is in fact a special case of Result 5.1, in that in Result 4.2 t^S
was set at 0.
[15]If, however, the two inequalities above are reversed, and the marginal benefit to the
sick low-taste type from joining the Gold Plan is lower than the marginal benefit to the
healthy rich type from joining that plan, there exists a payment policy that implements
the efficient allocation and for which $t_h^G = t_s^G$ and $t_h^S = t_s^S$.

6. DISCUSSION

Heterogeneity in demand for health care is one of the most well-established set of facts in health services research. Basic demographics and measured health status explain 10% or less of variation in health care utilization. Although provider-side factors also matter, much of the balance of the variation is linked to income, education, attitudes and other factors we refer to here as "taste" affecting demand for most goods and services. This paper derives the implications of the empirically important and systematic taste-related demand for health care for the regulation of competing health insurance plans. Health plans can be differentiated in a horizontal (think "location") as well as a vertical dimension. If, in addition, there are only one or a few plans at each location, another efficiency problem, monopoly power, is introduced. Our results on premium setting for efficient sorting on the basis of vertical differentiation are very likely to hold in this more general case. For example, consider a simple case of horizontal differentiation with a pair of Gold and Silver Plans located at each end of a line, with consumers distributed along the line. Suppose both the risk-adjusted plan payments and the premiums charged to consumers are regulated. The Regulator can raise the risk adjusted premiums high enough to induce the efficient quality of care, even with monopoly power. Then the Regulator would need to follow rules much like we laid out in the text, to ensure efficient sorting and fairness.

In the presence of a range of demands for health care due to taste, efficiency calls for plans with higher levels of service for the higher-demand groups. The key barrier to achieving efficiency is that the healthy among the high taste group will find the basic plan attractive. The discriminatory premiums necessary to sort consumers efficiently may not be feasible or fair. This paper identifies ways around this problem by showing how, when there must be a single premium for the Gold Plan, efficiency and fairness can be attained.

The emphasis in the literature on managed competition has been on regulation of the basic (our Silver) plan, describing the appropriate risk adjustment, defining the benefit, and limiting premium discrimination by health-related factors. The main conclusion of our paper is that a more active regulatory policy can improve both efficiency and fairness. Rather than letting the market set the premium for a Gold Plan, the Regulator should specify the premium for Gold Plans. Then, the Regulator should subsidize the poor and tax the rich if they go to the Silver Plan. If income taxes and subsidies do not capture enough of taste differences, targeted subsidies and taxes on health status measures may be necessary. These taxes and subsidies can be set so that the sick pay no more for a health plan than the healthy (our "weak solidarity").

As health care costs continue to increase, a viable Gold Plan may become an important element in national health policy. The extra costs in a Gold Plan are paid by consumers electing the plan. By permitting this outlet for higher demand, the publicly financed system can be kept at the basic level, conserving public funds. Health policy in a number of countries accommodates demand with some form of upgrade available to higher demand groups.

In Germany, most residents must choose among "Silver Plans" with specified benefits that compete on service and premiums (within narrow bounds).[16] Higher income groups can opt out of the Silver Plan choice and choose among "Gold Plans" competing on premiums and service and also subject to some regulation. In Israel and Switzerland, an "upgrade" consists of a complementary insurance policy to the basic plan.[17]

Questions of fairness are at the forefront of policy debates about health care and health insurance. Managed competition with differentiated plans is inherently less equal than a national policy oriented around a single plan for all, even if it attains equity in terms of "solidarity" principles. Other conceptions of fairness could be introduced into our analysis and may change the nature of the analysis and conclusions. To study tradeoffs between efficiency and other approaches to fairness, it is necessary to have a working model of managed competition with demand heterogeneity, and this paper describes a model that might be useful for such subsequent analysis.

ACKNOWLEDGMENTS

The authors are grateful to the National Institute of Aging for support through P01 AG032952, The Role of Private Plans in Medicare, J. Newhouse, PI and to the Institute of Business Research in Israel (Glazer). We are grateful to Martin Andersen, Kate Baicker, Sebastian Bauhoff, Michael Chernew, William Encinosa, Albert Ma, Nolan Miller, Joseph

---

[16]See Thomson *et al.* (2009) for a summary of the German health insurance system within the context of financing systems in Europe. Sen (2009) lauds systems in Western Europe that accommodate "those who have money and want to spend it [on health care]" through private practice and private insurance options.
[17]This is also possible in Germany.

Newhouse, Susannah Rose, Anna Sinaiko, Zirui Song and Xiao Xu for comments on an earlier draft.

APPENDIX A. BENEFITS AND COSTS IN SILVER AND GOLD PLANS — GENERAL EXPRESSIONS

	Healthy benefit	Cost	Sick benefit	Cost
Silver Plan				
Poor	$v_{hp}(x_{hp}^*)$	x_{hp}^*	$v_{sp}(x_{sp}^*)$	x_{sp}^*
Rich	$v_{hr}(x_{hp}^*)$	x_{hp}^*	$v_{sr}(x_{sp}^*)$	x_{sp}^*
Gold Plan				
Poor	$v_{hp}(x_{hr}^*)$	x_{hr}^*	$v_{sp}(x_{sr}^*)$	x_{sr}^*
Rich	$v_{hr}(x_{hr}^*)$	x_{hr}^*	$v_{sr}(x_{sr}^*)$	x_{sr}^*

APPENDIX B. EQUILIBRIUM IN MANAGED COMPETITION WITH A SINGLE PREMIUM

In the proposed equilibrium, the healthy poor and the sick poor join the Silver Plan and receive their first-best level of care. The sick rich join the Gold Plan and receive their first-best level of care. Only the healthy rich individuals do not receive their first best level of care, as they join the Silver Plan. In order to prove that this is indeed an equilibrium, all one has to show is that no plan can offer another policy that will attract some individuals and will make positive profit. One such deviation is to attract only the healthy rich individuals. Suppose that a plan offers another policy (y', x') that attracts only the individuals of type hr; then, in order for this to be a strictly profitable deviation, the following conditions must be satisfied:

$$3(x_h')^{0.5} - y' \geq 3$$
$$4(x_S')^{0.5} - y' \leq 8$$
$$6(x_S')^{0.5} - y' \leq 13$$
$$x_s' = 4x_h'$$
$$y' + 1 \geq x_h'$$

The left-hand side of the first condition above specifies the net benefit of an individual of type hr if she joins the new plan (y', x'). The first condition implies that type hr strictly prefers the new plan over the Silver Plan (which offers her a net benefit of 3).

Similarly, the second condition implies that type sp prefers the Silver Plan over the new plan and the third condition implies that type sr prefers the Gold Plan over the new plan. The fourth condition follows our assumption about how plans allocate their budget and the last equality simply implies that the new plan breaks even if it attracts only the healthy rich individuals.

One can easily verify that the conditions above can be satisfied only if $x'_h \leq 1$ and hence, no profitable deviation exists.

Another possible deviation is to offer a contract that will attract only types hr and sp. However, in a similar way, it can be shown that no such profitable deviation exists.

REFERENCES

Baumgardner, J., 1991. The interaction between forms of insurance contract and technical change in medical care. *RAND Journal of Economics* 25(2), 242–262.

Bundorf, M.K., Levin, J.D., Mahoney, N., 2009. Pricing and Welfare in Health Plan Choice. NBER Working Paper 14153. Available from: http://www.nber.org/papers/w14153.

Cheng, T., Reinhardt, U.E., 2008. Shepherding major health system reforms: a conversation with German Health Minister Ulla Schmidt. *Health Affairs* 27(3), w204–w213.

Cutler, D.M., Reber, S., 1998. Paying for health insurance: the trade-off between competition and adverse selection. *Quarterly Journal of Economics* 113(2), 433–466.

Diamond, P., 1992. Organizing the health insurance market. *Econometrics* 60(6), 1233–1254.

Ellis, R.P., McGuire, T.G., 1987. Setting capitation payments in markets for health services. *Health Care Financing Review* 8(4), 55–64.

Encinosa, W.E., 2001. The economics of regulatory mandates on the HMO market. *Journal of Health Economics* 20(1), 85–107.

Encinosa, W.E., Sappington, D.E.M., 1997. Competition among health maintenance organizations. *Journal of Economics and Management Strategy* 6(1), 129–150.

Enthoven, A.C., 1980. Health Plan. Addison-Wesley Publishing.

Enthoven, A.C., Kronick, R., 1989. A consumer-choice health plan for the 1990s: universal health insurance in a system designed to promote quality and economy. *New England Journal of Medicine* 320(1), 29–37.

Feldman, R.D., Dowd, B., 1982. Simulation of a health insurance market with adverse selection. *Operations Research* 30(6), 1027–1042.

Frank, R.G., Glazer, J., McGuire, T.G., 2000. Adverse selection in managed health care. *Journal of Health Economics* 19(6), 829–854.

GAO (2003) Private Health Insurance: Federal and State Requirements Affecting Coverage Offered by Small Businesses. United States General Accounting Office, pp. 1–63.

Glazer, J., McGuire, T.G., 2000. Optimal risk adjustment of health insurance premiums: an application to managed care. *American Economic Review* 90(4), 1055–1071.

Jack, W., 2006. Optimal risk adjustment with adverse selection and spatial competition. *Journal of Health Economics* 25(5), 908–926.

Kaiser Family Foundation, 2009. State Health Facts. Available from: http://www.statehealthfacts.org/ (site accessed 09.09.09).

Keeler, E.B., Carter, G., Newhouse,J., 1998. A Model of the Impact of Reimbursement Schemes on Health Plan Choice. *Journal of Health Economics* 17(3), 297–320.

Miller, N., 2005. Pricing Health Benefits: A Cost Minimizing Approach. *Journal of Health Economics* 24(5), 931–949.

Newhouse, J.P., 2002. Pricing the Priceless: A Health Care Conundrum. MIT Press.

Olivella, P., Vera-Hernandez, M., 2007. Competition Among Differentiated Health Plans Under Adverse Selection. *Journal of Health Economics* 26(2), 233–250.

Pauly, M., Ramsey, S., 1999. Would You Like Suspenders to Go with that Belt? An Analysis of Optimal Combinations of Cost Sharing and Managed Care. *Journal of Health Economics* 18(4), 443–458.

Pizer, S., Frakt, A., Feldman, R., 2003. Payment Policy and Inefficient Benefits in the Medicare+Choice Program. *International Journal of Health Care Finance and Economics* 3(2), 79–93.

Rothschild, M., Stiglitz, J., 1976. Equilibrium in Competitive Insurance Markets: An Essay in the Economics of Imperfect Information. *Quarterly Journal of Economics* 90(4), 629–649.

Sass, H.-M., 1995. The New Triad: Responsibility, Solidarity, and Subsidiarity. *The Journal of Medicine and Philosophy* 20, 587–594.

Sen, A., 2009. Capitalism beyond the crisis. The New York Review of Books 56 (March 5).

Smart, M., 2000. Competitive Insurance Markets with Two Unobservables. *International Economic Review* 41(1), 153–169.

Stock, S., Redaelli, M., Lauterbach, K.W., 2006. The influence of the labor market on German health care reforms. *Health Affairs* 25(4), 1143–1152.

Stone, D.A., 1993. The struggle for the soul of health insurance. *Journal of Health Politics, Policy and Law* 18(2), 287–317.

Thomson, S., Foubister, T., Mossialos, E., 2009. Financing Health Care in the European Union: Challenges and Policy Responses. Observatory Study Series, No. 17, World Health Organization.

Van de Ven, Ellis, R., 2000. Risk Adjustment in Competitive Health Plan Markets. In: Culyer, A., Newhouse, J. (Eds.), *Handbook of Health Economics.* Elsevier.

Chapter 7

MAKING MEDICARE ADVANTAGE
A MIDDLE-CLASS PROGRAM

Jacob Glazer[a,b] and Thomas G. McGuire[c,*]

[a] *Tel Aviv University, Tel Aviv, Israel*

[b] *Boston University, Boston, MA, USA*

[c] *Harverd Medical School, Department of Health Care Policy,
Boston, MA, USA*

This paper studies the role of Medicare's premium policy in sorting beneficiaries between traditional Medicare (TM) and managed care plans in the Medicare advantage (MA) program. Beneficiaries vary in their demand for care. TM fully accommodates demand but creates a moral hazard inefficiency. MA rations care but disregards some elements of the demand. We describe an efficient assignment of beneficiaries to these two options, and argue that efficiency requires an MA program oriented to serve the large middle part of the distribution of demand: the "middle class." Current Medicare policy of a "single premium" for MA plans cannot achieve efficient sorting. We characterize the demand-based premium policy that can implement the efficient assignment of enrollees to plans. If only a single premium is feasible, the second-best policy involves too many of the low-demand individuals in MA and a too low level of services relative to the first best. We identify approaches to using premium policy to revitalize MA and improve the efficiency of Medicare.

Keywords: health care policy; managed care; medicare; health insurance; enrollee premiums

1. INTRODUCTION

Beneficiaries in Medicare, the federal health insurance program for the elderly and disabled, have for some time chosen between two major options: traditional Medicare (TM) and a set of private health insurance plans,

*Corresponding author: mcguire@hcp.med.harvard. edu.

including managed care plans, offered under Medicare Part C. Presently, only about 27% of beneficiaries elect a Part C plan. The objectives of Part C, since 2003 known as Medicare advantage (MA),[1] are to expand health insurance options for beneficiaries while taking advantage of economies of managed care to save money for Medicare. Achieving these dual objectives requires that Medicare pay an MA plan less than what beneficiaries would cost Medicare in TM but more than cost for the beneficiaries in MA, leaving some savings to share with beneficiaries in the form of lower premiums/better coverage in MA to attract them to an MA plan. Research and policy have focused on the "risk adjustment" of Medicare payments to pay more for the sick and less for the healthy joining the MA plans.[2] In spite of improvements in risk adjustment technology and many other policy reforms, Part C has yet, however, to save Medicare money (McGuire *et al.*, 2011). As part of the Affordable Care Act (ACA), Medicare payments to MA plans are being cut, and, based on experience, plan and beneficiary exit will follow;[3] but, based on the same experience, these cuts are unlikely to move the MA program into the black for Medicare.[4]

We argue that a major contributor to the chronically poor performance of Part C is the inefficient sorting of beneficiaries between MA and TM caused by Medicare's premium policy. In this paper, we shift analytic focus away from plan payment and risk adjustment to the premiums and the incentives faced by heterogeneous beneficiaries when they elect MA or TM. To address normative questions around beneficiary choice between MA and TM, we propose a formulation of which beneficiaries *should* be in MA and in TM. Somewhat surprisingly, in light of the policy attention to Medicare and the Part C program, the Medicare policy literature says little about what socially efficient sorting looks like. The fundamental answer to who should be in MA underlies the title of the paper. We argue that MA should, from the standpoint of social welfare, draw beneficiaries from the thick central

[1]The Medicare Modernization and Improvement Act of 2003 renamed Part C plans as Medicare Advantage plans. Previously, plans were called Medicare+Choice plans.
[2]For reviews of the literature on risk adjustment, see Newhouse (2002) or Van de Ven (2000). Border themes regarding risk and variation are covered in Breyer *et al.* (2012).
[3]For recent analysis of payment changes from the ACA and plan response showing up in anticipation of these changes, see Afendulis *et al.* (2011).
[4]In addition to refining risk adjustment, Medicare has raised and lowered the overall level of payment to MA plans a number of times in the past 25 years depending on whether increasing access to MA plans or saving money were the dominant policy concern. McGuire *et al.* (2011) describe these changes and the plan and beneficiary response.

part of the distribution of preferences for health care, and in this sense make MA a "middle class" program.

Our approach is based on the observation that beneficiaries vary in their demand for health care for many reasons. Most attention has been directed to the heterogeneity related to "health status" and the risk adjustment technology designed to deal with it (Pope *et al.*, 2004). Health status-based risk adjustment explains a small share (10% or less) of the individual variation in health care spending, partly because health status is difficult to measure and predict. Another reason, and one that we call attention to here, is that factors other than health status — income, education, "taste" more generally[5] — also influence demand for health care, and therefore choice of plan.

From the standpoint of the beneficiary, anticipated demand for health care, together with the premiums for TM and MA, determine the best plan option. Premiums for TM are described below, and depend on the circumstances of the beneficiary. MA plans choose the premium beneficiaries pay (subject to Medicare regulation), and this premium is the same for all beneficiaries. There is a fundamental problem with this approach. Generally, efficient pricing of health insurance options requires beneficiaries be charged their incremental cost in the various options. Thus, at least some price discrimination according to incremental cost can improve efficiency. Furthermore, any single premium for MA cannot sort beneficiaries between MA and TM. We argue that some form of premium discrimination by non-health status factors affecting demand is necessary to rescue MA from its chronically poor performance. After our analysis, we discuss some ways to change premium policy in TM as well as MA to better achieve Medicare objectives and economic efficiency.

---

[5]Income effects, for example, have been studied in health care. Cross-sectional studies generally report a positive income elasticity of demand that is less than one. The Rand Health Insurance Experiment found income elasticities of between 0.1 and 0.2 (Newhouse, 1993). Studies using longitudinal variation in income find much larger elasticities, generally classifying health care as a "luxury good" with income elasticities exceeding 1.0 (see Fogel, 2008). Borger *et al.* (2008) reviewed over twenty papers and settled on a unit income elasticity to use in their simulation model. In a recent study, Acemoglu *et al.* (2009) use oil price shocks to estimate the income effect on demand for health care at 0.7. Those with higher income tend to be in better health, so adequate controls for health status are necessary to identify income effects. The same is true for education. The better-educated tend to be healthier, but once health status is controlled for, education increases health care demand.

2. TRADITIONAL MEDICARE AND MEDICARE ADVANTAGE

2.1. *Program Descriptions*

At age 65, most Americans become eligible for Medicare.[6] If beneficiaries do not elect an MA plan, they are automatically enrolled in Part A of Medicare at no cost to them.[7] Part A is financed largely by a payroll tax shared by employees and employers (Kaiser Family Foundation, 2008). Part A covers inpatient hospital services, some post-hospital stays in nursing facilities and home health care, and hospice care, but requires considerable beneficiary cost sharing. The most significant beneficiary cost sharing is the deductible ($1132 for 2011) per hospital episode ("benefit period"). Beneficiaries may also enroll in Part B, which covers doctors' visits, other ambulatory services and some drugs administered in physician offices. The standard Part B premium for 2011, which applies to new enrollees, is $115.40 per month. Many enrollees pay only $96.40 per month because of hold-harmless provisions applying to social security payments from which the Part B premium is deducted (CMS, 2010). Very few (3%) of beneficiaries pay a higher premium because of high individual or family income, and some (17%) have premiums all or partly covered by Medicaid.[8] Part B premiums cover only about 25% of Medicare's cost of Part B, the balance being paid for by general revenues (Kaiser Family Foundation, 2008). The vast majority of beneficiaries in TM enroll in Part B. Beneficiary cost sharing in Part B includes an annual deductible of $162 in 2011 and a 20% coinsurance on Medicare allowed charges. Since 2006, beneficiaries may also join a Part D plan covering prescription drug costs. Part D plans receive about 75% of their federal revenue from general revenues, are offered by private insurers, and vary in coverage. Part D premiums are set by a bidding procedure, the average premium for a stand-alone drug plan (taken as part of TM) was $38/month in 2011 (MedPAC, 2011b, Section 10). Low-income beneficiaries receive a premium subsidy (and lower

---

[6]Medicare also provides health insurance for qualified disabled beneficiaries below age 65. These beneficiaries may also choose to join the same MA plans on the same terms as the elderly beneficiaries.

[7]Beneficiaries with short Medicare work histories and not married to a beneficiary with a long work history may pay a Part A premium but this applies to about 1% of beneficiaries CMS (2011).

[8]In addition, there are penalties for delaying enrollment in Part B in the form of higher premiums (CMS, 2010).

cost sharing). Beneficiaries with Part A, and the optional Parts B and D, are considered to be in "traditional Medicare."

Most beneficiaries in TM avoid cost sharing in Parts A and B with medigap or some other supplemental coverage. Medicaid pays cost sharing for eligible low-income beneficiaries. Some employers buy wrap-around coverage for retirees. Finally, most beneficiaries in these groups do not buy medigap policies to cover some or all of the cost sharing. The average monthly premium for the most popular medigap policy (Plan F) was $167 in 2009 (MedPAC, 2011a). Given the pervasiveness of supplemental coverage, we think of TM as traditional health insurance with low cost sharing, with a premium for beneficiaries equal to the Part B premium plus what they pay for Part D and supplemental coverage.

Virtually all hospitals and practicing physicians accept Medicare payment, giving beneficiaries wide choice of providers. Medicare and its regional intermediaries make broad coverage decisions but do not interfere with (a.k.a. "manage") physician and patient choice of treatment. Health care in TM has been criticized as being uncoordinated and costly (Newhouse, 2002). TM contends with cost issues primarily by using its monopsony power to pay physicians and hospitals roughly 20–30% less than private plans on average (MedPAC, 2008).[9]

The Medicare Modernization Act of 2003 (MMA) created MA to replace the short-lived Medicare+Choice version of Part C. MA plans are private, must cover all Part A and B benefits, and may supplement these benefits by reduced cost sharing or coverage for additional services not part of TM, such as vision or dental care (Gold, 2008).[10] MA plans may or may not include drug coverage. Those that do are referred to as MA-PD (i.e., "Prescription Drug") plans. In total, 11 million beneficiaries, or 24% of all, were enrolled in an MA plan in 2010 (KFF, 2010a).

The MMA created new plan types within MA and the higher payments mandated in the legislation awakened dormant plan types established

---

[9]In traditional Medicare, physicians are paid for each procedure according to a fee schedule. Hospitals are paid according to the diagnosis-related group (DRG) in which a patient is classified at discharge. The hospital payment system is partly "prospective," embodying some incentives to the hospital to economize on resources during the hospital stay. For an overview of Medicare payment policies applying to physicians, hospitals and health plans, see Newhouse (2002).

[10]Gold and her colleagues at Mathematica Policy Research have tracked policy, enrollment, plan types and other data on Part C for a number of years in a useful series of publications (Gold, 2009; Gold *et al.*, 2004).

earlier. We distinguish between what we consider to be bona fide managed care plans and others. We regard Health Maintenance Organizations (HMOs), the oldest and largest plan type, and the mostly tightly managed, along with Local Preferred Provider (PPOs) and the small number of Provider-Sponsored Organizations (PSOs) as managed care. The other plan types, notably the Regional PPOs and Private Fee-for-Service (PFFS) plans, are not in this category.[11] Our model of MA plan behavior laid out below applies to managed care plans only; 78% of Medicare beneficiaries in MA were in bona fide managed care plans in 2010.[12] Coverage in MA managed care plans is more comprehensive than in TM, with smaller (or no) deductibles, less cost sharing, and some coverage of additional services. Beneficiaries in MA plans cannot purchase medigap coverage.

Beneficiaries in MA plans must pay the Part B premium (which goes to Medicare).[13] MA plans can charge a premium above this. Many plans, however, are "zero premium" plans, meaning they charge nothing above the Part B premium. A small percentage of plans reduce the beneficiary Part B premium obligation. More than half of beneficiaries in HMO plans pay zero premium. Most beneficiaries are in MA-PD plans. The average monthly premium for an MA-PD plan (across all plan types) was $51 per month, unweighted by enrollment (KFF, 2010b).

Medicare payments to plans are based on a Medicare "benchmark" rate set for each county and the plan's "bid." The benchmark is based on the maximum of the CMS estimate of Medicare costs for a typical beneficiary in Parts A and B, a minimum or "floor" payment, and the past payment rate for the county trended forward at national average Medicare cost growth rates. In the past several years, benchmarks have generally exceeded expected FFS costs in a county (GAO, 2011). For 2011, benchmarks were frozen at 2010 levels. Beginning in 2012, the ACA phases in a new formula by which the benchmark is a percentage of the estimated FFS spending based on a county's level of spending relative to other counties. For counties in the lowest spending quartile the new formula pays 115% of the benchmark, and this ranges down to 95% of the

---

[11] Part C also includes Special Needs Plans (SPNs) intended for beneficiaries in long-term care and with certain chronic diseases.

[12] Government Accountability Office (GAO) (2011), p. 14.

[13] Thus, the higher Part B premium charged to a small number of higher-income beneficiaries is like a tax, and does not affect the relative cost facing beneficiaries in MA and TM.

benchmark for the highest quartile counties (GAO, 2011). In most counties, these changes are expected to reduce Medicare payments (Afendulis *et al.*, 2011).

A plan's bid is supposed to be the plan's estimate of what regular benefits from Parts A and B would cost the plan for a beneficiary of average health status. If a plan bids above the benchmark, the plan is paid the benchmark. If the bid falls below the benchmark, Medicare pays the bid plus 75% of the difference between the bid and the benchmark. The idea is that Medicare gets 25% of any "savings" (difference between benchmark and bid) and the plan must use the balance of the difference to reduce beneficiary premiums or provide additional coverage and benefits. In 2010, the average plan bid was 98% of the benchmark, but HMO forms were the only plan type with an average below the benchmark (94%) (GAO, 2011). All others were greater than 100% of the benchmark. As a final step in figuring plan payments, Medicare then applies the CMS-HCC risk adjustment formula reflecting the measured health status of actual enrollees.

Figure 1 summarizes the typical 2011 monthly premium costs for a Medicare beneficiary in TM and MA. The beneficiary would pay the Part B premium to Medicare in either case. She buys a Part D freestanding drug plan for $38/month and a medigap plan for $167. If the beneficiary were to join a typical "zero-premium MA-PD plan, she pays nothing per month over Part B.

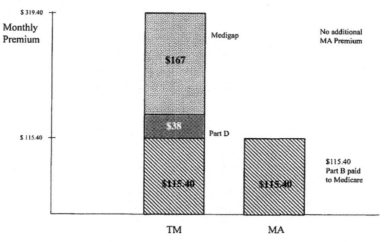

Figure 1.   2011 Monthly premiums for beneficiary in "typical" situation in TM and MA.

2.2. *Previous Research*

A large literature in public finance is concerned with the public provision
of private goods. Health care is a private good financed collectively for
reasons, among others, related to equity. In Besley and Coate (1991), rich
and poor consumers demand a good that could be provided by government
with an equal consumption requirement, or left to the market.[14] Some
redistribution to the poor can be achieved by providing a base level to
everyone financed collectively by progressive taxes, and letting the rich
opt out to the private system. Within a health care context, researchers
study resource allocation in public systems, and how a private sector fringe
affects public costs and efficiency (Barros and Siciliani, 2012). Grassi and
Ma (2008) analyze the interaction between a budget-constrained public
health care system that allocates by rationing and a private sector that
accommodates demand but may set prices. Consumers differ according to
wealth and cost. The analogy to our paper is that our MA plan has an equal
consumption feature, and the consumer has the option of choosing a TM
plan that accommodates heterogeneity. In our analysis of Medicare, however, the alternative system, TM, is also publicly financed and subject to
regulation.

A focus on the premiums paid by beneficiaries recalls Rothschild and
Stiglitz (1976) who recognized the premium as a powerful selection device.
In a Medicare context, the emphasis in the literature has been on skimping
on services as a tool for selection.[15] Other papers stress that plan choice of
benefits and premiums can serve beneficiary heterogeneity, as well as being
a device for selection.[16] The idea, as expressed by Pizer *et al.* (2003), is
that "Beneficiaries who highly value certain benefits can search for a plan
that offers those benefits and pay the marginal premium that corresponds
to their choice." One can imagine Medicare risk-adjusted plan payments
as a voucher, with plan-set premiums sorting beneficiaries by tastes for

---

[14]Government provision can give a private good the "equal consumption" characteristic
of a public good, as is the case in government provision of health insurance, education,
and other services.

[15]The early literature made overall cost comparisons between managed care and
traditional Medicare. The more recent literature on service-level selection studies
categories of expenditures. See Ellis and McGuire (2007) for review of some papers.

[16]Another use of the premium in the context of private health insurance is for an
employer to recover some of the inframarginal surplus health insurance benefits confer
on high-demand employees (Miller, 2005).

additional services.[17] However, as shown in Bundorf *et al.* (2012) and Glazer and McGuire (2011), except in special circumstances, a single premium for each plan does not sort beneficiaries efficiently among plans.[18]

Bundorf *et al.* (2012) show, in their theoretical analysis, that any uniform price for health plans will generally not lead patients to efficiently sort themselves across plans. They also estimate the efficiency loss due to this inefficient pricing in the context of a small group market in California. Glazer and McGuire (2011) model managed competition with demand heterogeneity to consider plan payment and enrollee premium policies in relation to efficiency and fairness. Specifically, this paper studies how to implement a "Silver" and "Gold" health plan efficiently and fairly in a managed competition context. The assumption shared with these two papers and the current one is that demand for health services and health insurance is driven by both tastes and need. The current paper introduces demand heterogeneity in the context of Medicare, with beneficiaries faced with a choice between TM and MA. This specific application allows us to demonstrate the fundamental inefficiencies in current Medicare policy, and to identify new approaches to address these inefficiencies.

3. UTILITY AND WILLINGNESS TO PAY FOR MA AND TM

Beneficiaries are heterogeneous in their demand for health care. A beneficiary's valuation of the quantity of health care, x, is positively related to a preference parameter, θ. Specifically, we assume that a beneficiary characterized by θ values health care at $V(x, \theta)$, with $V_x > 0$, $V_{xx} < 0$, $V_{xxx} \leq 0$, $V_\theta > 0$, $V_{x\theta} > 0$, and as a normalization, we assume $V_{\theta\theta} = 0$.[19]

---

[17]Restructuring the "choice architecture" in Medicare — limiting and clarifying the options — may be necessary for choice to serve beneficiaries. See McWilliams *et al.* (2011) for recent evidence for how too many choices may lead to ineffective decisions, at least for the substantial share of the elderly who have some impairment in decision making.

[18]Town and Liu (2003), following methods proposed by Berry (1994), use market share and premium (price) data to estimate consumer surplus and profits associated with Part C plans during the 1990s, when Part C rode the success of managed care throughout the US health insurance market, and plan and beneficiary participation was growing rapidly. They found that demand for HMO plans was inelastic to the premium, implying ample surplus to be divided between consumers and HMO plans. Beneficiaries had diverse tastes, but costs were assumed to be uniform, ruling out any selection issues by assumption.

[19]Most of our assumptions about the shape of $V(x, \theta)$ are intuitive and conventional. The assumption that $V_{xxx} \leq 0$ needs some discussion and this will be carried out after our presentation of Proposition 1, where it comes into play.

J. Glazer and T. G. McGuire

We also assume that $\theta \in |\underline{\theta}, \bar{\theta}|$, $F(\theta)$ is the distribution function and $f(\theta)$ is the density function of θ. We assume that $f(\theta)$ has full support over the interval $|\underline{\theta}, \bar{\theta}|$. Quantity x is measured in dollars so the cost of x is 1. Efficient x for beneficiary θ is $x^*(\theta)$, the solution to $V_x(x^*, \theta) = 1$.

In order to focus on heterogeneity in demand from sources other than health status, we interpret θ as representing elements affecting demand for health care that the MA plan does not or cannot accommodate. Such elements could include income, education, and other dimensions affecting taste, so long as these elements are not recognized and responded to by the plan. In our model, individuals differ only in θ, implying that demand varies only because of taste parameters. We make this assumption because we regard the clinicians in the managed care MA plan as trained and interested in gearing treatment to health status (more resources go to a patient with greater need), but not in accommodating differences in "taste" for health care. The "equal consumption" assumption about MA plans refers to heterogeneity with respect to taste.

The economic literature on managed care is concerned with rationing in the presence of heterogeneity in demand, which is most often associated with health status differences.[20] Rationing can avoid moral hazard problems and improve efficiency, but an equal consumption feature of rationing creates inefficiency by homogenizing services to those with heterogeneous preferences. Essentially, this paper is about how to use the efficiency gains MA plans can create to best advantage among Medicare beneficiaries with heterogeneous preferences for health care. We now describe more specifically our models of MA and TM.

In MA there are no copayments. Since (by assumption) individuals differ only on dimensions not accommodated by the MA plan, quantity in MA is the same for everyone in the plan at x^{MA}. Willingness to pay (or utility measured in dollars) for MA is simply:

$$U^{\mathrm{MA}}(x^{\mathrm{MA}}, \theta) = V(x^{\mathrm{MA}}, \theta) \tag{1}$$

U^{MA} is positive for every value of θ and, given our normalization on $V_{\theta\theta}$, for a given x^{MA}, it increases with θ at a constant rate.

---

[20]Papers that characterize rationing with a "shadow price" emphasize the responsiveness of rationing to variation in health status (see Keeler *et al.*, 1998: Frank *et al.*, 2000). Papers that characterize rationing as setting quantity emphasize that patients with different demands end up with the same use (see Baumgardner, 1991; Pauly and Ramsey, 1999).

We assume, in contrast to MA, TM does accommodate beneficiary demand due to heterogeneity in θ. In TM, beneficiaries pay a copayment $0 < c < 1$ for each unit of x, and choose quantity to maximize utility by setting the marginal valuation of x equal to c:

$$V_x(x, \theta) = c \tag{2}$$

We define $x^{\text{TM}}(\theta)$ to be the solution to (2) above. Note that our assumption that $V_{x\theta} > 0$ implies that consumers with higher θ demand more care in TM. Willingness to pay for TM is then:

$$U^{\text{TM}}(\theta) = V(x^{\text{TM}}(\theta), \theta) - cx^{\text{TM}}(\theta) \tag{3}$$

This is also everywhere positive, increasing in θ at an increasing rate.[21] Intuitively, this is because as demand shifts out, quantity increases (unlike in MA) and consumer surplus goes up approximately quadratically with quantity demanded.

Throughout the analysis we will focus on the case where x^{MA} is located in the interior; by "interior" we mean that the level of care provided under managed care is higher than the level of care consumed by the lowest type, $\underline{\theta}$, under TM and lower than the efficient level of care for the highest type, $\bar{\theta}$, individual:

Assumption 1.

$$x^{\text{TM}}(\underline{\theta}) < x^{\text{MA}} < x^*(\bar{\theta}).$$

Figure 2 depicts the two functions $U^{\text{TM}}(\theta)$ and $U^{\text{MA}}(x^{\text{MA}}, \theta)$ for an arbitrary level of x^{MA} that satisfies Assumption 1.

Efficiency involves both the level of managed care, x^{MA}, and the sorting of beneficiaries between MA and TM, given the efficient x^{MA}. We conduct our analysis in several steps. In Section 4 we take x^{MA} as given and study how to efficiently divide consumers between MA and TM. In Section 5 we keep the assumption that x^{MA} is fixed and characterize a premium policy to implement the efficient sorting. We show that, for any level of x^{MA}, a single premium cannot implement the efficient sorting whereas a premium policy with two levels of premium that depends on θ, can implement the efficient

---

[21]Dropping the elements inside the parentheses we have: $dU^{\text{TM}}/d\theta = V_\theta + [V_x - C][dx^{\text{TM}}/d\theta] = V_\theta > 0$. $d^2U^{\text{TM}}/d\theta^2 = V_{\theta\theta} + V_{\theta x}(dx^{\text{TM}}/d\theta) + [V_{x\theta} + V_{xx}(dx^{\text{TM}}/d\theta)](dx^{\text{TM}}/d\theta)(dx^{\text{TM}}/d\theta)$. Since $V_{\theta\theta} = 0$ and $dx^{\text{TM}}/d\theta = -V_{x\theta}/V_{xx}$, by $V_x = c$, we get $d^2U^{\text{TM}}/d\theta^2 = -(V_{x\theta})^2/V_{xx} > 0$.

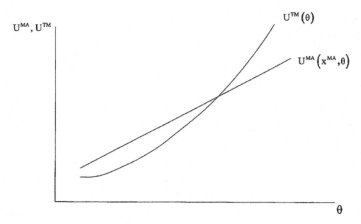

Figure 2.   Utility in TM and MA for a fixed level of x^{MA}.

sorting. In Section 6 we allow the regulator to choose x^{MA} and analyze the first-best and second-best levels of managed care (x^{MA}) depending on whether the regulator can condition premiums on θ (the first-best case) or use only a single premium (the second-best case).

4. EFFICIENT SORTING

We consider how to efficiently divide consumers between MA and TM for a given x^{MA}. We establish (Proposition 1) that the optimal division of consumers between MA and TM is characterized by consumers in a single range of θ in MA with the others in TM. We will first present our result formally and then discuss the interpretation. Maximizing social welfare (efficiency) requires dividing beneficiaries into the two insurance types based on social welfare defined as utility less cost.[22]

---

[22]Recently, perspectives from both "value-based insurance design" and behavioral economics have questioned the conventional welfare framework based on utility, adding to long-standing doubts about whether consumer choices should be regarded as a guide to welfare. See Chernew *et al.* (2007) for the proposal for the value-based approach, and Pauly and Blavin (2009) for an integration of the Pigouvian subsidy perspective into the conventional moral hazard framework. In a related point connected to behavioral economics, Newhouse (2006) illustrates how time-inconsistent preferences could lead to choices by consumers not in their best interest. As Pauly and Blavin (2009) show, however, consumer over or undervaluation can be integrated with traditional considerations of optimal health insurance. In this paper we take the conventional approach that utility is also the measure of his social welfare.

Given an x^{MA}, welfare in MA as a function of θ is given by:

$$W^{MA}(x^{MA}, \theta) = V(x^{MA}, \theta) - x^{MA} \qquad (4)$$

And welfare in TM is given by:

$$W^{TM}(\theta) = V(x^{TM}(\theta), \theta) - x^{TM}(\theta) \qquad (5)$$

Proposition 1. *For every x^{MA} there exists θ_1 and θ_2 with $\theta_1 < \theta_2$ such that $W^{TM} = (\theta_i) = W^{MA}(x^{MA}, \theta_i)$ for $i = 1, 2, W^{TM}(\theta) < W^{MA}(x^{MA}, \theta)$ if $\theta_1 < \theta < \theta_2$ and $W^{TM}(\theta) > W^{MA}(x^{MA}, \theta)$ otherwise.*

Proposition 1 says that the efficient division of beneficiaries can be expressed in terms of two cutoff values θ_1 and θ_2. All individuals below θ_1 and all individuals above θ_2 should be TM. Beneficiaries between θ_1 and θ_2 should be in MA.[23] (Proofs of all results in this paper are contained in the Appendix.)[24]

For the person on the boundary between TM and MA, the social net benefits (welfare) in MA and TM are equalized. Figure 3, Panel A shows demand for type θ_1, defining the lower boundary of those who should be in MA. For this beneficiary, consumption in TM, x^{TM} just equals the given x^{MA}. Obviously, social welfare in MA and TM for this beneficiary must be the same in both MA and TM. Depicted in terms of the welfare loss against the first best level of care for this beneficiary, the shaded triangle welfare loss must be the same when $x^{MA} = x^{TM}$. For any θ lower than θ_1, the beneficiary is still "over consuming" in both systems, but since x^{TM} for a θ less than θ_1 would be less than x^{MA}, the welfare loss in TM would be less than in MA. Thus, for any demand to the left of θ_1, the beneficiary belongs in TM. For θ just greater than θ_1, the welfare loss in MA is strictly less than the loss in TM. To see this, imagine shifting the demand shown in Panel A slightly to the right. The higher θ type is over consuming, but since $x^{MA} < x^{TM}$, the welfare loss due to over consumption is less in MA.

---

[23] Notice that the θ_1 and θ_2 cutoffs depend on the x^{MA} chosen. Rather than writing the cutoff as a function of x^{MA} we stipulate that the discussion here applies for a particular value of x^{MA}.

[24] As can be seen in the proof of Proposition 1, the fact that there are only two cutoffs follows from the convexity of $\Delta W(x^{MA}, \theta)$, which follows from, along with other assumptions about utility, our assumption that $V_{xxx} \leq 0$. If V_{xxx} was sufficiently greater than 0, there could be some special cases where there would be more than two levels of θ at which welfare in TM was equal to the welfare in MA. We do not discuss these special cases here.

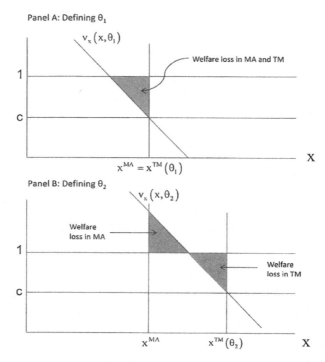

Figure 3. The socially efficient cutoffs.

Panel B of Fig. 3 shows demand for beneficiary θ_2, defining the upper boundary of efficient assignment into MA. For the given x^{MA}, there is a second level of demand in TM for which the welfare loss is the same as it would be if the beneficiary were in MA, the θ for which the two shaded triangles in Panel B, the welfare loss in MA and the welfare loss in TM, are equal. The loss from "under consumption" in MA for type θ_2 just equals the loss from over consumption in TM. As θ increases beyond θ_2, the loss from over-consumption in TM goes up by less (and, in fact, could even go down) than the increase in the welfare loss in MA. Thus, anyone with $\theta > \theta_2$ belongs in TM. A similar argument applies in the opposite case as θ decreases below θ_2. These beneficiaries belong in MA.

Figure 4 depicts the cutoffs in terms of welfare and the distribution of demand for care. As shown in Panel A, for a fixed level of x^{MA} welfare in MA increases as a constant rate, whereas welfare in TM is concave. Panel B depicts a plausible distribution of θ among beneficiaries, with the bulk of the population falling in the "middle class" in terms of demand.

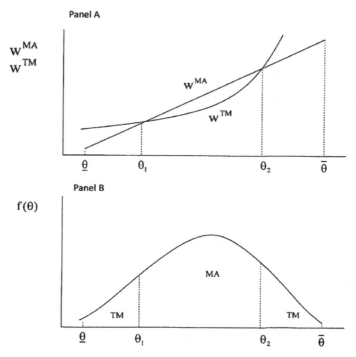

Figure 4. Optimal division between MA and TM for fixed x^{MA}.

The single range of θ result in Proposition 1 is due to fundamental properties of demand. Only one MA plan offers the same level of care for everyone serving a population with heterogeneous tastes. The offered care is just right for a certain type of consumer but as more and more people are included in the MA plan, on either side of the distribution of tastes, the fit becomes worse and worse. Indeed, the welfare loss from being in the MA plan goes up approximately quadratically as less well-suited consumers are included. It is this rapidly increasing welfare loss with more inclusion on either side of the "right" θ that puts a bound on each side of the efficient range of θ in MA.

Our single-range result is robust to reasonable modifications of our assumptions about underlying demand. Our main requirement is that the quadratic property of loss as the taste parameter, θ, moves in either direction from the MA plan it is just right for, eventually dominates the MA-TM comparison. One could alter our assumptions and assume the loss from moral hazard in TM goes up more than proportionately with θ, but responsiveness proportional to the square of θ seems implausible.

5. IMPLEMENTATION OF EFFICIENT SORTING

We now consider the premium policy required to implement the optimal division of beneficiaries between MA and TM, for a given x^{MA}.

Beneficiaries sort themselves between MA and TM based on their willingness to pay for each alternative and the relative premiums. The difference in willingness to pay for MA and TM, which we refer to as ΔU, is a function of θ:

$$\Delta U(x^{MA}, \theta) = V(x^{MA}, \theta) - (V(x^{TM}(\theta), \theta) - cx^{TM}(\theta)) \qquad (6)$$

Beneficiaries compare this difference to the difference in premiums between the two options and choose the option with the highest net benefit.

The following Lemma regarding ΔU is central to our results about premium policies and beneficiary sorting.

Lemma 1. *The beneficiary whose utility in MA exceeds TM by the maximum amount is θ_1 (as given by Proposition 1), the marginal beneficiary defining the lower bound of the types who are more efficiently served in MA.*

In other words, the beneficiary for whom *social welfare is equal* in MA and TM defining the low end of the θ distribution belonging in MA is the beneficiary for whom the *difference in utility (before any premiums) is the maximum* between the two options. The advantage of TM in comparison to MA is the beneficiary's ability to choose quantity. For one type of beneficiary, that defining θ_1, this advantage counts for nothing — the beneficiary would choose x^{MA} in any case. MA absolves the beneficiary of cost sharing, and thus for this beneficiary the utility advantage of MA is cx^{MA}. The point of Lemma 1 is that this is as good as it gets: cx^{MA} is the maximum any beneficiary gains from being in MA. Figure 5 shows why (with proof in Appendix). For a beneficiary with $\theta < \theta_1$, the gain from MA is less since some of the services are valued at less than c. For a beneficiary with $\theta > \theta_1$, there is a cost sharing gain of cx^{MA} but then a deduction because of the services lost with a value greater than c to the beneficiary. Thus, as θ moves away from θ_1 in either direction, the gain from MA is falling.

The unusual relationship between the private and social rankings of the alternatives poses a challenge for premium policy and sorting. Choice is

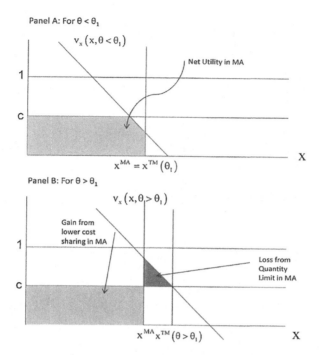

Figure 5. Net utility in MA.

based on utility and efficiency is governed by social welfare. The challenge is this: of the beneficiaries with the same net private utility in MA (those just to the left and right of θ_1), some (those to the left of θ_1) should be directed into TM, and some others (those to the right of θ_1) should be directed into MA. As we will show, no single premium can achieve this desired sorting. It should be emphasized that the result presented in Lemma 1 is quite general as it follows only from our assumptions about the shape of the individual's utility function, $V(x,\theta)$, which are conventional, and on the way the level of service is determined in MA and in TM.

By Lemma 1 we know that for all $\theta > \theta_1$, $U^{\mathrm{TM}}(\theta)$ increases at a rate faster than $U^{\mathrm{MA}}(x^{\mathrm{MA}},\theta)$ and, hence, there exists a $\theta' > \theta_1$ such that U^{TM} is equal to U^{MA} at θ'. In general, θ' can be either smaller or larger than θ_2 depending on the level of the copayment c. In our analysis, hereafter, we focus on the relevant case where c is not too large and hence, U^{TM} intersects U^{MA} at a θ less than θ_2. This situation is depicted in Fig. 6 if there were no premiums for either alternative. The bolded (red) regions of

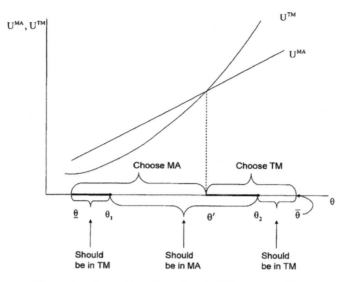

Figure 6.   Comparing efficient and utility max sorting.

the θ-axis flag the discrepancy between the beneficiaries who should be in MA and those who via utility maximization choose MA.

We consider now how the ranges of sorting can be affected by premium policy. Let $y(\theta)$ denote the premium paid by an individual of type θ if she joins TM (without loss of generality we normalize the premium in MA to zero). We allow for $y(\theta)$ to be either positive or negative. Premiums paid to TM are like a tax and do not affect services received by a beneficiary in TM. With a premium the net utility of type θ joining the MA plan is, therefore, $\Delta U(x^{MA}, \theta) + y(\theta)$.

A premium schedule $y(\theta)$ *implements the efficient sorting (assignment)* if, given x^{MA}, $\Delta U(x^{MA}, \theta) + y(\theta) \geq 0$, for all θ, $\theta_1 \leq \theta \leq \theta_2$, and $\Delta U(x^{MA}, \theta) + y(\theta) < \theta$ otherwise. That is, a premium schedule implements the efficient sorting if, given that schedule, all individuals of type θ, $\theta_1 \leq \theta \leq \theta_2$ prefer MA over TM, and all other individuals prefer TM over MA.

5.1. *Failure of Any Single Premium*

The following proposition follows directly from Lemma 1:

Proposition 2. *A single premium cannot implement the efficient sorting.*

The proof is based on the following logic. According to Lemma 1, the premium beneficiary θ_1 pays for TM should make him indifferent between TM and MA so that beneficiaries with lower values of θ will not be willing to pay this premium and (efficiently) stay in TM. However, given Lemma 1, if type θ_1 is just indifferent between MA and TM, then all other beneficiaries strictly prefer TM over MA and they will all choose TM, which is obviously not what the first best calls for.[25]

With the premium for MA set at zero, as we raise the single premium for TM, the first beneficiary willing to join MA is at θ_1, but then, as the premium is raised further, MA attracts beneficiaries on both sides of θ_1; those on the right who we want in MA, and those on the left who we do not. Lemma 1 identifies the severe handicap constraining the MA program based on a single premium policy. Any (single) premium attracting enrollment to MA brings in beneficiaries who would be more efficiently served in TM.

Figure 7 shows the effect of a positive single premium for TM, shifting upward the net utility in MA. The positive premium moves some beneficiaries who should be in MA from TM (those just to the right of

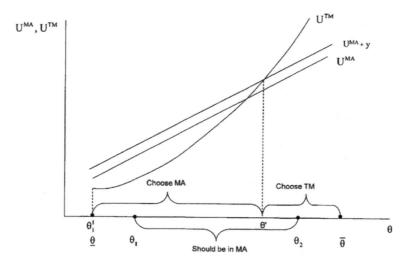

Figure 7. Sorting with a single premium.

---

[25] If the density function of θ did not have a full support over the interval $|\underline{\theta}, \bar{\theta}|$ then there could be a case where only the upper cutoff, θ_2, was in the support of $f(\theta)$ and, in such a case, a single premium could implement the efficient sorting. This case is very special and we do not discuss it.

the θ' in Fig. 6), initially improving efficiency. Beneficiaries to the left of θ_1 continue to make the wrong choice. Eventually, further increases in the single premium for TM will lead to inefficient choices in the range above θ_2 as well. There is no way to manipulate the single premium (positive or negative) to attain the efficient sorting.

5.2. *Implementing Efficient Sorting Requires Two Premiums*

From Proposition 2 we know that at least two premium levels are necessary to implement the efficient sorting. In Proposition 3 we describe how premiums need to depend on θ to lead to an efficient division between MA and TM. The premium policy uses two premium levels y_1 and y_2, where $y_1(y_2)$ is the level of premium that would make type $\theta_1(\theta_2)$ just indifferent between MA and TM. The premium $y_1(y_2)$ is paid by all individuals of type $\theta < \theta_1$ ($\theta \geq \theta_1$) if they choose to be in TM.

Proposition 3. *Let x^{MA} be given, let $y_1 = -cx^{\mathrm{MA}}$, and let*

$$y_2 = V(\theta_2, x^{\mathrm{TM}}(\theta_2)) - V(\theta_2, x^{\mathrm{MA}}) - cx^{\mathrm{TM}}(\theta_2) \qquad (7)$$

The premium policy: $y(\theta) = y_1$ if $\theta < \theta_1$, and y_2 if $\theta \geq \theta_1$, implements the efficient sorting.

Figure 8 illustrates the two-level premium policy. (see Appendix for a formal proof.) Beneficiaries below θ_1 would pay the negative premium $y_1 = -cx^{\mathrm{MA}}$ (be subsidized) to join TM; this subsidy is large enough to keep all beneficiaries in this range in TM. Everyone else pays a positive premium for TM, calculated so as to make the beneficiary at the upper end of the efficient range just indifferent between the two options. This premium, y_2, is high enough to keep all the beneficiaries between θ_1 and θ_2 in MA, but is not enough for the very high-demand types, those with $\theta > \theta_2$, and they go to TM (where they belong).

There are obviously other premium policies that would also sort beneficiaries efficiently (for example, the subsidy for TM need not be equal to y_1 for all the beneficiaries below θ_1, but the (y_l, y_2)-policy we describe is the simplest — the only two-premium policy that does the job.

5.3. *Second-Best Sorting Using a Single Premium*

The two-premium policy described in Proposition 3 relies on the regulator using θ as a basis for premiums. Such a policy may not be feasible as the factors behind θ, e.g., education, attitudes towards health and health

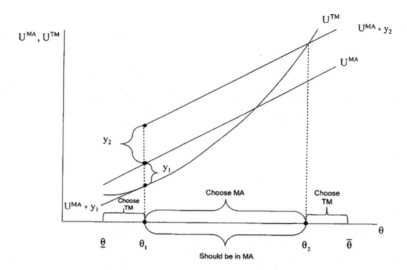

Note: y_1 is negative; y_2 is positive

Figure 8.   Efficient sorting with two premiums.

care, are not easily observable by the regulator and even if observable, cannot be used as a basis for a premium policy. If θ cannot be used to set premiums, the regulator must pick just one premium to sort beneficiaries, and we know from Proposition 2 that the socially efficient sorting cannot be implemented. The question then becomes what is the optimal (second-best) single premium to sort beneficiaries between MA and TM?

When the regulator chooses a single premium for TM, y, and the level of care is x^{MA}, two distinct possibilities arise. The first is when the premium is positive and, hence, there exists a single cutoff θ' such that all individuals with $\theta < \theta'$ choose MA and all individuals with $\theta \geq \theta'$ prefer TM. The second is when the premium for TM is sufficiently negative, so that there are two cutoffs θ_1' and θ_2' with $\underline{\theta} \leq \theta_1' < \theta_2' \leq \bar{\theta}$, such that all individuals with $\theta_1' \leq \theta \leq \theta_2'$ choose MA and all other individuals choose TM. In the first case the cutoff θ' is given by $-\Delta U(x^{MA}, \theta') = y$. In the second case the two cutoffs are given by $-\Delta U(x^{MA}, \theta_i') = y$, for $i = 1, 2$.

The first case is of more practical significance, since Medicare's single premium policy leads to a positive premium for TM, when the medigap and Part D premiums are factored into the picture. This is the case we select for analysis. How should consumers be divided between MA and TM in this case? We characterize the second-best sorting in Proposition 4.

Proposition 4. *Assume that x^{MA} is given and let θ' denote the second-best efficient cutoff given that a positive premium is implemented for TM (i.e., $y > 0$). Then, $\theta' = \theta_2$ where θ_2 is the first-best cutoff given by Proposition 1.*

The second-best policy must accept that the low-demand beneficiaries (with the lowest willingness to pay for TM) will be in MA. With x^{MA} given, the tradeoff on the upper end of the distribution of demand is unaltered from the first-best case, the same cutoff, θ_2, will be the target of the TM premium. Thus, the single-premium (given an x^{MA}) is y_2 from Proposition 3.

6. EFFICIENT LEVEL OF CARE

Now suppose that Medicare can set the level of x^{MA} by altering the level of its payments to plans.[26] How should x^{MA} be set if Medicare's objective is to maximize social welfare? We will first consider the first-best where we assume that Medicare can implement efficient sorting by using a premium policy such as the one discussed in Proposition 3. We next restrict Medicare to use a single premium and, hence, the best it can achieve is a second-best sorting as described in Proposition 4.

6.1. *The First-Best Level of Managed Care*

Suppose that Medicare can implement efficient sorting as given by Proposition 1. We can then express social welfare as the sum of three integrals, and the efficient outcome is given by the solution to the following problem:

$$
\mathrm{Max}_{(\theta_1,\theta_2,x^{\mathrm{MA}})} \int_{\underline{\theta}}^{\theta_1} (V(x^{\mathrm{TM}}(\theta),\theta) - x^{\mathrm{TM}}(\theta))f(\theta)d\theta
$$

$$
+ \int_{\theta_1}^{\theta_2} \left(V(x^{\mathrm{MA}},\theta) - x^{\mathrm{MA}}\right) f(\theta)d(\theta)
$$

$$
+ \int_{\theta_2}^{\bar{\theta}} (V(x^{\mathrm{TM}}(\theta),\theta) - x^{\mathrm{TM}}(\theta))f(\theta)d(\theta) \tag{8}
$$

---

[26]The relation between payment level (the benchmark) and services available in MA, x^{MA}, depends on the market structure of MA plan supply. Competition among MA plans implies they will make zero profit by maximizing the welfare of a representative beneficiary choosing MA. If the sector is not competitive, there will still be a positive relationship between Medicare payment and services chosen by the MA plans. In this paper we are focusing on premium policy and so do not introduce a particular model of plan behavior and MA sector equilibrium.

Three first-order conditions (FOC) define the solution, $(\theta_1^*, \theta_2^*, x^*)$, to (8). Consider the FOC with respect to x^{MA} describing the x^* best for the beneficiaries in MA:

$$\int_{\theta_1^*}^{\theta_2^*} (V_x(x^*, \theta) - 1) f(\theta) d(\theta) = 0 \tag{9}$$

Condition (9) is a public good-like condition stating that at x^*, the sum of the marginal valuations of x less marginal cost, weighted by the frequency of θ in MA, equals zero. x^* is the efficient care for just one value of θ (the value that solves $V_x(x^*, \theta) = 1$)), but the efficient sorting puts beneficiaries with θ in a range above and below this value into MA (because of the overconsumption for all beneficiaries in TM). The compromise on x^* reflects the relative frequency among beneficiaries between the θ_1^* and θ_2^* cutoffs.

The FOCs describing the optimal cutoffs between MA and TM are characterized in Proposition 1 and the two panels of Fig. 3 when x^{MA} is chosen optimally at x^*. The same modification could be made to Panels A and B of Fig. 4, adding stars to depict θ_1^* and θ_2^* to indicate that x^{MA} is chosen optimally. There is a welfare gain in MA for a range of beneficiaries to avoiding the over-consumption in TM. The value of x^* maximizes this gain. One consideration in this choice is the frequency of θ among the population of beneficiaries. With a plausible distribution of θ, maximizing social welfare implies setting the level of services in MA to serve the large bulk of the population.[27]

6.2. *The Second-Best Level of Care with a Single Premium*

Suppose now that $y > 0$ and the premium implements a single cutoff.

Proposition 5. *When a single premium is implemented, the (second-best) efficient level of care is lower than the first-best level of care.*

When the single premium is positive there is a single cutoff and beneficiaries with a low θ are in MA, whereas in a first best these low-demand types would be in TM. This will lower the efficient x^{MA}, implying

---

[27] Another consideration is the relative welfare cost of over-consumption for beneficiaries with different values of θ. If higher θ individuals had more elastic demand, there would be more social gains to including them in MA and θ_2 would be higher. In the proof of Proposition 1, we need to rule out cases in which there are "islands" of unusual demand elasticities for some values of θ. For example, if there were a bunch of beneficiaries with perfectly inelastic demand, they could be safely put in TM with no welfare cost. The assumptions above about third derivatives of utility rule out these unusual islands.

that the second-best high-end cutoff will fall below θ_2. Thus, in this case, services in MA will be lower than in the first best and too few higher θ beneficiaries will be in MA.

7. DISCUSSION

Part C of Medicare has been a disappointment for more than 25 years. Our paper identifies one fundamental reason for this. Policies governing the premiums for MA plans and TM lead to inefficient distribution of beneficiaries between the options. Although our model does not generate quantitative conclusions, the character of the optimal equilibrium is so different from what we see in practice that we are confident that the welfare losses associated with current policy are large. Enrollment in MA has vacillated between 10 and 27% in the past 15 years, and is likely to be driven down from its recent highs with cuts in plan payments set in the ACA. Each MA plan sets its own "single premium." Premiums for TM are highly subsidized and also do not vary according to demand-related factors.

We argue that MA should be directed to serve the large middle part of the distribution of demand for health care — what we refer to as the "middle class." Instead, current premium policies encourage MA plans to attract beneficiaries with lower demand, both for reasons of better health status and for non-health status factors.[28]

Increasing pressure on public budgets mean two things for Medicare advantage (MA): first, it is even more important for Medicare to achieve the savings potential of managed care plans; second, in one form or another, beneficiary premiums (rather than tax-supported payments) will play a larger role in financing Medicare, both on the TM and the MA side. Premium policy will inevitably be reformulated for financing reasons, yielding an opportunity to get more and more of the right beneficiaries in improved MA plans.

---

[28]After adjusting for health status, there is an inverse relationship between income and other indicators of socioeconomic status and the likelihood that beneficiaries join an MA plan. Balsa *et al.* (2007) studied enrollment choices of 65+ Medicare beneficiaries not on Medicaid using 5 years of data from two sources, the National Health Interview Survey and the Medicare Current Beneficiary Survey. Lower income groups, lower education groups and members of racial/ethnic minorities were more likely to join MA, after adjustment for self-assessed health status, the presence of a series of other health conditions, age, gender, and other factors. The Kaiser Family Foundation, with more recent data, reports that MA enrollees are more likely to be poor (and report poor health) than beneficiaries in TM (KFF, 2008).

A comprehensive discussion of restructuring Medicare policy towards MA requires consideration of issues not addressed in this paper, including: the cost-effectiveness and quality of care in MA plans compared to TM; the desirable forms of MA plans; the level of the benchmark payment and bidding; the role of medigap and employer plans; regional differences in patterns of care; the "choice architecture" for MA plans and the setup of the default option; the broader (spillover) effects of Medicare MA policy on health financing systems; and equity-distributional concerns in terms of rich-poor, healthy-sick and young-old.

While noting these concerns, we point out here two practical implications of our analysis of premiums and beneficiary sorting. First, our main message is that the premium for joining TM should be higher for higher-demand beneficiaries. Socially, there is more to be gained by keeping these high-demand types in MA. Currently, the Part B premium is mildly income-related, but the beneficiary pays the same premium whether they join an MA plan or stay in TM. We recommend that the income-related portion of the Part B premium be waived if the beneficiary elects MA. This step would introduce a simple version of a two-level premium based on income and may open important options for further differentiating premiums down the road. In the future, as more is asked of beneficiaries in terms of premium, widening the premium differences by income will work towards the premium discrimination called for in our analysis.

Second, the structure is also in place to create options attractive to low-demand beneficiaries. Low income/asset Medicare beneficiaries qualify for special premium and cost sharing subsidies through state Medicaid programs. These expensive "dual eligible" would likely benefit most from coordination of care in MA, but face no premiums at all. Furthermore, their cost sharing in TM is paid by Medicaid, biasing their choice toward TM. Translating some of the subsidy for this group into income support if these beneficiaries choose economical Medicaid managed care plans could make beneficiaries better off, improve sorting, and reduce public health care spending.

More broadly, our analysis implies that Medicare should take a direct hand in setting premiums for MA plans. Although it would represent a big change for Medicare, there is nothing radical about a sponsor setting premiums for plan options. Virtually all large private employers do this, setting the price employees pay for any health plans offered through employment. Employers recognize their interest in affecting incentives employees face in deciding about plans. Like private employers,

Medicare should take charge of the premium paid by beneficiaries to join health plans, and set those premiums in order to forward Medicare objectives.

Our model is not well-suited to making a comprehensive estimate of the welfare effects of a more efficient premium policy. There would, however, be an immediate impact on Medicare costs of moving more beneficiaries into MA plans. A doubling of MA enrollment (to, say, 50%) would move about 25% of Medicare costs into managed care — at a 10% saving over TM, health costs would fall about 2.5%, corresponding to over $13 billion in the $565 billion (in 2011) Medicare program. Recent research finds that the MA program affects practice style in TM and commercial populations, leading to additional savings (Baicker *et al.*, under review).

The more important beneficial effect, however, of revitalizing MA in Medicare comes in the longer term. Medicare is evolving to a system in which there are more than two types of plans. In addition to TM and MA, practice groups can now organize into Accountable Care Organizations (ACOs) and accept payment from Medicare with some prospective features. No premium-side policies work along with this provider-side payment reform. Efficient premium policy should complement new provider payment policies in Medicare, not continue to sort beneficiaries inefficiently among plan options.

Pursuit of efficiency in health insurance when serving a heterogeneous population runs up against concerns for fairness. Health care policy in the U.S. leaves much more room for gradations in health insurance (e.g., the Bronze-to-Platinum range in the ACA) than in most other countries. Nonetheless, targeting MA plans to groups across the range of socioeconomic status raises fundamental positive and normative questions about serving taste heterogeneity in health insurance, and about the role and fairness of collective methods of finance.

Our analysis leaves a number of questions unanswered. Incorporation of an explicit analysis of MA plan behavior should be high on the agenda. Within a population of heterogeneous beneficiaries, many MA plans setting different levels of services will better serve diverse tastes than a single MA product.

In this paper we abstract from heterogeneity in health status and issues related to risk adjustment and MA plan resource allocation according to health need also need incorporation. MA plans obviously do respond to some dimensions of beneficiary heterogeneity. This form of heterogeneity has been recognized in the literature, and raises a different set of issues than our concern in this paper. A comprehensive analysis would include consideration of heterogeneity which plans respond to in resource allocation (e.g., health status), and heterogeneity which plans do not (e.g., income-related tastes). One could ask our question: who *should* be in MA along dimensions of health status as well as taste for health care. With new data becoming available on what goes on inside the black box of managed care plans, empirical patterns of care in MA and TM, and how they respond to these factors can be assessed empirically. This can be a basis for theory development and policy application.

ACKNOWLEDGEMENTS

The authors are grateful to the National Institute of Aging for support through P01 AG032952, The Role of Private Plans in Medicare, J. Newhouse, PI. This paper grew out of discussions with Rhema Vaithianathan. Chris Afendulis, Kate Baicker, Mike Chernew, Richard Frank, Nolan Miller, Joe Newhouse, Steve Pizer, Zirui Song, and Alan Zaslavsky provided helpful comments on an earlier draft. Guest editor David Dranove and two reviewers redirected our initial analysis into more fruitful directions. We thank members of the BU/Harvard/MIT Health Economics Workshop and seminar participants at Duke University and the University of Pennsylvania for helpful discussion. The opinions and conclusions in this paper are the authors' alone.

APPENDIX

Proof of Proposition 1. We define the difference between social welfare in MA and social welfare in TM to be:

$$\Delta W(x^{\mathrm{MA}}, \theta) = W^{\mathrm{MA}}(x^{\mathrm{MA}}, \theta) - W^{\mathrm{TM}}(\theta)$$

The change in ΔW as θ changes is given by (recall that $V_{\theta\theta} = 0$):

$$\frac{d\Delta W(x^{\mathrm{MA}}, \theta)}{d\theta} = V_\theta(x^{\mathrm{MA}}, \theta) - V_\theta(x^{\mathrm{TM}}(\theta), \theta) - \left[V_x(x^{\mathrm{TM}}(\theta), \theta) - 1\right] \frac{dx^{\mathrm{TM}}}{d\theta}$$

$$= V_\theta(x^{\mathrm{MA}}, \theta) - V_\theta(x^{\mathrm{TM}}(\theta), \theta)$$

$$+ [V_x(x^{\mathrm{TM}}(\theta), \theta) - 1]\left[\frac{V_{\theta x}(x^{\mathrm{TM}}(\theta), \theta)}{V_{xx}(x^{\mathrm{TM}}(\theta), \theta)}\right]$$

The second equality follows from our definition of $x^{\mathrm{TM}}(\theta)$.

The curvature of the ΔW is given by:

$$\frac{d^2 \Delta W(x^{\mathrm{MA}}, \theta)}{d\theta^2} = \frac{dx^{\mathrm{TM}}}{d\theta} \left[-V_{\theta x} + (V_x - 1)\left(2\frac{V_{\theta xx}}{V_{xx}} - \frac{V_{xxx}V_{\theta x}}{(V_{xx})^2} \right) \right] < 0$$

The inequality follows from the fact that

$$V_{\theta\theta} = 0, \quad V_{\theta x} > 0, \quad \frac{dx^{\mathrm{TM}}}{d\theta} > 0, \quad V_{xx} < 0, \quad V_{xxx} \leq 0,$$

$$V_x(x^{\mathrm{TM}}(\theta), (\theta) < 1.$$

$V_{\theta\theta x} = 0$ and $V_{\theta xx} = V_{xx}\theta$ by our assumption that $V_{\theta\theta} = 0$.

Given x^{MA} there exists a θ, call it θ^{MA}, for which, x^{MA} is socially efficient, that is $V_x(x^{\mathrm{MA}}, \theta^{\mathrm{MA}}) = 1$ and, hence, $\Delta W(x^{\mathrm{MA}}, \theta_1) > 0$. Furthermore, there exists another $\theta < \theta^{\mathrm{MA}}$, call it θ_1 for which $x^{\mathrm{MA}} = x^{\mathrm{TM}}(\theta_1)$ and, hence, $\Delta W(x^{\mathrm{MA}}, \theta_1) = 0$. By the concavity of ΔW, we know, therefore, that there exists at most one more θ, call it θ_2, such that $\theta_2 > \theta^{\mathrm{MA}}$ and $\Delta W(x^{\mathrm{MA}}, \theta_2) = 0$.

Proof of Lemma 1. Using the envelope theorem one can see that:

$$\frac{d\Delta U}{d\theta} = V_\theta(x^{\mathrm{MA}}, \theta) - V_\theta(x^{\mathrm{TM}}(\theta), \theta)$$

We know that at $\theta_1, x^{\mathrm{TM}}(\theta_1) = x^{\mathrm{MA}}$, and thus at $\theta_1, \Delta U/d\theta = 0$. Furthermore, by the linearity of U^{MA} and the convexity of U^{TM} we know that ΔU is convex with respect to θ. Thus, ΔU is maximized at θ_1.

Proof of Proposition 2. Assume a single premium y for TM. For the premium to implement the efficient sorting it must be that $-y + \Delta U(x^{\mathrm{MA}}, 0) \leq 0$ for all $\theta < \theta_1$ and $-y + \Delta U(x^{\mathrm{MA}}, 0) \geq 0$ for $\theta > \theta_1$. However, since with $\underline{\theta} < \theta_1 < \bar{\theta}$ and $\Delta U(x^{\mathrm{MA}}, \theta)$ is maximized at θ_1, the two conditions above cannot be met simultaneously.

Proof of Propositions 3. Since $y_1 = -cx^{\mathrm{MA}} = \Delta U(x^{\mathrm{MA}}, \theta_1) > \Delta U(x^{\mathrm{MA}}, \theta)$ for all $\theta < \theta_1$, all individuals with $\theta < \theta_1$ will prefer TM over MA. Since $\Delta U(x^{\mathrm{MA}}, \theta)$ is decreasing with θ, for all $\theta > \theta_1$ and since $y_2 = -\Delta U(x^{\mathrm{MA}}, \theta_2)$, it must be that $\Delta U(x^{\mathrm{MA}}, \theta) + y_2 > 0$ for all θ, $\theta_1 < \theta < \theta_2$ and $\Delta U(x^{\mathrm{MA}}, \theta) + y_2 < 0$ for all $\theta > \theta_1$.

Proof of Proposition 4. When $y = 0$ there is a single cutoff to the left of θ_2. By increasing the premium the single cutoff moves towards θ_2 and welfare is increased. Once the cutoff reaches θ_2, welfare will be decreased if the premium is further increased (see Fig. 7).

Proof of Proposition 5. When $y > 0$, and there is a single cutoff between MA and TM, the second-best outcome is given by:

$$\text{Max}_{(\theta',x)} \int_{\underline{\theta}}^{\theta'} (V(x,\theta) - x)f(\theta) + \int_{\theta'}^{\bar{\theta}} \left(V(x^{\text{TM}}(\theta),\theta) - x^{\text{TM}}(\theta) \right) f(\theta)d(\theta) \tag{10}$$

The first-order condition implies:

$$V(x',\theta') - x' = V(x^{\text{TM}}(\theta'),\theta') - x^{\text{TM}}(\theta') \tag{11}$$

and:

$$\int_{\underline{\theta}}^{\theta'} (V_x(x',\theta) - 1)f(\theta)d\theta = 0 \tag{12}$$

Condition (11) is similar to the result obtained in Proposition 4, namely that $\theta' = \theta_2$. Using the fact that $\theta' = \theta_2$ and $\underline{\theta} < \theta_1$, where θ_1 is the first-best lower cutoff, (12) implies:

$$\int_{\theta_1}^{\theta_2} (V_x(x',\theta) - 1)f(\theta)d\theta > 0$$

Thus, when the cutoffs can be chosen efficiently (i.e., at the first-best), welfare at x' is increasing in x. Thus, $x^* > x'$.

REFERENCES

Acemoglu, D., Finkelstein, A., Notowidigdo, M., 2009. Income and Health Spending: Evidence from Oil Price Stocks, NBER Working paper No. 14744.

Afendulis, C., Landrum, M.B., Chernew, M., 2011. The Impact of the Affordable Care Act on Medicare Advantage Plan Availability and Enrollment. Working paper, November.

Balsa, A.I., Cao, Z., McGuire, T.G., 2007. Does managed health care reduce health care disparities between minorities and whites? *Journal of Health Economics* 26(1), 101–121.

Baicker, K., Chernew, M.E., Robbins, J. The spillover effects of medicare managed care: medicare advantage and hospital utilization. Journal of Health Economics (under review).

Barros, P., Siciliani, L., 2012. Public and private sector interface. In: Pauly, M., McGuire, T., Barros, P. (Eds.), *Handbook of Health Economics*, Vol. 2. Elsevier, pp. 927–1002.

Baumgardner, J., 1991. The interaction between forms of insurance contract and technical change in medical care. *RAND Journal of Economics* 22(1), 36–53.

Berry, S.T., 1994. Estimating discrete-choice models of product differentiation. *RAND Journal of Economics* 25(2), 242–262.

Besley, T., Coate, S., 1991. Public provision of private goods and the redistribution of income. *American Economic Review* 81(4), 979–984.

Borger, C., Rutherford, T.F., Won, G.Y., 2008. Projecting long term medical spending growth. *Journal of Health Economics* 27(1), 69–88.

Breyer, F., Bundorf, M.K., Pauly, M.V., 2012. Health Care Spending Risk, Health Insurance, and Payment to Health Plans. In: Pauly, M., McGuire, T., Barros, P. (Eds.), *Handbook of Health Economics*, Vol. 2. Elsevier, pp. 691–762.

Bundorf, M.K., Levin, J.D., Mahoney, N., 2012. Pricing and welfare in health plan choice. *The American Economic Review* 102(7), 3214–3248.

Centers for Medicare and Medicaid Services, 2010. Fact Sheet: Premiums and Deductibles for 2011, November 4, 2010.

Centers for Medicare and Medicaid Services, 2011. Medicare & You.

Chernew, M.E., Rosen, A.B., Fendrick, A.M., 2007. Value-based insurance design. *Health Affairs* 26(2), w195–w203.

Ellis, R.P., McGuire, T.G., 2007. Predictability and predictiveness in healthcare spending. *Journal of Health Economics* 26(1), 25–48.

Frank, R.G., Glazer, J., McGuire, T.G., 2000. Adverse selection in managed health care. *Journal of Health Economics* 19(6), 829–854.

Fogel, R.W., 2008. Forecasting the Cost of U.S. Health Care in 2040. National Bureau of Economic Research Working Paper 14361.

Glazer, J., McGuire, T.G., 2011. Gold and silver health plans: accommodating demand heterogeneity in managed competition. *Journal of Health Economics* 30(5), 1011–1020.

Gold, M., 2008. Medicare Advantage in 2008, Issue brief 7775, Henry Kaiser Family Foundation, June 2008.

Gold, M., 2009. Medicare's private plans: a report card on medicare advantage. *Health Affairs* 23(1), w41-w54.

Gold, M., Achman, L., Mittler, J., et al., 2004. Monitoring Medicare + Choice: What Have We Learned? Findings and Operational Lessons for Medicare Advantage. Mathematica Policy Research, Washington, DC.

Government Accountability Office, Medicare Advantage Plan Bids, GAO-11-247R, February 4, 2011.

Grassi, S., Ma, C.-T.A., 2008. Public Sector Rationing and Private Sector Selection. Department of Economics, Boston University.

Kaiser Family Foundation, 2008. Medicare Fact Sheet: Medicare Spending and Financing, Publication # 7305-03 at www.k_.org

Kaiser Family Foundation, 2010a. Medicare Chartbook, 4th edn.

Kaiser Family Foundation, 2010b. Medicare Advantage 2011 Data Spotlight: Plan Availability and Premiums, October, 2010.

Keeler, E.B., Carter, G., Newhouse, J., 1998. A model of the impact of reimbursement schemes on health plan choice. *Journal of Health Economics* 17(3), 297–320.

McGuire, T., Newhouse, J., Sinaiko, A., 2011. An economic history of Medicare Part C. *Milbank Quarterly* 89(2), 289–332.

McWilliams, J.M., Afendulis, C.C., McGuire, T.G., Landon, B.E., 2011. Complex Medicare advantage choices may overwhelm seniors — especially those with impaired decision making, Health Affairs.

MedPAC, 2008. Report to Congress; Medicare and the Health Care Delivery System, June.

MedPAC, 2011a. Report to Congress; Medicare and the Health Care Delivery System, June.

MedPAC, 2011b. A Data Book: Health Care Spending and the Medicare Program, June, 2011.

Miller, N., 2005. Pricing health benefits: A cost minimizing approach. *Journal of Health Economics* 24(5), 931–949.

Newhouse, J.P., 1993. Free for All: Lessons from the Rand Health Insurance Experiment. Harvard University Press, Boston, MA.

Newhouse, J.P., 2002. Pricing the Priceless: A Health Care Conundrum. MIT Press.

Newhouse, J.P., 2006. Reconsidering the moral hazard-risk avoidance tradeoff. *Journal of Health Economics* 25(5), 1005–1014.

Pauly, M., Blavin, F., 2009. Moral hazard in insurance. Value-based cost sharing, and the benefits of blissful ignorance. *Journal of Health Economics* 27(6), 1407–1417.

Pauly, M., Ramsey, S., 1999. Would you like suspenders to go with that belt? An analysis of optimal combinations of cost sharing and managed care. *Journal of Health Economics* 18(4), 443–458.

Pizer, S., Frakt, A., Feldman, R., 2003. Payment policy and inefficient benefits in the Medicare + choice program. *International Journal of Health Care Finance and Economics* 3(2), 79–93.

Pope, G.C., Kautter, J., Ellis, R.P., Ash, A.S., Ayanian, J.Z., Iezzoni, L.I., Ingber, M.J., Levy, J.M., Robst, J., 2004. Risk adjustment of medicare capitation payments using the CMS-HCC model. *Health Care Financing Review* 25(4), 119–141.

Rothschild, M., Stiglitz, J., 1976. Equilibrium in competitive insurance markets: an essay in the economics of imperfect information. *Quarterly Journal of Economics* 90(4), 629–649.

Town, R., Liu, S., 2003. The welfare impact of Medicare HMOs. *RAND Journal of Economics* 34(4), 719–736.

Van de Ven, W.P.M.M., Ellis, R.P., 2000. Risk Adjustment in competitive health plan markets. In: Culyer, A., Newhouse, J. (Eds.), *Handbook of Health Economics*, Vol. 1. Elsevier, pp. 755–846.